Praise for

Bonobo Handshake

ॐ

"Funny, adventurous, and heartbreaking. Woods takes us with her to darkest Africa to meet our nearest relative, the nearly extinct bonobo. This must-read book illuminates extraordinary courage in both people and animals."
—Sara Gruen, bestselling author of *Water for Elephants*

"Gain insights into both the darkness and altruistic sides of our own emotions by getting to know chimpanzees and bonobos in an African sanctuary. This book is both shocking and hilarious."
—Temple Grandin, author of *Animals in Translation*
and *Animals Make Us Human*

"Don't think that this is just a book about apes. It's a love story, an adventure story, and a political education about a country that has seen more tragedy and inhumanity than you can imagine. Above all, it's an introduction to creatures who have every claim to being more human, in the best sense of the word, than we are." —Adam Hochschild, author of *King Leopold's Ghost*

"This is a startling book. Page after page astonished me. A beautifully written journey into the tangled jungle of the human mind, it also brings us movingly into intimate, loving contact with our extraordinary cousins. This is a compelling story, told with striking honesty, humor, and intelligence."
—Alan Alda, author of the *New York Times* bestsellers
Things I Overheard While Talking to Myself and *Never Have Your Dog Stuffed*

"This is a thoughtful, eloquent memoir, well written and well researched, alternately charming and horrific." —*Minneapolis Star-Tribune*

"Woods's account of her time with the bonobo apes is a story to savor."
—*People*

"[Woods's] book about her work in the Congo is exciting, informative, and personal. It is hard to come away without a soft spot for these frisky cousins of ours." —*St. Louis Post-Dispatch*

"When Woods describes her daily interaction with the bonobos, her account takes on a warm charm. Woods's personable, accessible work about bonobos elucidates the marvelous intelligence and tolerance of this gentle cousin to humans." —*Publishers Weekly*

꩜

Vanessa Woods is a research scientist, a journalist, and an author. A member of the Hominoid Psychology Research Group, she works at Duke University as well as Lola Ya Bonobo in Congo. She is also a feature writer for the Discovery Channel, and her writing has appeared in publications such as *BBC Wildlife* and *Travel Africa*. Her first book, *It's Every Monkey for Themselves*, was published in Australia in 2007. Woods lives in North Carolina with her husband, scientist Brian Hare. Ten percent of the profits of this book will be going to Lola Ya Bonobo.

Bonobo Handshake

A Memoir of Love and Adventure in the Congo

VANESSA WOODS

GOTHAM BOOKS

GOTHAM BOOKS
Published by Penguin Group (USA) Inc.
375 Hudson Street, New York, New York 10014, U.S.A.

Penguin Group (Canada), 90 Eglinton Avenue East, Suite 700, Toronto, Ontario M4P 2Y3, Canada (a division of Pearson Penguin Canada Inc.) • Penguin Books Ltd, 80 Strand, London WC2R 0RL, England • Penguin Ireland, 25 St Stephen's Green, Dublin 2, Ireland (a division of Penguin Books Ltd) • Penguin Group (Australia), 250 Camberwell Road, Camberwell, Victoria 3124, Australia (a division of Pearson Australia Group Pty Ltd) • Penguin Books India Pvt Ltd, 11 Community Centre, Panchsheel Park, New Delhi–110 017, India • Penguin Group (NZ), 67 Apollo Drive, Rosedale, North Shore 0632, New Zealand (a division of Pearson New Zealand Ltd) • Penguin Books (South Africa) (Pty) Ltd, 24 Sturdee Avenue, Rosebank, Johannesburg 2196, South Africa

Penguin Books Ltd, Registered Offices: 80 Strand, London WC2R 0RL, England

Published by Gotham Books, a member of Penguin Group (USA) Inc.

Previously published as a Gotham Books hardcover edition

First trade paperback printing, June 2011

10   9   8   7   6   5   4   3   2   1

Gotham Books and the skyscraper logo are trademarks of Penguin Group (USA) Inc.

LIBRARY OF CONGRESS CATALOGING-IN-PUBLICATION DATA

Woods, Vanessa, 1977–
  Bonobo handshake / by Vanessa Woods.
    p.   cm.
  ISBN 978-1-592-40546-6 (hc)   978-1-592-40634-0 (paperback)
  1. Bonobo—Behavior—Congo (Democratic Republic) 2. Bonobo—Congo (Democratic Republic)
3. Wildlife rescue—Congo (Democratic Republic) 4. Woods, Vanessa, 1977– 5. André, Claudine. I.
Title.
  QL737.P96W655   2010
  599.884096751—dc22   2009040721

Printed in the United States of America • Set in Bembo • Designed by Elke Sigal

Penguin is committed to publishing works of quality and integrity.
In that spirit, we are proud to offer this book to our readers;
however, the story, the experiences, and the words
are the author's alone.

For Malou

Au Congo la guerre est finie
Oh, mon ami,
Alors pourquoi de la forêt
Ils inondent notre nursery?

A Lola
A Lola ya Bonobo
C'est leur paradis.

Kikwit et Lomami, comment aux arbres grimper
Sans les doigts que les sorciers vous ont coupé?
Kikongo et Lomela, comment oublier
La peine et la douleur?

A Lola
A Lola ya Bonobo
C'est leur paradis.

—CHANSON DES MAMAS, LOLA YA BONOBO

In Congo, the war has ended
Oh, my friend,
Why then from the forest
Do they flood our nursery?

At Lola
At Lola ya Bonobo
It is their paradise

Kikwit and Lomami, how do you climb trees
Without the fingers the witch doctors severed?
Kikongo and Lomela, how can you forget
The pain and suffering?

At Lola
At Lola ya Bonobo
It is their paradise

—SONG BY THE MAMAS, LOLA YA BONOBO

Chapter 1

*I*t's 2:17 A.M. in a Paris hotel room and my sweat is bleeding into the sheets. I've been staring for hours at the popcorn ceiling, little balls of stucco poised to drop like concrete rain. The walls boxing me in are as thick as a bomb shelter, built to keep out the noise of landing planes and overzealous couples in neighboring rooms.

Anxiety is drilling holes into my chest, because I have to sleep and I can't. In a few hours I'm going to a place where bad things happen. I need to be rested. I must be alert.

But instead I'm shivering and clammy. I have never done anything as stupid as this journey I have already begun. My eyes are almost swollen shut but I can't keep them closed. I am curled and crushed under this fear that I've been carrying around, like a hernia, for so many days.

There is a man sleeping next to me. His curls fall over his face and his cheeks are flushed because the room is too warm. His eyelashes are obscenely long, his lips too full. He could be a woman except for his prognathic jaw, his Neanderthal brow. His breath sails in and out of his lungs without effort. His sleep is so deep that his fingers are twitching and his eyes flicker behind his eyelids.

It's because of him that I'm here. He is on a treasure hunt. Chasing shadows of our simian past to answer the greatest question of all time.

I want to slap him awake. I can't believe he can sleep when I'm obviously freaking out. I want to push him off the bed with my feet and hear the satisfying thud when he hits the thinly covered concrete. But we've already fought for an hour tonight. Or rather, I screeched at him like a harpy with my fists twisted into the covers so they didn't punch him in the face.

I want so desperately to go home, to go back to my family and tell them it was a horrible mistake, this new life with him.

His tongue falls back against his throat and a small snore escapes. It reverberates through this jail cell I'm in and rakes its fingernails across my nerves.

We're supposed to get married and I've never hated anyone so much in my life.

Chapter 2

I didn't always want to push my fiancé off a balcony. Twelve months ago I would have jumped off a balcony for him. But a lot can change in a year.

We met in Uganda at the house of Debby Cox, the founder of a chimpanzee sanctuary called Ngamba Island. Debby and I had been friends for years. I first met her when I was twenty-two and fresh out of college. I was volunteering for Taronga Zoo in Sydney when I heard about the chimp island she had started for orphan chimpanzees whose parents were killed by the bushmeat trade.

Part of Debby's conservation program was counting the chimpanzees in Budongo Forest. The world's biggest population of chimpanzees was in Congo, but they were rapidly being butchered and eaten. The Ugandans had traditional taboos against eating apes, and they had the second-biggest population. But no one knew how many chimpanzees were left or where they were. My job was to lead a team of Ugandans on a census, for which I had zero qualifications. Debby hired me only because the real primatologist got malaria and pulled out at the last minute.

Those were interesting times. It was 1999 and eight gorilla tourists had been hacked to death with machetes in Bwindi National Park. Their bodies were found covered in deep slashes, their skulls smashed to pieces. The 150 rebels who surrounded their camp were part of the genocide in Rwanda in 1994 and used the mountains as a base.

Debby wrote three days before I was supposed to arrive and told me it was too dangerous and I should cancel my trip, but being young and stupid I told her I didn't care about rebels and I was coming anyway. In return, Debby threw me into the jungle like a football and hoped I would come out alive.

I envisioned myself slicing through the foliage with my hair swept into a glossy ponytail and stylish smudges of dirt underneath my cheekbones. I would walk among forest elephants in the glittering sunlight. I would adorn myself with pythons and gain a reputation among the rebel warlords as some kind of goddess. Perhaps I would even find my own personal Tarzan whom I could take home and show the wonders of civilization.

All I found in the jungle were bugs and a lack of personal space. The vegetation pressed in thick and close, and hacking your way through it wasn't as easy as Indiana Jones makes it look. We barely even saw chimpanzees, and when we did, they screamed their heads off and clearly wanted to rip our guts out.

After four months, I was ready to get out but I didn't want to go home. So I started helping Debby with the education programs around the office.

Then one afternoon, a pet pack was dropped on the doorstep and changed my life. Shivering in the back of the pet pack was Baluku, a two-year-old chimpanzee. Hunters had shot his mother and locked him in a coal shed for two months. When the Ugandan police confiscated him, he was as white as paper beneath his hair from lack of sunlight, and two slashes in his groin oozed pus where he had struggled against the rope that tethered him.

Debby took Baluku out of the pet pack and plastered him to my chest. And that is where he stayed for a month. Debby wasn't trying to give me the experience of a lifetime. Baluku needed someone to cling to and Debby needed a giant petri dish to inform her of the diseases he was carrying. If I got worms, it meant Baluku had worms. If I got giardia, Baluku had giardia.

But from the moment his tiny fingers latched onto my T-shirt, I was never the same. Before Baluku, I loved selfishly. I took my family for granted, my boyfriends were an extension of my vanity, and my friends were a fun way to pass the time. That wasn't enough for Baluku. He needed all of me. He didn't let go. I cooked, showered, slept, and went to the toilet with his frail arms wrapped around my neck. If I tried to give him to someone else even for a minute, he dug his fingers into my arms and didn't let go. If I did manage to pull him off, he would fall to the floor, hit his head on the ground, then finally wrap his arms around his knees and rock with a terrible blank look in his eyes.

It was the first time I had to give myself so completely. But I didn't feel trapped or resentful because I never had a moment's rest or a solid night's sleep. Baluku's love was its own reward.

Every day we sat under an old mango tree, playing tug-of-war and hide-and-seek. I chased him around the gnarled trunk and when I caught him, I blew raspberries into his belly and listened to his hoarse laughter. I watched him grow from a shattered husk to a youngster full of mischief. Despite the pee I occasionally slept in, the poop I combed through looking for parasites, and the bottles of milk I had to warm every two hours throughout the night, I woke each morning happier than I had ever been. I was making a difference. I was making Baluku's world a better place.

That was when I decided I was going to be just like Debby, who was part chimpanzee herself. Tough as a brick, proud, and stubborn, she had fits of temper that would send everyone diving under the furniture. But her life was full of meaning and purpose. There were more than forty chimps on Ngamba Island living on a hundred acres of forest, and every one of them had arrived in the same state as Baluku: shivering, terrified, and motherless.

I was going to dedicate my life to saving chimps. I would snatch them from the arms of death and bring them to a sanctuary I would call

Chimp Paradise. I would be on good terms with the president of wherever we were and he would listen attentively to my plans for chimpanzee conservation. I would stop deforestation. End global warming.

Unfortunately, I had run out of cash. Debby found me a job with a zebra project in Kenya. I didn't get paid, but we were fed and we slept in tents in the savanna. I counted zebra all the way from Nairobi to Ethiopia and back again, until I was really and truly broke.

I went home to Australia, intending to save up enough money to go back to Uganda, but life kept getting in the way. I took odd jobs. I was a secretary, a receptionist, and a pizza waitress. I managed to move on to more interesting employment, but I had no follow-through.

I went to Antarctica to measure the temperature of the ocean currents but I never published. I wrote a children's book and some magazine articles but I never got serious about writing. I worked in television but I never did any training so my camera work was only ever mediocre. I was a goldfish, swimming until I bumped the glass and then changing direction until I hit glass again.

After a bad breakup with a boyfriend, I decided what I needed was to go back to where it all started—the jungle. I wanted to work with chimpanzees in Africa, but the closest I could get was chasing monkeys in Costa Rica. I took it. And when I got there I remembered everything I hated about the jungle. Bugs. Vines. Four A.M. starts.

It didn't surprise anyone when I bailed out early. I was twenty-eight years old and I hadn't accomplished anything. I was bewildered and slightly traumatized by the whole monkey-chasing experience, so I bumped the glass and flipped again.

I had just finished a filming contract with Disney to film five-minute video postcards of animals in Central America. I talked them into another contract, this time filming animals in Africa. I asked Debby if I could come back to Uganda to film Baluku and the other chimps on Ngamba Island. She said yes, and I booked a plane and was on my way.

My plan was this:

I would make my pilgrimage to the island and call Baluku in from the forest. I would find him with one hand on his belly, serenely contemplating the distance. He would remember me, of course, and when he saw me, he would take both my hands in his, lean close, and whisper my destiny.

That was the plan, anyway.

DEBBY'S HOUSE WAS IN ENTEBBE, a forty-five-minute boat ride from the island. She wasn't home, and I was dirty and exhausted. My plane had been delayed for fifteen hours in the Nairobi airport. My bag, with my filming equipment, was lost somewhere between Uganda and Zanzibar. I dragged myself up the stairs and stumbled into the living room. Sitting on the sofa was a young man reading a book.

I did a double take. Men were uncommon in the chimp house. It was usually filled with giggling girls with hairy legs, like I used to be.

He lowered the book and looked at me. His blue eyes glittered through a mess of curls. I was acutely aware that I resembled something that had crawled out of a gutter. He raised an eyebrow that was as sharp as a crow's wing.

"Hi," he said. "I'm Brian."

He had an American accent with a faint Southern twang.

"What are you doing here?" I blurted out.

"I'll be working here soon, I hope."

"Volunteer?"

"Researcher."

"Ph.D.?"

"Just finished."

He pushed his curls back from his forehead. The way he looked at me could have set off a fire alarm.

You are not to fall in love with him, I told myself sternly. And you are definitely not going to sleep with him.

Of course I did both.

. . .

IT TOOK TWO DAYS to have sex with him and three to fall in love. Fast, even by my standards.

Debby took us to Jinja, the source of the Nile, where a friend of hers ran a guesthouse. From the balcony we could see the Nile flowing past on its way to Egypt. The chocolate-cake riverbank crumbled over the edges. The strength of the water pouring over the falls was enough to power the city. The whole place was a giant metaphor for sex.

Resist, I hissed at my erogenous zones, which were poking their heads out of a six-month coma. Everything about him, from his careless charm to his easy smile, made it clear I'd get more commitment from a stray cat.

"Ngamba is so different from what I'm used to," he said massaging my foot, oblivious to how wrong we were for each other. "You know I used to work in a biomedical lab?"

All inner dialogue screeched to a halt. I scrambled backward, appalled. I knew a little of what went on in biomedical labs and I couldn't believe he had slipped under Debby's radar. She would never let a biomedical researcher near her chimps. Brian held up his hands, as if to show me he wasn't hiding any tortured monkeys in his pockets.

"It's okay, Debby knows. I only started working in a lab because I was so nuts about chimps."

When Brian was nineteen, he went to college at Emory because he knew he could work with the chimps at the Yerkes National Primate Research Center. On his first day, he went on a tour with one of the lab assistants. She rolled her eyes while Brian babbled about how excited he was to see the chimps, how they were the most amazing animals ever and he couldn't wait to hug one.

The lab assistant led him into a corridor. On either side, there were rows and rows of concrete runs. Each run had a room inside and a room outside that were connected by a door. Reinforced metal bars protected people standing in the corridor. Almost.

"Okay," said the lab assistant. "Stand here."

She went into the next room and watched Brian through a window. Suddenly, unearthly screams flew into the corridor, so loud they nearly knocked him over. Brian saw black flashes as a dozen two-hundred-pound chimpanzees ran in from outside. They were almost as tall as he was and their thighs were as thick as tree trunks. Their hair stood on end as they howled for his blood. They bashed on the metal grille and bared their teeth, drooling in rage.

The first pile of shit hit Brian square in the face. This started a volley of shit balls that transformed Brian into a putrid mud pie. Shit splattered in his ears and in his mouth. Then Brian watched in horror as a chimpanzee jerked himself off, slurped up the cum, and spat it out. The missile dribbled down Brian's chest as the chimp screeched maniacally.

The lab assistant brought Brian out, watching smugly as he cleaned himself off as best he could.

"*Those*," she said, "are chimpanzees."

Brian's supervisor at Yerkes was studying reproduction. During one experiment, a probe was inserted into the chimpanzee's anus, then electricity was shot through the probe to make the chimpanzee ejaculate. The tissue around the anus is extremely sensitive, and the chimps could bleed for days. Brian's job was to clean the anal probes.

Occasionally, Brian passed the HIV unit, where the chimps were in crush cages. Each cage was just big enough for the chimp to stand up and turn around. The cages had a crank that moved one wall of the cage forward, jamming the chimps against the wall so a researcher could give them injections. The chimps spent their entire lives in these crush cages. They could see each other, but they weren't allowed to touch. The only contact they had was with humans who were covered head to toe in white fabric, goggles, a face mask, Kevlar gloves, and gum boots.

Brian didn't last much longer than a month at the medical station. He transferred to the field station and started working with a famous psychologist called Mike Tomasello. Mike was interested in intelligence, and Brian's new job was to figure out how chimpanzees think.

The chimps at the field station were better off than the ones at the medical station. They lived in social groups in enclosures that were no worse than those at most zoos. Brian convinced himself that this was as good as things were going to get. He loved the chimps, and he knew they looked forward to his experiments to break the monotony of the day.

Then he started working with a group of chimps called FS3. The other chimps at the field station were allowed to spend part of each day outside, but FS3 didn't have an outdoor area. Their "enclosure" was a concrete cage with some Plexiglas benches. There was one toy, a metal pole, and a swing made for a three-year-old chimp called Abby.

As Brian got to know FS3, he became bothered by their lack of freedom—not in terms of space but in terms of choice. Brian knew of a progressive research institute in Japan run by Professor Tetsuro Matsuzawa. Matsuzawa's chimps didn't have much space either, but the chimps had a lot of choices. Their enclosure was high and full of climbing structures, so the chimps could choose to go up or down. There were hiding places so the chimps could choose whom they wanted to hang out with. They could choose from a wide variety of food. Mothers could choose to be tested with their infants. Infants could participate in the research.

In the novel *1984* by George Orwell, the worst part of the dystopia wasn't Big Brother always watching or the drab postwar world or the dreary work. It was the absence of choice. The people had all their decisions made for them. They were told when to eat, how to behave, whom to love. And it was this dehumanizing lack of choice that made life so unbearable.

At Yerkes, the chimps had only one choice—inside or outside—and FS3 didn't have even that. They couldn't avoid their cage mates or hide from researchers. In the wild, chimps eat hundreds of different foods. By U.S. law, the only food you are required to feed a captive chimpanzee is "monkey chow," which has all the required nutritional components but tastes like cardboard. In a show of benevolence, Yerkes added half an orange to the diet.

Then there was the commercial side. Every part of the chimps could be bought and sold, their minds, their organs, their blood. It was $30 a day per chimp for the kind of behavior work that Brian did, and much more for any kind of medical testing.

After five years, Brian had had enough. His undergraduate degree was finished, and his supervisor, Mike Tomasello, was moving to Leipzig to become the director of psychology at the Max Planck Institute. The Germans were building Mike a $14 million facility at the Leipzig Zoo, inspired by Matsuzawa's institute in Japan. There would be spacious indoor and outdoor enclosures with grass and trees and climbing structures. When the Max Planck Institute told Mike he could get twenty-five chimps from anywhere he wanted, Brian started hatching a plot to bust out FS3.

Yerkes was already in trouble because it had too many chimps. In 1997, the National Institutes of Health banned the breeding of chimpanzees and demanded that Yerkes reduce its population. So when Mike asked for twenty-five chimps, including FS3, the director of Yerkes was thrilled. He hastily agreed and even promised to see the chimps off at the airport. All the plans were in place. Then Dr. Death stepped in.

The most powerful person at a biomedical center is not the director—it is the head vet. The head vet makes the rules about research, animal health, and animal management. Dr. Death was so obsessed with the physical health of her animals that she made their environment as sterile as possible. One of the keepers wanted to put honey between the pages of a phone book to give to the chimps as enrichment. No, said Dr. Death, honey can carry botulism. Rope in the cages for them to play with? No, they might strangle themselves.

Dr. Death was hated by anyone who cared about the chimps. Keepers used to fantasize about keeping her in a crush cage and feeding her monkey chow for a month.

With a purse of her thin lips, she blocked Brian's FS3 transfer. There was a biomedical lab in Louisiana that wanted Yerkes's excess chimps. FS3 would go there.

Brian was devastated. He wrote to the board at Emory, pleading for the decision to be overturned. But Dr. Death was too powerful. FS3 went to Louisiana.

The final straw for Brian was Abby. Several years after he left Yerkes, he met a malaria researcher at a conference who said she had tested some of the chimps in FS3. It turned out she had ordered Abby's spleen to be removed.

"Did you ever meet Abby?" asked Brian, desperate for news. "She's amazing. Really sweet. And super smart."

"No," said the researcher. "I never met any of the chimps."

Brian paused in his story as the sunlight winked on the Nile like a thousand golden eyes.

"I know how many people malaria kills. I think research should be done to stop it and that if necessary, research should be done on chimps to find a cure. But there is no reason for the chimps to live in concrete cages their whole lives. No reason they can't have ropes and toys and honey in phone books. And in 1997, only three hundred chimps out of the fifteen hundred in biomedical centers were being used in any kind of research. The rest were just sitting there, digging out their eyeballs in boredom and throwing shit.

"I put five years into Yerkes, telling myself it was okay. But it wasn't. And people like me, who study behavior, we tell ourselves that there's nowhere else we can do the research. We can't study them in the wild—we need to interact with them to figure out how they think. We need controlled conditions like a lab so we can be sure of the results. Apart from Leipzig, zoos aren't usually set up for research. And even if they are, most of them don't have a large enough sample to run the most powerful statistics.

"But paying biomedical labs to use their chimps means we are supporting how they operate and the conditions those chimps live in."

He pushed his hair back from his forehead and his eyes were all the colors of a shattered glacier.

"And there is somewhere else we can go. My Harvard adviser, Richard Wrangham, has a wild chimpanzee field site up-country, in

Kibale. He told me about Ngamba. We can work at sanctuaries. There are over a thousand chimps in sanctuaries all over Africa. They have night buildings we can run our experiments in. There are heaps of subjects, of all different ages. After we work with them for a couple of hours, they go out to a huge forest. They live like chimps, not rats in a cage."

He broke off and leaned in conspiratorially.

"I just applied for a million bucks from the Germans. If I get it, I'm going to make three sanctuaries, world-class research facilities. I'm going to build buildings better than any biomedical lab, where people can do the best studies ever. This is where we belong, in Africa, giving back more than we take away."

He was so passionate, so hungry, that I forgot everything. I stopped calculating how I could lose less than he would. How I could come out of this less broken, more intact. He had an intense frown creasing his forehead, and those glacier eyes were full of purpose. His dream lay between us, spilled and uncorrupted.

And right there and then, I wanted to fold myself up like a letter and deliver myself to his hands.

DESPITE MY BEST EFFORTS, the next morning I was naked and in bed with him. I squeezed my eyes shut to delay facing the opponent I'd given in to with such pitiful resistance.

I opened my eyes a little, so I could just see him through my eyelashes. He was watching me, a crooked smile tugging at his lips. I pulled up the sheet to cover myself, but frankly, it was a little late for such modesty.

"You asshole," I whispered. "You took advantage of me."

"*You* took advantage of *me*."

We grinned at each other stupidly.

"You've ruined my career," he said. "Debby's never going to let me work here once she finds out about this."

"What about me? I'm never going to live it down."

"I don't care. It was worth it."

"No, it wasn't. Get out of my room. Quick, before anyone knows you're here."

HE LEFT ON THE THIRD DAY. We said good-bye at the airport security gate. I had to pretend I didn't care. Falling in love with someone straight after you have sex is so not cool.

He waved and smiled. I did my best to smile and wave back.

Well, I thought as I walked out the door, guess I won't be seeing him again.

Chapter 3

"Check this out," Brian says, slamming a piece of paper on the kitchen table. It's four P.M. on a Thursday in Leipzig, Germany. A sparkling engagement ring is on my left hand, and six boxes of clothes are spilling onto the bedroom floor of our apartment.

I'm still jet-lagged, if that's possible after three months, and still getting used to the idea that I've moved halfway across the world to marry a man I barely know.

After the initial three days in Uganda, he flew me to Germany for two weeks. Five months later, he flew to Australia for two weeks. Two weeks after that he flew back to Australia and asked me to marry him. The whole process took a year, six hundred megabytes of e-mail, and almost a thousand hours on the phone. But the time we had spent face-to-face before we decided to get married amounted to thirty-one days.

I quit my job at the Discovery Channel in Sydney, which wasn't such a hard decision since I was about to be fired anyway. My job was scheduling programs, and I had a television on my desk, but instead of watching nature documentaries, I switched to *Buffy the Vampire Slayer* every day at three P.M., followed by *Baywatch Hawaii* and *90210*. I wasn't exactly a stellar employee. Then I screwed up a $3 million advertisement deal and I was pretty much finished.

Moving to Germany was almost a relief. Brian got his million bucks from the Germans and he had just spent three months at Ngamba Island. The chimps loved the tests, the keepers were amazingly helpful, and the results were better than he had hoped. He promised if I came to Germany I could go on his trips with him and help him with his research.

I pictured us in matching safari outfits, striding through the Ngamba forest, baby chimpanzees dangling from our arms. I would make insightful and intelligent comments that would revolutionize his research. He would introduce me as the inspiration behind his ideas and I would lower my eyes modestly in a way that made everyone realize it was true.

But Brian has suddenly changed the game plan. We aren't going to Ngamba anymore. We're going to Congo, to study bonobos.

"Bonobo? Is that some kind of tree?"

Brian looks at me incredulously. "I can't believe you don't know what a bonobo is. They're a different species of chimpanzee."

"How come I've never heard of them?"

Brian sighs. "No one has. They're ignored by everyone, especially chimp people, who should know better. I guess I shouldn't be surprised they escaped you too."

Now I'm on the defensive. "You said we were going to Ngamba. Why are we going to Congo to study some weird chimp?"

"They aren't chimps. They're a different species. You know how chimps hunt and kill each other? How they have war and kill babies? Well, bonobos don't do any of that. They're more peaceful."

"They sound boring."

"They have a lot of sex."

"So do rabbits."

Brian opens his mouth as if to go on, but the look on my face changes his mind. "Trust me, you're going to love them."

IN THE FOLLOWING WEEKS, I refuse to listen to why Brian's so excited about bonobos, despite his pointedly leaving journal articles and research papers around the flat. I feel gypped. I'm a chimp girl. The idea that there's another primate cousin out there somewhere is as interesting as finding another freckle on my arm.

I want to go to Ngamba to see Baluku. I spent a few days with him last year after Brian left. He looked remarkably like a Buddha, with a belly the size of a watermelon. Instead of leaning forward and telling me my destiny, he whooped and yelled and grabbed my hand and shook it frantically. We were so happy to see each other, I didn't want to leave.

Brian said Baluku was one of the smartest chimps he had ever met, and though I obviously had nothing to do with this, I couldn't help feeling smug. I wasn't exactly sure what Brian's research was about, but I knew it involved playing fun problem-solving games. I wanted to play them with Baluku and the other chimps on Ngamba, not some weird chimp strangers on the other side of Africa.

I halfheartedly pick up the piece of paper Brian has left on the kitchen table. It's an article about Congo. I'm not really interested but I read it anyway. It tells the story of Zainabo Alfani, a widow from Kisangani in the east. She was on her way to Bunia with her two daughters and her six-month-old baby to sell some diamonds. She was on the bus with fourteen other women when they heard gunfire. The bus driver told everyone to get off the bus and hide in the jungle. As soon as they got off he drove away, abandoning them in the forest.

Soon after, eighteen soldiers appeared. They ordered the women to take off their clothes. One by one, the soldiers examined the women's genitals. A witch doctor had told them that long vagina lips would protect them from bullets. Zainabo's were the longest. The soldiers shot the other women and cut off Zainabo's vagina lips. The soldiers raped her while she was bleeding until she fainted.

When she woke up, the soldiers were eating part of her thigh. They cut her right foot, her left arm, and her right breast to collect her blood. They drank her blood mixed with water and ate pieces of her flesh.

The soldiers brought Zainabo and her children farther into the jungle, where a cook was preparing human flesh skewered over a fire. While Zainabo watched, they drowned her daughters, ten-year-old Alima and eight-year-old Mulassi, in a barrel, then pierced their stomachs. They ate one daughter with *foufou* (mashed manioc powder) in front of her, then saved the other one until later in the night.

A man approached Zainabo. She begged him to leave her dead body with her baby on the road so someone might bury them. He didn't answer. Instead, he took a knife and cut her stomach open. She fainted.

When she woke up, she was in a hospital with her baby. It was two years before she could leave. One of her rapists had given her AIDS. She traveled to Kinshasa to tell her story to the U.N. and died a month later. Her son was three years old.

By the time I finish reading, the blood has drained from my face and I am shaking.

"Fucked-up shit, huh?" Brian says, nodding as though he is pleased he's finally got my attention.

"I'm not going."

"What?"

"If you want to go to a country where they eat people, you go ahead. But I'm not coming."

"You have to come. You speak French. I can't do it without you."

I am baffled by Brian's logic. "And that convinces me how? Why can't you study bonobos somewhere else?"

"They don't live anywhere else. Just Congo."

"I don't understand. You say you love me. You want to marry me. And then you want to take me to a country where they cut off women's vagina lips. You're not making any sense."

"Okay," he says. "You don't have to come. But what are you going to do while I'm gone? Stay here in Leipzig by yourself?"

I look out the window. It's August, the end of summer, and it has been raining for three weeks. The clouds hang so low, they float on the same plane as our apartment on the fifth floor. It's already turning cold.

Leipzig isn't exactly a barrel of laughs. The East Germans had to deal with the aftermath of World War II in the forties, the Russians in the fifties, and the Stasi in the eighties, when one in four civilians was a spy. Our secretary's father had been kidnapped by the secret police for listening to the Beatles. Our baker's uncle was shot. Not surprisingly, there is a heaviness to the place. An air of suspicion.

I don't know anyone. I don't speak German. I'm so homesick for Australia that I just spent three days on the sofa, crying. This isn't at all working out how I expected. I contemplate being alone in the apartment for a month and try to think of a reason to go to Congo. I can think of only one.

My father was in the Vietnam War. To say he came back shattered doesn't really cover it. There were nights when he would barricade himself in the bedroom, stacking up the furniture against the door, making machine-gun noises and hollering for backup. During New Year's Eve fireworks, he hit the ground in the middle of astonished holiday crowds, covering his head with his hands. There were stints in mental institutions and rare but explosive outbursts of violence.

He left my mother when I was five and my sister was two. Eventually, when I was nineteen, he left all of us for Southeast Asia. Not back to Vietnam, but to Cambodia, Thailand, and Laos. He teaches young men landscape gardening and sends them to college to get an education. Never young women, always young men. I wonder if it's some kind of penance.

I've tried, over the years, to patch things up. I've been alternately furious, distant, and miserable. But I could never understand how he can put so much into the lives of children who don't even belong to him and remain so emotionally unavailable to his own family.

Why have I never heard about this Congo war? I know about Iraq and Afghanistan. Thanks to George Clooney, I even know a little bit about Darfur. But for almost a decade, Congo has suffered the bloodiest war since World War II. By 2005, almost four million people have died, from either disease, or starvation, or bullets. And no one talks about it.

I've never lived through a war. I don't know for sure whether what happened to my father happened to everyone or if we were just unlucky. And part of me wants to know. I want to see what my father lived through. I want to believe that what happened was not his fault. That if he could have, he would have been a better man.

And that is how I end up in a Paris hotel room before the ten a.m. flight to Kinshasa, shivering and dehydrated, thinking I just made the biggest mistake of my life.

Chapter 4

$\mathscr{B}$rian and I sit in the Kinshasa airport with his Harvard adviser, Professor Richard Wrangham, in complete darkness.

"Well," says Richard in his tallyho English accent. "This is a good start, isn't it?"

I've given our passports and U.S.$150 to a man the size of a house called Jean Marie Baston. We hired him as an "*homme de protocol*," which roughly translates to someone who bribes you through customs. I'm contemplating the wisdom of handing over our identities, given that two seconds after he disappeared, the lights went out. But I didn't have much choice. When an ex-boxer with the physique of the Incredible Hulk demands your passports and 150 bucks, you give them to him.

I hug my backpack to my chest. I'm suspicious we are about to be robbed but I'm unsure of what to do about it.

I was duly warned before we arrived. Congo just made the top ten most dangerous countries list of the U.S. State Department. I've been warned to expect pillaging, vehicle thefts, carjackings, extra-judicial killings, rapes, kidnapping, ethnic tensions, and continued military operations. Every foreign office I've spoken to said we would definitely be robbed and would almost certainly be killed. Excellent.

The lights flicker on and Baston comes barreling down the corridor with our passports and four massive bags. I stand up and smile, relieved, but his eyes are wild and his fierce jaw is clenched.

"*Cours,*" he says in French. *Run.*

"Excuse me?" I begin, but Baston has already turned and is running back down the corridor, hauling more than 170 pounds of luggage with him.

"What's going on?" Brian asks.

I grab his arm and say, "Run!"

Brian, Richard, and I catch up to Baston, breathless. He explains that $150 wasn't enough, and the customs officials wanted more. He refused and effectively stole our bags. I look at the men lounging around with AK-47s and run faster.

In the parking lot, Baston hands us our passports, checking furtively over his shoulder. Children surround us with their arms outstretched.

"Madam, madam," they beg.

"Beat it," says Baston, batting his giant hand. Then he starts walking away.

"Wait," I cry, "you can't leave us here! Where are you going?"

"I'm done," he says, tossing his head toward the driver of a minivan. "This man will take you to your hotel. Tomorrow you will be taken to the sanctuary."

And then, like the Hulk, he vanishes.

THE NEXT MORNING, our driver, Papa Sedico, seems to be doing his best to drive us off a cliff.

Part of the problem is that the road is more a postmodern abstraction of a road than a functional strip of tarmac you can drive a car on. Rain has eroded sections of the roadway into giant chasms that drop off into nothing, so that as the car swerves around corners, we are treated to glimpses of the valley below. Overturned shells of vehicles are scattered by the wayside, stripped of mechanical parts and electrical wiring.

As we pass through villages, hordes of children run after us.

"Papa Sedico! Papa Sedico!" they cry, cheering raucously. Papa Sedico tosses handfuls of sweets out the window. I close my eyes and pray for him to keep both hands on the steering wheel.

Finally we come to a bridge held together with rusty iron barrels and covered in railroad planks. It looks barely strong enough for a goat, much less a car.

Papa Sedico eases onto the bridge. Every few seconds we tilt violently to one side. Through the window, I have a disturbing view of the river rushing beneath us. Plank by plank, we crawl across, until by some miracle, we are on the other side and a sign greets us like a placard for heaven:

LOLA YA BONOBO SANCTUARY

"*Nous sommes arrivés!*" Papa Sedico announces cheerily as the car rolls to a standstill. I jump out of the deathmobile as fast and far as my trembling legs will take me.

I look around, and the first surprise is the forest. Besides mango trees, we have barely seen a single tree since we arrived in Kinshasa. The sanctuary is covered in them. Feathered palm trees, wide-leafed umbrella trees, trees with weird curling seed pods. In the distance, a giant forest with languid vines and flocks of birds stretches as far as the horizon.

The sanctuary is built on a hill that slopes toward a large lake. Tall red flowers bloom around its edges. Water lilies float on the surface. Below us, the river snakes over small rapids. Above us, a stone path leads to several colonial houses. It is more a resort than an orphanage for the world's most endangered ape.

"*Bonjour!*" calls a voice above us. A woman descends the stone steps. Her hair is the most extraordinary color I have ever seen. It is the burning amber of a setting sun. It is the electric orange of copper wire. The light catches it and sends sparks flying in every direction.

"I'm so glad you are here," she says in a sultry French accent.

"*Mon Dieu.*" Self-consciously she touches her face, which is not the unfortunate blotchy complexion of most redheads but a smooth olive. "I must look such a mess."

She looks like no such thing. Her eyes are kingfisher blue, and her long lashes have been carefully combed with mascara, her eyebrows smoothed with russet pencil. She exudes Chanel No. 5. Standing next to her, I am doing a fair impression of a sweating bushpig.

"Semendwa is pregnant and we have been up all night waiting for the baby." She extends her hand to Richard first. "Claudine André."

We introduce ourselves.

"You must be hungry," says Claudine, as if she has guessed my stomach is devouring itself. "Come and eat."

LUNCH IS BY THE RIVER. Our pagoda is built on the sand and a cooling breeze fans the tablecloth. The fare is mouthwatering. Fried sweet bananas (the edges crispy and caramelized), moambe chicken (cooked in a kind of curry sauce with hints of peanut, cayenne, and sesame), *foufou* (mashed cassava), and saka saka (boiled cassava leaves).

"All this," she says, waving her hand around the sanctuary, "is the last forest in Kinshasa. Mobutu used to come here on the weekends."

I nearly choke on my chicken. Mobutu is a secret fascination of mine. Being here, where he walked, slept, and ate, is as good as being in Elvis Presley's Graceland.

Brian would be thrilled if he knew about my clandestine obsession with the man they called the Leopard. He would be even more smug if he knew he was the one who started it, one rainy afternoon in Leipzig.

I was watching *Strange Love,* a reality television show starring Flavor Flav from the hip-hop group Public Enemy. In the show, Flav was running around Italy with the washed-up actress Brigitte Nielsen, who was in the barbarian movie *Red Sonja* with Arnold Schwarzenegger circa 1985. Anyway, Flav was wearing a metallic Viking hat and baring his teeth in a gold-plated grin. A giant diamond-studded clock hung around his neck and bling dripped from every possible appendage.

"He looks like Mobutu," Brian commented.

"Who?"

Calling politics my weak point is an understatement. I can barely point to Iraq on a map and I only just figured out that North and South Korea are different countries. Brian, who reads the news obsessively, sees my disinterest in world politics as a disease he's going to cure me of.

"Mobutu Sese Seko was the Congolese dictator who stole a four-billion-dollar fortune before he died."

I made a noncommittal grunt.

"Really," said Brian, trying desperately to interest me. "He was a celebrity nightmare."

Strange Love cut to a commercial. I turned to Brian.

"Celebrity? As in diva? As in tantrums? As in Mariah?"

Mariah Carey and I transformed from virgin to whore to happily engaged roughly on the same timeline. In fact, Mariah and I are practically identical twins separated at birth. Except for her eight-octave range, $225 million fortune, and ability to throw the kind of tantrums in public I can only dream about.

"Mariah is nothing. Mobutu hired jumbo jets to fly to Disneyland. He spent millions on shopping sprees. If he didn't like someone, he didn't fire them, he had them killed."

When Brian left for work, I found a video of Mobutu on YouTube in a documentary called *When We Were Kings*. When no one in the United States would foot the $10 million bill to bring the two legendary fighters Muhammad Ali and George Foreman together, Mobutu flew them over for the fight of all fights, the Rumble in the Jungle. Mobutu *did* look very Flavor Flav. He wore a leopard-skin hat that Flav would definitely covet and geek-chic glasses.

I did more research and found out Mobutu's father was a cook who worked for a Belgian judge. When Mobutu's father died, the judge's wife took Mobutu under her wing and educated him. As a young man he was bright and passionate, influenced by the writings of Winston Churchill, Charles de Gaulle, and Niccolò Machiavelli.

Mobutu befriended the handsome, charismatic Patrice Lumumba, who, after the long Belgian regime, would become Congo's first democratically elected president and great hope in 1960. But Lumumba was no puppet; he spoke out viciously against Belgian colonial rule and the West and threatened to cooperate with the Soviets. It was the height of the Cold War, and the CIA paid Mobutu to keep an eye on Lumumba and his communist links with Russia.

As soon as he could, Mobutu betrayed Lumumba and provided intelligence that led to Lumumba's assassination by the Belgians and the Americans. Lumumba's body was cut up into pieces and dissolved in acid so there would be no martyr's grave. Mobutu, backed by the West, stepped into his place and ruled supreme for more than three decades.

Money poured from Europe and the United States into Congo in exchange for concessions to mine its vast, rich mineral deposits. And Mobutu began to spend it in a way that did make Mariah seem like celebrity small fry.

He renamed Congo Zaire and renamed himself Mobutu Sese Seko Kuku Ngbendu Wa Za Banga, which translates to "Mobutu the all-powerful warrior who goes from conquest to conquest leaving fire in his wake." He also went by "the Messiah." At the beginning of television programs, he was shown descending from parted clouds.

On a typical day, he would wake up at seven A.M. and go straight to a team of Chinese masseurs. He ate breakfast on the terrace of his palace that he built in the jungle of Gbadolite. Surrounding the palace were plantations of oranges and grapefruit, along with a ranch for the five thousand sheep he had flown in from Venezuela. Around nine he would start drinking Laurent-Perrier pink champagne from his fifteen-thousand-bottle wine cellar.

Lunch might be mussels flown in from Belgium. After lunch, he had appointments with his hairdresser, flown in from Paris; his barber, flown in from New York; and his stylist, flown in from Italy. The palace was a United Nations of high-class employees that would have made any Hollywood celebrity green with envy. His lavish dinners were attended by relatives waiting for cash, which he handed out by the truckload.

When his daughter got married, her dress was worth $70,000, but her jewels were worth $3 million. The wedding cake, flown in from Paris, cost almost as much as the dress. He had palatial vacation homes in Portugal, Madrid, Switzerland, and Paris, not to mention a luxury cruiser on the Congo River that had oyster-shaped couches swathed in pink silk. Seriously.

To maintain power, he ordered the execution and torture of his enemies. His soldiers stood by the election polls with guns to ensure that people made the right decision. But in the end, bribery was his weapon of choice. His drawers were stuffed with $100 bills. His attendants followed him with enough cash to fill several garbage bags. He paid off his ministers, his attendants, his civil servants. Everyone who was anyone drove a Mercedes.

During his thirty-two-year rule, Mobutu stole between $4 billion and $15 billion. Though he paid his generals lavishly, his solders were starving. The roads were unpaved, garbage lay rotting in the streets, and the health system was on the verge of collapse. Unpaid teachers demanded gifts from boy students and sex from the girls. The most cosmopolitan cities rarely had electricity. The water was polluted. The national economy, which before 1974 had grown 7 percent every year, began to fall and did not stop falling.

In 1989, Mobutu visited President George Bush, who greeted Mobutu as among America's "most valued friends." But a year later, the Cold War ended, and so did the financial support of the United States. Zaire was bankrupt. Its foreign debts ran into the billions, and its people were completely destitute.

I smooth my hands over the side of my chair. So this is where he sat, the man whose leopard-skin hat was fashioned in Paris, who ordered cargo planes filled with haute couture, champagne, and chandeliers.

I wondered if he had ever walked around the lake, his hands behind his back, and contemplated the cost. Or if he thought of nothing, just breathed in the heady scent of the water lilies, $100 bills floating on the air behind him.

AFTER LUNCH, we hold our bloated bellies and sigh. Claudine is adept at entertaining. She gracefully fills in the conversation, asks how our trip was, how we found the sanctuary, whether we need anything.

"Well, of course," she says, getting down to the reason why we have come. "Now you must see the bonobos."

Chapter 5

⁊⊘

*F*or thousands of years, people have wondered what makes us human.

There is no doubt that as a species, we are pretty spectacular. When I was nineteen, I went to visit my father in Cambodia. He took me to Angkor Wat, the kingdom built for Suryavarman II in the twelfth century. On one of the temples beneath vines prising apart the sandstone bricks, I found an engraving of a dancing *aspara*. She was one sculpture among thousands, but her face was so beautiful, the cheekbones and full lips so exquisitely carved, that I stared at her for half an hour.

I was struck with wonder that even a thousand years ago, humans were capable of creating something so incredible as that face in the jungle. We can fly like birds and swim like fish. We can trawl volcanoes on the ocean floor and crack the ice on the Antarctic shelf. We can break through Earth's atmosphere and stare at our world from space.

Each day of our life is a miracle, from the cars that drive us to the computers on our desks to the buildings we sit in. Even our sandwich bread is a complicated orchestra of wheat grown in vast fields, protected by chemicals, harvested by machines, processed in factories, and shipped to our stores.

How is it that humans have come so far, and our closest living relatives are still barely out of the trees?

Humans didn't evolve from chimpanzees or bonobos. Instead, we all shared a common ancestor around six million years ago. Slowly we changed. We stood up. We got smarter. We tamed fire. And millions of years later, here we are.

But which change happened first? Which change led to all the other changes? Was it language? Was it culture? Was it intelligence?

When I was a kid, we played this game called Spot the Difference. There were two pictures almost exactly the same, and you had to figure out what was in one that wasn't in the other. Maybe in one of them a lady was wearing a hat, or there was a cat with a blue tail instead of a pink one.

Scientists use chimpanzees as a Spot the Difference for what makes us human. If we have something and chimpanzees don't, then that might be what makes us special. It sounds like an easy exercise, but for forty years, chimpanzees have been confounding us. It turns out chimpanzees have a type of culture. They make tools. They use gestures to communicate. They have sophisticated political systems and emotions that can only be described as love, grief, and jealousy.

Even the dark side of our nature that we thought was exclusively ours, such as hunting and war, is found in chimpanzees too. A chimpanzee community, similar to many human communities, is male-dominated. Females can be raped; infants might be killed. As a chimp, you have more chance of being killed by another chimp than by anything else.

When thinking about what makes us human, we turn to chimpanzees for inspiration, insight, and solace. They are the mirror we hold to our face to search for recognition. They are the model of how our ancestors may have lived all those years ago.

But we have another closest living relative. Bonobos look almost exactly like chimpanzees, except they have black faces, pink lips, and hair parted down the middle. They live in only one country, the Democratic Republic of the Congo. Their populations are so scattered that it is impossible to know how many there are, although current estimates are between ten thousand and forty thousand. They were never brought to America to be tested on in laboratories. They were never sent into space. There are very few of them in zoos.

Even people like me who are familiar with chimps barely even know there are two "closest living relatives" to humans. Like an embarrassing relative, bonobos are frequently missing from the family tree. According to Microsoft Word's spell-checker, "bonobo" isn't even a word.

Bonobos were discovered late one afternoon in a little town called Tervuren in Belgium. An American anatomist called Hal Coolidge was rifling through a tray of bones stored in the museum. He picked up a skull from south of the Congo River that he first thought was an adolescent chimpanzee. But the cracks, or sutures, along the skull were fused, which meant it was an adult. Coolidge knew he was holding in his hands a different species altogether.

However, his rival Ernst Schwarz published that the strange juvenilized skull was nothing more than a subspecies of chimpanzee. And so ever since bonobos were recognized in 1933, a full 150 years after the discovery of chimpanzees, they have lived in the shadow of their more famous cousins. They were even given the name "pygmy chimpanzee," implying that bonobos are a cute miniature of the real thing.

There is scarcely any research published on bonobos. They pop in and out of scientific history like a streaker running naked through a baseball game. Robert Yerkes was one of the first people to study chimpanzees, in the 1920s. He had a chimpanzee called Prince Chim that he swore was a "genius among apes," who turned out to be a bonobo.

But the world's most famous bonobo is Kanzi. Born in a biomedical laboratory, Kanzi knows more than two hundred words of Yerkish (a language of iconic symbols named after Robert Yerkes) and understands novel sentences to a degree that shows that in many cases he can comprehend spoken English. He can light a fire and cook hamburgers, and he loves playing Pac-Man. Together with other signing apes, Kanzi has proven that complex forms of communication are not unique to humans.

There are at least ten field sites in East and West Africa at which groups of chimpanzees have been studied for more than twenty years. In 2005, there were more than a thousand chimpanzees in laboratories in America where researchers study their physiology, biology, and cognition.

There is only one long-term bonobo field site, called Wamba, which is run by the Japanese. In 1973, a young Japanese man called Takayoshi Kano set off into the Congo basin for a five-month survey of bonobos before he arrived at Wamba. Kano rode his bicycle for hundreds of miles and waded through the swamps, sometimes alone, to reach his field site. He walked the survey area between the Congo and Luilaka rivers. He traveled to villages and talked to the native Mongo people, trying to get an idea of the number of bonobos in the area.

Since Kano began his study, for thirty-five years, the Japanese have told us almost everything we know about bonobos: their diet, their habitat, their social structure. Wamba is still the only place you can get a good look at bonobos in the wild. But there was never a Jane Goodall or a Dian Fossey for bonobos. And Western mainstream media were not willing to focus on a young man who spoke only Japanese.

It wasn't until the 1980s that Frans de Waal published a study of bonobos in the San Diego Zoo. He saw tongue kissing, fellatio, and a *kama sutra* of sexual positions. Before de Waal, people thought that nonconceptive sex, or "sex for fun," was unique to humans. But bonobos were having sex in all sorts of crazy ways, including the missionary position, which no one had ever seen in an animal. De Waal also concluded that bonobos were female-dominated and that compared to chimps, they committed very little violence. He suggested that here was another model for human behavior, one that didn't include war and bloodshed.

The media sensation surrounding his discovery riled other scientists, especially since his data was based on observations of bonobos in a zoo and not wild bonobos. In fact, de Waal's findings generated such a backlash that even bonobo researchers started saying that de Waal's image of the "make love not war" hippie ape was an exaggeration.

With the tiny amount of data on wild bonobos compared to chimpanzees, there was no way of knowing what was really going on. Maybe bonobos do kill each other, only no one has seen it yet. Maybe their sex isn't as frequent or ingenious in the wild. Others went farther and said that de Waal's observations were worthless because they were based on a handful of wacky bonobos in a zoo.

When Brian took Frans de Waal's class at Emory, he was fascinated by bonobos. But there were no bonobos in zoos for three hundred miles, and the only bonobos at Yerkes were two males who lived in a concrete run and threw shit. So Brian joined everyone else and played Spot the Difference with chimpanzees.

When Brian's professor Mike Tomasello moved to Leipzig, Brian did his Ph.D. with Richard Wrangham at Harvard, who studies wild chimpanzees at Kibale National Park in Uganda. Richard is unusually broad-minded for a field primatologist. Most people who observe primates in the wild are purists. They think if you interfere with the animals at all, then what you see isn't real. For instance, when Jane Goodall first saw chimps killing each other, the purists suggested she had turned them into psychopaths by feeding them bananas. So you can imagine what they think of experiments where the setting is unnatural and the animals are manipulated.

When Brian wanted out of Yerkes, Richard, who was a good friend of Debby's, suggested Brian study the chimps at Ngamba Island. When Brian said he wanted to study bonobos, Richard suggested Brian continue his experiments at Lola ya Bonobo.

LOLA YA BONOBO is the only bonobo sanctuary in the world. More than sixty orphans live in a seventy-five-acre forest just outside of Kinshasa.

All ape sanctuaries, including Lola, exist because of the bushmeat trade. In many African countries, where livestock is scarce and expensive, the easiest way to get protein is to shoot it.

Some tribes in the Congo Basin eat more meat than the French—more than a million metric tons a year, or three times the weight of the Empire State Building. Up to 80 percent of the meat they eat comes from wildlife. Hunters prefer large mammals because there is a lot of meat per kill. Apes are especially targeted because they live in communities, so if you find one, you've probably found thirty you can kill at the same time.

In every African country, it is illegal to kill or sell bonobos, chimpanzees, and gorillas. All three great apes are endangered species and are protected by law and CITES (Convention on International Trade in Endangered Species). If hunters are caught, the meat is confiscated and destroyed. But after killing an ape community, the hunters usually find one or two infants clinging to their dead mothers. The infants don't have enough meat on their bones to make a good meal, but the hunters might try to sell them as pets to a wealthy family or to a wildlife trafficker.

If the authorities confiscate the infant, what do they do with it? Apes live for sixty years and grow many times stronger than a grown man. With no mother and no community, the infant can't be thrown back into the wild. The infant could be put in a local zoo, but in countries where the average citizen is starving, the zoos are little better than torture chambers. They could be sent to a zoo overseas, but this has a nasty smell to it, since in the past, foreign zoos have encouraged the traffic of wild apes for their exhibits. They could be euthanized, but killing an endangered species, even an infant who won't survive in the wild, has its own dilemmas.

As you run through the options, only one solution presents itself. There needs to be a facility within the country where the infants can go, where they can grow up with their own kind and live out their natural lives.

Sanctuaries can take many forms. They can be an island, like Ngamba, or an ex–presidential retreat, like Lola. Generally sanctuaries have a large forest where the apes can play during the day and a building nearby where the apes come in to sleep at night.

Most African countries are in no position to fund sanctuaries, so sanctuaries rely on private donations from people in Europe and the United States, as well as grants from NGOs.

Claudine started her bonobo sanctuary in 1994. She has lived in Congo since she was three years old and has had several successful careers, including selling haute couture and African art. She waited until most people her age were getting ready for retirement before she started on her last, most challenging project.

AFTER LUNCH, Claudine guides us along the river, between the ponds, and up a path that is bordered on one side by a wall of trees and on the other by a large lake. Soon we come to a stadium, a kind of amphitheater that looks out onto a natural stage. The backdrop is a thick-leaved forest with vines looping from the branches. An electric fence snakes around the forest, occasionally crackling in the heat. To the right is an inlet that joins the lake where wild lilies stand as tall as people. In the foreground, there is a grassy lawn covered in tropical fruit and sugarcane. It is here that we get our first glimpse of the creatures we have come so far to see.

In the dead center of the food patch is Mimi. At twenty-four years old, Mimi is the oldest bonobo at the sanctuary. Claudine calls her La Princesse because she led a pampered life with a human family until she was fifteen. Mimi slept in a bed and was perfectly toilet-trained. She made herself snacks from the refrigerator and ate with a knife and fork. She was an avid reader of fashion magazines and scoured the pages as intently as if she were deciding on her next season's wardrobe. Most apes who are raised by humans don't realize they are apes. When Mimi arrived at Lola, she couldn't understand why Claudine wanted her to live outside with savage, hairy beasts.

"A fifteen-year-old bonobo virgin," says Claudine ruefully. "Can you imagine? When the other bonobos tried to make sex with her, she screamed and ran away."

Mimi may have entered Lola as La Princesse, but there is nothing frilly about her now. She reminds me of Empress Dowager Cixi, the original dragon lady, who ruled China in the nineteenth century. In the notoriously male-dominated Chinese society, where women could be bought and had fewer rights than a horse, Empress Dowager outwitted every one of her enemies and ruled supreme for almost half a century.

Mimi even looks like the empress dowager, with a low, sloping mouth wrinkled toward the lips. Her big ears are flaccid with age. She has a thousand creases around her eyes and a droopiness to her mouth that might trick you into thinking she is a harmless old lady, but her eyes are as bright as flint. They sweep like laser beams over the group, scanning the subjects in her kingdom to ensure everything is to her liking.

Next to Mimi is Semendwa, a beautiful, full-bodied bonobo with curves in all the right places. She reclines on the grass like a painting of Venus, her round breasts sloping voluptuously toward her nipples. She is heavily pregnant, and her swollen belly only makes her more of a goddess. Her eyes are wide but slanted exotically toward the corners, and she is covered with flowing black hair. All bonobos have pink lips, but Semendwa's could have been painted on with the finest coral pigment. All she needs is a boy fanning her with feathers, and she would be the bonobo reincarnation of Cleopatra.

On the other side of Mimi is a young female called Isiro. She has boyish long limbs, and the lines of her body are cut like a knife. She has a sharp face, with high, angular cheekbones and ears pointed toward the tips like an elf's. Isiro is known as the testosterone police because she keeps the boys under control.

It is strange that the food patch is monopolized by females. Among chimps, females have to wait their turn and beg for scraps. Where are the males?

There is a loud, high-pitched whinny as a charging bonobo heads straight for me, sliding on a small branch.

When I was in the jungle in Uganda, I was once surrounded by a group of male chimpanzees. They crept up so silently that I didn't realize I was trapped until it was too late. At that moment a chorus of bloodcurdling cries filled the forest. They pounded the trees, their enormous hands echoing off the solid mahogany trunks. Branches broke like cracking thunder and shook like they were possessed by demons. The screams went on and on, until my hair stood on end and I was trembling. Through the leaves I saw fierce glinting eyes. I smelled something sharp and rotten. It was my own fear.

This bonobo has nothing on them. He just charged me with a twig. He lifts his chin as though he's assessing the impact his display has had on me.

"Oooh," I tell him. "Scary."

He stares at me in dead seriousness.

Claudine lowers her voice, anxious not to embarrass him.

"Tatango was recently…corrected, by the females."

Three months ago, Tatango was in another bonobo group on the other side of the sanctuary. There was a bonobo called Max, also known as "the gorilla" because he spent a few years at the gorilla sanctuary in Brazzaville before he came to Lola. If Max were human, he would be a gay fashionista. He has the most perfect hair you can imagine. Even though grooming one another is an integral part of bonobo society, Max doesn't let anyone touch his hair. No way, no how. It grows in a glossy mane straight from a shampoo commercial.

Max is a favorite of the females and Tatango was wild with jealousy. Tatango started to attack Max. He pulled his hair and sank his teeth into whatever body part was available. This is pretty normal behavior for chimpanzees, and if Tatango had been a chimpanzee, he would quickly have found himself at the top of the hierarchy, and Max and his glorious hair would have been a cowering, bloody mess in the corner.

But a group of female bonobos called the Terrible Five, led by Semendwa and Isiro, decided they'd had enough of Tatango and his big chimpanzee ideas. So one day, after Tatango's attack left Max screaming in distress, the Terrible Five turned on Tatango. And their wrath was vicious. They bit chunks out of his leg and his arms. They tore off one of his fingernails and tried to bite off his testicles.

"Since that day," Claudine says, "Tata has never made a problem. But also I think he is a little bit sad."

By the edge of the lake in front of us, a bonobo called Kikongo is doing headstands in a pile of moss. His feet are covered in green mossy shoes and he waves them around while he stands on his head, laughing.

I walk farther still and find a bonobo called Mikeno sitting in the posture of Rodin's thinker, his fist beneath his chin and his elbow resting on his knee. Now here is an interesting face. His lips are full and plump, as though evolved for kissing. Long black hair parted down the middle. Muscular, graceful limbs. Thickly lashed eyes the color of beaten copper.

I hold my camera so the lens sits between the wires. I must be careful. Every second, eight thousand volts pulse through the silver fence encircling the forest. It is high noon, and the heat snaps on the electricity like a whip.

"Mikeno is so beautiful," says Claudine behind me, her red hair flaming in the midday light. "So gentle and kind, even for a bonobo."

"Where did he come from?" I ask.

"He was my first bonobo. I took him from my friend Denise because of her grandson, Paul."

Denise's daughter lived in Angola with her husband. She was heavily pregnant and Denise was waiting for her to arrive in Kinshasa to give birth to the baby. Two days before Denise's daughter was to leave Angola, the rebel army passed through the village.

They stabbed her to death with a machete and slit open her stomach. They threw the baby to one side. Her son, Paul, saw everything. "They tortured him. His body was covered in burns, but in the end, they let him live."

I stand up slowly, feeling sick. This part of the world is totally fucked up.

"I was helping at the Kinshasa Zoo. The animals were starving and I brought them food. Denise and I had known each other for years; we were very close. I wanted to help her, give her something else to think about besides what had happened. All Paul would talk about was his mother's death. He was only two years old and he wouldn't stop talking about how the rebels killed his mother. He kept saying over and over, 'The knife, the knife, they cut her, they cut her open.' It was driving Denise mad. The family doctor told her it was better to let him say it, that it needed to come out. But you can imagine what it would do to you, hearing day after day how your pregnant daughter was slaughtered."

Denise loved animals. Her backyard was a refuge for all sorts of injured and orphaned creatures. Claudine asked Denise to come to the zoo and help her feed the starving animals.

It was around that time that Mikeno arrived. He was almost dead. The director of the zoo told Claudine and Denise not to bother, that they'd had bonobos before and they all died. But Denise was an emergency nurse. She brought Mikeno to her house and slowly nursed him back to health.

Mikeno had also seen his parents killed, although it is impossible to say how. Perhaps they had been eaten by starving soldiers in the forest or shot so that Mikeno, who might bring several thousand Congolese francs at the market, could be captured.

"Denise thought Mikeno might help Paul. They were about the same age," Claudine said. Denise lavished love on both Mikeno and her grandson while she grieved for her daughter.

Then, strange things started to happen that the Congolese would call black magic. Mikeno started to behave like a little boy. He wore Paul's clothes. He never left Denise's side. At the same time, Paul would only be naked. He screamed if they tried to dress him. He talked like a bonobo. He spent all day outside climbing trees and would not come down.

"Eventually the family doctor and Denise's husband told me I had to take Mikeno away. That it was frightening what was happening to the little boy. So I told Denise that Mikeno needed a forest, that I was going to put him somewhere safer than her backyard. Of course, she didn't believe me. She didn't understand why I would want to take Mikeno from her; she loved him so much already.

"One morning, her car pulled up at my house. She dropped Mikeno off and drove away without a word. She didn't see him again. Or me. But what could I do?"

Her question is soft and has no answer. She has a lovely voice. Ahead, the long line of bonobos starts moving. It is hot and they want to get to the pond, where they can slip into the water and forage for roots along the bank.

Mikeno watches us calmly. In his eyes, I see our shadows.

Chapter 6

❧

Our house at Lola is built from stone blocks the color of jewels, fitting for the weekend retreat of a dictator. There is satellite television, air-conditioning, hot water, and a flushing toilet. From the patio there is a sweeping view of the grounds down to the river.

Papa Jean is our cook. He used to work for Mobutu as a gardener, which of course drives me wild with curiosity.

"He was a nice man," Papa Jean says as I stare at him with my mouth open. "He loved his family. When he was with his grandchildren, he would squat on the floor and let them tumble all over him."

"But he was a thief. He ruined Congo."

Papa Jean shakes his head.

"People here loved him. He would go down to the water and talk to the fishermen. He would stop by people working in the fields and ask them about their crops. When he spoke, hundreds would come to listen. He was like a father to us."

Papa Jean is a handsome man, around fifty years old. I search for signs of the war on his face, in his eyes. There is nothing. In fact, no one at Lola seems to have any trace of it. They shout joyfully at each other. They crack jokes and slap palms and sing.

Did I read the news right? Didn't millions of people die here, like, yesterday?

Richard and Brian are already setting up initial experiments for the bonobos, to get a feel for what is possible. While they are occupied, I have been left to my own devices.

I thought being here would give me insight into war. I thought someone would pop up and say, "This is what turned your dad into such an asshole."

But so far, nobody has been forthcoming.

I climb the stone path that stretches up the hill from our house to the office. When the path ends, I take a right into the forest, which opens up and reveals, of all things, a jungle gym. It was donated by the legendary actress Brigitte Bardot and looks like any playground. There are ropes, wooden platforms, climbing netting, and even a little swimming pool.

But instead of children, running around are tight little balls of fuzzy fury. They swing from the trees, grab each other by the arms and feet, and fall to the ground wrestling. Next to the jungle gym, a miniature Bruce Lee does a kamikaze leap from his bamboo stalk and kung fu–kicks another bonobo in the head.

Supervising the mayhem are four women called the Mamas, with a capital "M." In Congo, anyone old enough to reproduce can be called "Mama." It's not an affectionate term, implying someone warm and huggable. It's a sign of deference and respect. At Lola, only these four women are privileged with the prefix. The name seems to be applicable to all four of them, even though the youngest is nineteen and the oldest must be over a hundred. Yelling "Mama!" from anywhere in the sanctuary will bring one of them sashaying insolently around the corner. If they are in a group, the correct protocol seems to be to attach their actual name after the Mama title, as in "Mama Esperance" or "Mama Yvonne." These four women are the power source of Lola. They are Macbeth's witches, the Greek Fates—everything begins and ends with them.

Claudine quickly discovered that baby bonobos die without constant attention. In the wild, they stay attached to their mother until they are five years old. So when the orphans arrive at Lola, sick and terrified, they need a warm body to cling to.

Every bonobo who arrives at the sanctuary is given to one of the Mamas, who treats the orphan like one of her own children. They spend all day in the Brigitte Bardot playground until they are brave enough to descend from their Mama's bosom and play with the other infants. The orphans who arrive at Lola are usually around three years old, young enough to have been clinging to their mothers when they were shot. They can spend years in the nursery, and their Mama is the center of their world. There is always a fight for lap space, which is usually won by the smallest, and every time a Mama stands up to get a snack or go to the toilet, a cluster of baby bonobos clings to her like fleas.

When a hundred-pound male bonobo doesn't come back from the forest, it's not the male keepers who go out to look for him, it's his Mama. When one of the grown females falls sick and refuses to take medicine, it's the Mamas who mix the dose into tea with honey and lemon and bring it to her bed of straw.

If one of the Mamas decides, for some reason, to walk around the sanctuary, the bonobos she raised go absolutely bonkers. They stand on the edge of the lake, hold out their arms, and peer over the fence, trying to figure out a way to leap into her bosom.

But the Mamas hardly ever leave the nursery. With eight baby bonobos running completely riot, it takes all four of them to keep the situation under control. While the other sixty staff members, from the gardeners to the keepers, are always ready with a smile and a cheery wave, the Mamas look like they will bitch-slap you at the first opportunity. They seem perfect for questioning. Surely they have seen more of the war than anyone else.

"Maniema! Maniema!" the big-bosomed Mama Henriette calls out furiously. Maniema has stolen her shoe and run off into the bushes. Next to Mama Henriette is Mama Micheline, a wizened old woman with only two teeth left that I can see. Mama Yvonne is an Amazon, and Mama Esperance is the youngest, with a face like the dancing *aspara* I saw at Angkor Wat.

"*Salut,*" I say, sitting on the ground. Out of nowhere a bonobo leaps from the trees onto my head. He wraps his arms around my face. "Um…" I can't really talk with the bonobo's fur in my mouth. Finally, I prise the baby off me. Apparently leaping from bamboo kung fu style is his specialty. He grabs my arm and pulls as hard as he can, punctuating my next question with sharp tugs.

"I just wanted"—*jerk*—"to talk to you guys"—*jerk*—"I mean, were you guys here during the war?"

The silence that follows is uncomfortable due to my newly dislocated shoulder and the unreadable expression on Mama Henriette's face. At her feet sits another bonobo, who is as tall as her knee. He is older than the other infants, but he clutches the material of her pants like a baby. I scramble to fill the silence.

"What's his name?"

Mama Henriette begins her sentences with a gangster flick of her chin.

"Lomami."

I hold out my hand to Lomami. He shrinks behind her leg. His hand curls around the front of her pants and I see that all five fingers on his right hand are stubs.

"What happened to his hand?"

"*Fetisheurs,*" says Mama Henriette. *Witch doctors.* In certain parts of Congo, witch doctors use body parts of a bonobo for spells. According to superstition, if a pregnant woman drinks soup with a bonobo finger in it, she will have a healthy baby. If a baby is bathed in water with a bonobo bone, they will become strong.

Lomami was found in Kisangani, the diamond capital of Congo. The director of a Congo airline company saw the bonobo for sale at the airport and pretended he wanted to buy it. The director got in touch with Claudine, who arranged for inspectors from the Ministry of Environment to confiscate the bonobo.

Lomami had been kept in a cage for weeks. Every now and then someone would cut off a finger, leave him screaming and bleeding, come back a few days later, and cut off another one. He is also missing bits of his groin and a little slice of his penis. His eyes are the eyes of

Holocaust survivors. While the other bonobos play rambunctiously around him, no one touches him. He is alone, hugging Mama Henriette's trouser legs.

A bonobo leaps from the bushes and sinks his fangs into my knee. The Mamas stare off into the distance, apparently unconcerned that a bonobo is eating my leg.

"Maniema," Mama Henriette says. Maniema looks up at her, his mouth full of my trousers. She frowns as though he has brought her a present she doesn't quite like. "*Laisse.*" *Leave it alone.* He doesn't listen to her. So I struggle to my feet, Maniema attached to my knee, and shake him off. Then I say good-bye and head despondently down the hill.

Chapter 7

❧

The next morning I wander aimlessly by the river, watching villagers tend their fields on the other side.

"Maniema!" Mama Henriette's voice comes booming through the bushes above. It's the kind of voice that implies that the back of her hand feels like a ton of bricks. An impish fur ball commandos out of the bushes. Two beady little eyes look right and left, high on adrenaline from his nursery jailbreak. He sees me and calculates whether he should bite me, run, or both.

"Maniema." It's a different voice this time. Low and soothing, the bass string of a guitar. A man steps out from behind the building. He offers his hand. Maniema takes it and climbs into the man's arms.

The man nuzzles Maniema's neck.

"*Mon ami.*" It's a personal moment and I feel awkward. The man sees me. He has a gentle smile, a high forehead, and almond-shaped eyes.

"*Bonjour.*"

"*Bonjour.*"

"I'm Vanessa."

"Jacques."

"You like Maniema?"

"He's a friend of mine."

We smile at each other.

"Where are you from?"

"The east."

From my meager research, I know this is where the worst fighting took place. I decide to take a shot in the dark. "Did you see much of the war?"

He becomes very still. He searches my face for the reason I have asked him this question.

"My father was in a war," I say. "I want to know . . ."

I trail off, feeling clumsy. It occurs to me what a raw, brutal demand I have just made of this man, a stranger.

"I've never told anyone what happened," he says quietly. "Not all of it."

"I'm sorry," I say, backing out.

He watches me as I scurry back to safer ground.

EVERY MORNING MANIEMA busts out of the nursery, his face blazing with glee. If I follow him, he always leads me to Jacques, who scoops Maniema in his arms and carries him back to the fuming Mamas.

Maniema safely delivered, Jacques and I exchange pleasantries. If he isn't busy, he takes me around and tells me about the bonobos.

"Do you still want to know?" he asks me suddenly one day.

I duck my head in shame. I asked him for his story so carelessly, and now I see it in the deep creases of his forehead. The hollow curve of his cheekbones. The recessive skin around his eyes, as though someone has pushed their fingers into his sockets.

I'm afraid of what shaped his face. But it is too late. Before I can nod, he has already begun.

I wanted money. I wanted to be rich.

My father and mother split up when I was four years old. They both remarried. My little brother and I couldn't live with either of them—my mother's husband was a bad man. She didn't want me to stay with her and I never saw her again. And my father, I wanted to live with him but his new wife didn't want us. So we lived with my uncle and our cousins.

I was determined I would never be poor. I didn't want to be dependent on people. I lived with my uncle until I was fourteen, then I started to grow vegetables to sell at the market: potatoes, maricot, and maize.

When I had enough money, I bought a plane ticket to Kisangani. I went to look for gold. In the forest, deep in the forest, there are many minerals. I wanted to be rich. I walked so far into the forest that I was two days away from the nearest village, but there must have been ten thousand people living beneath the trees. They came from everywhere, cities, villages—everyone had gold fever.

THE CONGO IS FULL OF RICHES. The diamond fields of Kasai to the southeast of Kinshasa rise nearly two thousand feet above sea level and stretch for 7,700 square miles.

These plains rest on layers of crystalline rock, the foundation of the Congo Basin, that were compressed and folded 2.7 billion years ago. The composition of this rock reads like a poem: granite, gneiss, migmatites, syenites, quartzites, amphibolites, and itabirites. On top of this, runoff from glaciers in the last ice age left traces of quartzites on the Precambrian floor. The Jurassic era left its own footprints, rocks carried by a long-gone river, rich in the elements that form precious stones.

But it was the Cretaceous that brought the diamonds. A layer of purple sandstone 650 feet tall, soaked with heavy minerals. This layer would make Congo the biggest producer of diamonds in the world. In 1961, more than eighteen million carats of diamonds left the country to adorn the third fingers and slender necks of women all over the world. A million carats still leave Congo every year.

But the ebbing and flowing of rivers, the crawl of glaciers across the earth, did not bring just diamonds. And the mineral wealth is not limited to Kasai. In Tshinyama there is copper that was used for wiring in the Vietnam War. Along the southern arch of Lubumbashi there is uranium that was used in the atomic bomb. If you ascend from Shaba, you will come across granite threaded with tin. Kipushi mines yield zinc and germanium. In the north of Congo, in the Oriental Province, there is gold. Lower, toward Congo's feet, there is zinc and lead.

There are minerals with fantastical names: stanniferous pegmatite of Manono, columbite-tantalite in Kalima, the rich pyrochlore deposits of Lueshe. In the Mountains of the Moon, the lava from the volcanoes has yielded several new kinds of silicates found nowhere else in the world.

This Aladdin's cave of treasure is Congo's great fortune, but it is also her greatest blight. The profits from these minerals were what kept Mobutu in power for so long. The money streaming out of Congo into the pockets of mineral companies from Europe, Australia, Canada, and the United States was so plentiful, it was just a fraction of the money these countries poured back into Congo as aid.

It was a dense, thick forest. So thick, there were only two hours of daylight. At noon, the sun came. Then it vanished.

We ate wild animals. Chimpanzees, rhinoceros, monkeys. I saw a leopard once. It saw me and ran away. Tortoises with great shells that were half as big as you. We boiled them in water to make soup. There were hunters in the forest who killed these animals and sold them for gold. We had no paper money, just gold.

The forest was full of it. I had five friends and we worked together and divided everything we found. We marked out an area as big as a swimming pool, then we dug with shovels. All day we dug. The hunters brought us food and we dug from five in the morning until six at night. We slept under a payote—*a hut made out of sticks, covered with leaves to protect us from the rain. We dug and sifted through the dirt. There were nuggets as big as your finger and nuggets as big as your fist. I dug hundreds of dollars at a time out of the earth.*

There were diamonds in the forest too; many people were searching for diamonds, but they were much harder to find. If you found a diamond, you could sell it for ten thousand dollars.

It was just the five of us. Life was good. We made friends with everyone. We had three good years. I had seven thousand dollars' worth of gold. That was so much money. I could have lived my whole life on that money.

Then I lost it. I lost everything.

In 1990, the Cold War came to an end. The United States abruptly pulled the plug on aid to Congo. Mobutu was warned by everyone—cabinet ministers, foreign diplomats, and politicians—that his spending sprees would have to stop. But everyone knows the story about the leopard and his spots. It took six years for an armed force to be mounted against Mobutu, and even then he didn't see it coming.

THE TRIGGER WAS PULLED IN RWANDA, after the genocide.

For centuries, the elite ruling class, the Tutsis, have been locked in a power struggle with the working-class Hutus. In 1994, the assassination of the Hutu president gave the Hutus the excuse they needed to wipe out the aristocracy. A systematic massacre was led by the Hutu extremist group called the Interahamwe.

The Interahamwe were cold, calculating, and meticulous. They trained in secret camps run by Hutu members of the government. They dispersed into the villages to compile lists of Tutsis, much like the Nazis registered the Jews.

When the moment arrived, there were thirty thousand Interahamwe members throughout Rwanda. They were given weapons, including machine guns and grenades, from massive caches. But the weapon of choice was the machete.

On April 6, 1994, the Hutu president of Rwanda, Juvénal Habyarimana, was assassinated and all hell broke loose. Messages were broadcast over the radio for Hutus to pick up the weapon closest to them and kill every *inyenzi,* or cockroach, they knew or could find. Any Hutu who refused to kill Tutsi, who hid them, or who tried to protect them was killed.

The Rwandan genocide was a vicious and intensely personal war.

The killing was perpetrated not by foreign armies or guards in camps, but by people who knew their victims. Neighbors killed their neighbors, hacking off body parts with machetes, knives, and studded clubs. Local politicians killed whole families. Even priests joined in. At a town called Musha, 1,200 Tutsis were killed from eight A.M. till midnight. When the Tutsis fled onto holy ground, churches became the scenes of the worst massacres. When they cowered in their houses, the Hutus broke in and killed them. When they fled into the forest, they were struck down when they came out to find food.

The international community refused to respond. After ten Belgian peacekeepers were tortured and killed, Belgium pulled out. The French evacuated organizers of the genocide and left the Tutsi employees of the embassy behind to be killed. Bill Clinton refused to use the word "genocide" or send in troops. He swore he knew nothing about the slaughter, despite daily CIA reports uncovered in 2004 that showed he, Al Gore, and Defense Secretary Madeleine Albright knew the moment the first machete came down on the Tutsis.

IN THREE MONTHS, as many as a million people were killed. Piles of bodies with missing limbs and smashed skulls lay rotting in the streets.

Finally, a Tutsi resistance took control of the country. Once the Tutsis were back in power, two million Hutus fled Rwanda, afraid the Tutsis would take revenge. And they did. Unlike the genocide, the killings by the Tutsi army were scattered and discrete. They trusted nobody. They even killed Tutsis who managed to survive the genocide, because they suspected that they had helped the Hutus.

More than 1.5 million refugees fled across the Rwandan border to eastern Congo. Among them, the Interahamwe began to set up camps and send out raiding parties to terrorize villages in both countries. Mobutu did nothing. He was plagued by prostate cancer, a fast-acting, painful disease, and was constantly flying to France for treatment. Congo has a large Tutsi population, and they were enraged that Mobutu was allowing the murderous Hutus to shelter on Congo soil. The time was right for an attack on Mobutu's regime.

The war. Mobutu's war.

I heard it was coming, but I didn't believe it. I thought it was hap-
pening somewhere else, somewhere far away. I didn't think it would
ever find me.

The bombs began to fall. Everywhere, all around. They bombed
and bombed and bombed us. For a week I dodged them in the forest.
I stepped over piles of dead bodies and waded through rivers red with
blood. It was 1996, and the bombs were Kabila's.

Mobutu had a good army, a vicious army. I didn't think Kabila
would ever get through. But Kabila's troops came over the gorilla
mountains, the Mountains of the Moon. The Rwandans won Kisan-
gani, and the army swept all the way to Kinshasa.

Laurent Désiré Kabila was a thug. He owned a brothel in Tanzania and a gold mine in the Kivus, where he smuggled gold to the
army. In 1975, he kidnapped three Stanford students who were studying chimpanzees at Jane Goodall's research site in Gombe. He held
them hostage for two months until $40,000 was paid in ransom.

In 1965, the Marxist revolutionary Che Guevara turned up at
Kabila's camp to help him lead a revolution against Mobutu, but
Guevara left soon after, disgusted with Kabila's boozing and wom-
anizing. By the 1990s, Kabila was a nobody. He ran his little band of
rebels, his gold-smuggling operation, and his brothels, but had it not
been for a turn of events, he would have died in obscurity in the
mountains.

After the Rwandan genocide, most of the two million Hutu refugees, some of whom had slaughtered thousands of Tutsis, fled straight
into Congo. It was the largest exodus in modern history. The Hutus
lived in squalid refugee camps, and within them, the Interahamwe
Hutus, who started the genocide, began to regroup. This was made
possible by well-meaning aid organizations such as the UNHCR
(United Nations High Commissioner for Refugees) donating tons of
food that could be controlled by the Interahamwe and bartered and
sold for weapons and ammunition. The Interahamwe sent out raiding

parties and terrorized Congolese and Rwandan Tutsis on either side of the border.

When the Tutsi government was back in power, they wanted these Interahamwe stamped out. Not to mention they had their eye on the vast richness of Congo's resources. Mobutu was clearly losing it, and they wanted someone in power who would be sympathetic to their interests.

So they found Kabila. Kabila was already friends with Yoweri Museveni, the president of Uganda. Uganda had its own problems with Congo. Rebel groups such as the Lord's Resistance Army were also hiding in the rain forests of the Uganda-Congo border, wreaking havoc on the government. And again, there were all those riches. Museveni introduced Kabila to Paul Kagame, the president of Rwanda, and the band of brothers was formed.

Mobutu's army was useless. His generals had been corrupt for so long, they didn't know how to organize a defense. They sold everything they could get their hands on, including Mobutu's fleet of fighter jets. They even sold weapons to Kabila's advancing army.

When Mobutu ordered them to gather their eighty thousand troops and attack, they ignored him. Desperate, Mobutu hired mercenaries from Serbia, Russia, and France. He paid them from his dwindling funds, at $2,500 a month. Kabila's Tutsi Rwandans fought against the Hutu Interahamwe who were holed up in camps. The Interahamwe sent out reconnaissance missions to continue killing Tutsi soldiers and Congolese Tutsis who had been living in Congo for generations. The slaughter was bloody and prolific, and it was mostly ordinary people who got caught in the middle.

Suddenly the forest was full of armies. The first day was terrible; I will never forget it. The noise, the huge, frightening noise. They poured into the forest, the Belgians, the Chinese, the Serbians—Kabila and Mobutu had them all. There were so many of them.

When they came upon us, they started cutting off heads. I will never forget it. That woman [he points to a woman in a pink sarong;

she has a basket balanced on her head and sashays gracefully along the riverbank]. There was a woman just like that, I remember her; they cut off her head.

There were bodies everywhere. Thousands and thousands of bodies. A friend I knew from school was killed right in front of me. Friends, families, people I loved. There were so many dead.

I hid in the forest for seven days with two of my friends. We had nothing to eat. Just a little fruit. Water is everywhere in Congo, so we had enough to drink. We ran all the way to Kisangani. I found my little brother, but I had no money, nothing. So I left him and went to Butembo and found shelter with one of my father's cousins. He owned a nightclub and I started working in the bar.

But the war followed me there. The soldiers arrived and started killing everyone they saw. They stopped short of coming into houses. The whole village was locked inside their houses. If you stepped outside, the soldiers would kill you.

In Butembo, these Rwandans of Kabila, they stayed for five days. We couldn't go out to the toilet. Through the window I saw sick people trying to get to hospital; the Rwandans killed them. I saw starving people leave their houses to find food; the Rwandans killed them.

I was in the nightclub when it started, so I was stuck there for five days. Five days, nothing to eat. I drank beer. Nothing but beer, Fanta, and a few peanuts.

There were eight of us in the bar. Bullets flew outside the window. Rockets. Not one white person was there to witness it. Not one journalist to tell the story.

After five days, the army left. I was sick for three days after that. I went to Goma. I went to Rwanda. I crossed back and forth over the border.

I had nothing. I left everything in the forest. I was empty.

Kabila's victory was swift and merciless. It took four years for Paul Kagame to take over Rwanda, six years for Museveni to win Uganda.

Kabila won the Congo in less than twelve months. His troops stormed Kinshasa and won the city with barely a shot fired. Ravaged by cancer, Mobutu fled to Morocco and died four months after Kabila took over the capital.

Kabila inherited a national debt of $9.6 billion and a country already tired of fighting. There were desperate shortages of food and gasoline. But the worst was yet to come.

When Kabila took over power, I joined the army.

It was just an administration job. I had it for two years. Working for the same people who attacked us in the forest. Kabila's Rwandans. They are evil. I hate them. They killed so many of us, right in front of my eyes. You see, Rwandans have nothing. They are poor. They have no family here. They have nothing to lose by invading. They own nothing, so they steal from us.

I joined them because I needed work, but I didn't kill a single person.

Each month I earned ten dollars. But sometimes they didn't pay me. The army has no money. When you can, you steal. To live, you must steal. I stole a little. Just enough to eat. I didn't want to become a thief, but I couldn't stay honest. It could be months in between paychecks.

I looked for other work in Kinshasa. For seven months I was not paid. I worked in horticulture. Rural services. I drove a goods truck to and from Kinshasa. I slept in my office.

Finally I got a job at the prison.

With Kabila in power, Western countries were hopeful that they could continue to plunder Congo's resources. Aid money poured in. Kabila squandered it. He seized successful businesses and drove them to bankruptcy. He banned miniskirts. He idealized Communism and became hostile to the West.

Then he made a serious miscalculation. The Congolese were suspicious he was nothing but a Rwandan puppet, which, of course, he was. To gain public support, he turned on the Rwandans and threw them out of the country. In a chilling echo of the Rwandan genocide, he got on the radio and implored the Congolese to take up whatever arms they had in their homes and chop the Rwandans to pieces.

For a few days, frenzied Congolese threw car tires around Tutsis and set them alight. Kabila also threw out the Ugandans. Anyone who resisted him he threw in jail.

The prison was huge, with many rooms. There were twenty-five hundred prisoners. I guess the rooms were fifteen feet by fifteen feet. Ten people crammed into a tiny cage. Sometimes fifty. Sometimes a hundred. There were no beds. Some people spent a year in these rooms. Without a breath of fresh air. Bathing, sleeping, eating, in the same room. Some women delivered children.

Almost everyone was sick. They only had beans and maize twice a day, as much as you could fit in two hands. Rice, once a day. No meat. Who would give them meat? Sometimes, very rarely, they would give the sickest people a little fish. Some saca saca.

At four in the afternoon, they went to sleep and were not allowed to wake or make any noise until the morning. There were over three hundred and fifty women, mostly mothers and young girls kept separate from the soldiers and young men. The women were always ill.

I knew everyone. Thieves, politicians, murderers. I walked in and among them. I listened to their stories. There were so many stories; it was another world. There were soldiers who had deserted and were thrown in prison. There was a twenty-two-year-old girl who had killed her boyfriend for being with another woman. A woman who sold her family home when it didn't belong to her.

But mostly it was people Kabila had turned on. He called them traitors and threw them into prison. No court, no trial, no law. Whoever he wanted, he put them in jail.

The prisoners were executed publicly. Soldiers tied them to a tree, with their arms behind their back, and shot them.

I remember one of the executions. The boy was very young, only

nineteen. There were boys who fought who were twelve, thirteen, four-
teen years old. Even ten or eleven. They were Kabila's little army, called
the Kadogo. Some say it was the Kadogo who liberated the Congo.

This boy, the guards held out his arms like a crucifixion. His
woman was crying, but it was too late. They shot him many times.

After five months, it was too much for me. I was fond of the pris-
oners, but I was so tired. And they didn't pay me.

The Ugandans and Rwandans were furious that the man they
had put in power had betrayed them. They immediately seized most
of eastern Congo. Kabila asked Angola, Zimbabwe, and Zambia for
help. They greedily agreed, in exchange for oil concessions and the
right to mine and export diamonds and other minerals. And so began
an even bloodier war than the first, one that would see the death toll
rise to the millions, that would see Zainabo gang-raped and her children eaten in front of her. The war that would create millions of refugees and shatter the lives of millions more. But that is not part of
Jacques's story.

I left for Equateur. I worked on a boat, a supply barge that traveled
from Kinshasa to Bandaka. We had soap, sugar, cocoa, maize. I was
the cashier. I handled the money, but I could be honest again. I never
stole any of it.

The journey to Equateur was five hundred miles along the Congo
River. The journey took seven days, but we were always gone for two
months. For most of the dry season, it was calm, but in the wet sea-
son when the rains arrived, the river swelled and the waves could
reach over thirty feet. Rapids could capsize a boat. If the river became
too rough, we had to carry the boat through the forest.

Then, after twelve months, I was in Bandaka, where I met some-
one from my village who was the director of a monkey project. He
used to work for the Japanese bonobo researchers, at Wamba. Now he
was running an ecological study. He asked if I wanted to work for
him, so I left for the forest.

I was in a big forest again. The trees were gigantic. It was so dark, like night even during the day. I was there for three months; I studied the animals. I told the villagers about conservation. There were so many monkeys. And bonobos. For the first time, I saw wild bonobos. It was good. I wasn't paid much but I had enough to eat.

But soon I returned to Kinshasa. I worked in the office of the boat managers and stayed with a friend of mine. One day, when this friend was out, Crispin, the vet at Lola, came to visit me. He said he knew I enjoyed working with animals and had done a good job in the forest. Crispin is from my tribe in the east. He offered me a job at Lola. And now, here I am.

It is late, and the mosquitoes are eating me alive, but I don't care. Jacques reminds me so much of my father. Dad was always dreaming of riches and hatching crazy schemes to make a million.

Before the war, they were ordinary young men. Life wasn't perfect. Their parents were divorced. They were poor, and Dad had to work on a farm while Jacques was hauling vegetables to the market.

But all that death, all the blood and butchery. The Rwandans have a name for it—*bapfuye buhagazi*. It means "the walking dead." They use it to describe those who have survived the genocide, for what they carry in their eyes. They carry it with them and they will carry it always. And as with Lomami, the bonobo with the mutilated hand, no one will ever know how bad it was out there. Or how much it still hurts.

Chapter 8

❧

*K*ikongo clutches the bars and wails, his long pink penis arching longingly toward my hand.

"I'm not touching that," I say, but my words are lost in the high-pitched screeches reverberating off the concrete walls. Kikongo, the bonobo I saw doing headstands in the moss, thrusts his penis through the bars.

I reach over and pat his head, hoping this will suffice. No effect. His teeth are bared in a ghoulish grin and he gives a few thrusts for good measure. He sure is making a racket. Chimp calls are low and long, like the hoot of an owl. If they scream, chances are someone is going to bleed. They don't scream for no reason. And here Kikongo sits, screeching at the top of his lungs because I won't touch his penis.

His penis is the width of my index finger. It is so long and skinny that it droops toward the end. I can't believe he wants me to touch it. He has spent the last hour spinning around and around in circles. He has developed a break-dancing move where he puts his tongue on the floor, then propels himself around with his feet. As though I were his doctor, he opened his mouth as wide as he could and said, "Ahhhhh. Ahhhhh."

Then, all of a sudden, Kikongo decided he desperately needed his penis touched and he was not going to do anything else unless I fondled it.

I turn around and give Brian the dirtiest look I can manage. Richard left Kinshasa yesterday, mission accomplished. After a few tests, both he and Brian agreed that it was possible to run experiments here. With Richard gone, Brian summoned his cutest smile and said, "Will you help me with some experiments?"

At no point did he mention fondling bonobo penises. But from his bewildered face, I can see this is not something he expected either.

The volume and pitch of Kikongo's cries are cutting into my brain like a chainsaw. When the Japanese first heard bonobos, they compared them to tweeting birds. Bonobos do have a chirruping quality to their food peeps and social calls, but I don't know any bird that sounds like Kikongo.

"Fuck it." I reach over, close my eyes, and give the penis a few pats. It has a rubbery texture. He gives me a screechy grin and calms down immediately.

Next to Kikongo is Tatango, the adult male who was "corrected" by the Terrible Five. I tickled him for at least half an hour to make him smile, without success. His deep-set eyes gaze at me mournfully.

Poor Tatango. He is a bonobo trying to be a chimpanzee, and it isn't working out too well for him. With his strong limbs and manly jaw, he wants to be in charge. He knows, with his superior muscle power, that it is nature's law that he dominate females basically half his size. They barely even have canines. You can almost hear him grinding his teeth. Those damn females and their alliances are ruining his plans.

With Richard gone and preliminary tests over, Brian wants to get down to business. In trying to figure out what makes us human, Brian is concentrating on cooperation. Cooperation is the foundation of our society. It allowed us to build Angkor Wat, the pyramids, the Empire State Building. It gives us our justice system, our police force, our government.

The amazing thing about human cooperation is that it is so spontaneous. People don't need to be taught to cooperate or ordered to by a higher authority. We just do it.

A famous example is in World War I when British soldiers were fighting the Germans on the Western Front. They were ordered by their officers to shoot to kill. The British knew they outnumbered the Germans, and all they had to do was continue a steady offensive to win.

But in the trenches, where soldiers were so close that they could see their enemies' eyes, occasionally something very peculiar occurred. By a silent mutual agreement, neither side would fire during mealtimes. Then it was between the hours of eight and nine P.M. Flags were put up to mark areas that were "out of bounds" for snipers. There were cease-fires during bad weather. Then came the Christmas Truce of 1914, when both sides came out of the trenches and exchanged gifts and sang carols.

This kind of cooperation requires a certain amount of intelligence. You have to understand that you need the other side to cooperate. You have to guess what the other side is thinking and whether they are willing to cooperate with you. Finally, you have to be prepared to retaliate if the other side betrays you, so you don't find yourself on the losing side of a raw deal.

These rules apply to every situation, from dating to business to politics. Civilization is founded on our ability to cooperate and we would never have gotten far without it.

There are a hundred theories why humans began cooperating. Maybe we were hunters and had to work together to hunt down prey much larger than us. Maybe we were the hunted and had to put our brains together to outwit predators. Maybe we started cooking, and cooking led to bigger brains.

But what was the very first change, in our nature or in our minds, that allowed us to cooperate so much more flexibly than other animals? Some say we got more intelligent, so we knew we could get more done with the help of other people. Others say the change was emotional, and as social animals, we felt the need to help our own kind.

Animals cooperate all the time. Bees gather nectar for the hive. Ants work together to fatten up the queen. But this kind of cooperation is explained by family relations—all the insects in the colony are siblings. Evolutionarily, it makes sense to cooperate if it helps you pass on your genes. But not all cooperation can be explained by family ties, especially in humans.

The ultimate form of cooperation is the hunt. When a pack of hyenas hunts down an antelope, are they communicating with one another while they do it? Or is everyone just running toward the antelope and then by accident, someone catches it? Just because it looks like cooperation doesn't mean it is.

In the wild, chimpanzees hunt monkeys for meat. These hunts seem highly organized, and Richard, along with many field researchers, wondered if they involved sophisticated communication and organization.

The problem was, no one could get chimps to cooperate during an experiment, so others argued it was difficult to know how much thinking is going on behind the cooperation. Are they communicating with one another? Do they know they need everyone to work together, or is it just a mad dash for the monkey? And if there is cooperation going on, how sophisticated is it? How much do chimps understand? Most important, what constrains their cooperation and prevents them from developing a more humanlike ability?

Say there is a long red plank, six feet long. At each end, there is a dish full of food. Next to each dish is a metal loop. A long rope threads through the loops so that in order to pull the plank, you have to pull both ends of the rope at the same time. If you pull only one end, the rope comes unthreaded from the plank like a shoelace. To succeed, two chimps have to cooperate and pull both ends of the rope at the same time to drag the plank toward them and get the food.

This very elegant apparatus was designed by Brian's friend at Kyoto University, Sitoshi Hirata. To succeed, first, you have to know that you need a partner, and second, you need to work together.

But Sitoshi had only two pairs of chimps, and they didn't succeed until they had been trained for a long period of time. And when the chimps finally did cooperate, there was no evidence that they realized when they did and didn't need a partner, whether they knew who was a good partner, or if they remembered when someone screwed them over.

Soon after we met, Brian spent three months at Ngamba. There, he had something special—a social group of more than forty chimpanzees. And with this group of chimps, Brian and his student Alicia Melis swapped and mixed the chimps into pairs until they were able to do things no one else had done. The chimps cooperated to pull the plank on the first trial. They opened doors to let in different partners depending on their skills. They remembered who betrayed them on previous trials and betrayed them in return. In short, chimpanzee cooperation was showing a level of complexity that we have only ever seen in humans.

For example, Mawa, the dominant chimpanzee, was not a very good cooperator. He was loud and impatient and often yanked the rope from the tray. My little Baluku, naturally, was a great cooperator. He always waited for his partner and was nearly always successful in getting the food. At first, the chimpanzees chose Mawa and Baluku equally, but when the chimpanzees learned how useless Mawa was, most chose Baluku on the next trial.

But there was one thing that constrained chimpanzee cooperation, something no one had taken into account—tolerance. If the chimps liked each other, they cooperated, often on the first trial. If the chimps hated each other, or if one was scared of the other one, then you got the situation everyone else had encountered—one chimp monopolizing the rope and the other one sitting in the corner, refusing to play the game.

Chimpanzees become incredibly emotional, especially over food. Richard's theory (although he doesn't explain it in terms of chocolate) is that the natural environment of chimps is like an Easter egg hunt. Anyone who has been to one that doesn't quite have enough eggs can attest to how quickly sweet-natured children become savage beasts. Like Easter eggs, chimpanzee food is limited and spread over a large area. Females have to forage alone, so they never form strong friendships, and males quickly realize that whoever controls the food holds the power.

The test for tolerance is very simple. The chimps have to be able to share a meal. So Brian took the rope out of the long red plank and filled the ends with food. If the chimps were tolerant of each other, they could sit down without any problems and eat together. If they were intolerant, one of the chimps would take all the food while the other chimp watched, sulking.

So now we come to bonobos. If chimpanzees live in an Easter egg patch, then bonobos live in a chocolate factory. Relative to chimpanzee food, bonobo food is plentiful. And unlike chimpanzees, bonobos do not have to share their food with gorillas, who only live north of the Congo River, while bonobos live to the south. Because there is so much to go around, bonobo females don't have to compete for the sake of their children. That means females can become friends and stand up to the males who try to threaten them.

If Brian is right, and tolerance is what allows for cooperation, then bonobos should be able to do the cooperation test much more flexibly than chimpanzees. But no one has seen bonobos cooperate to obtain food in the wild before. They don't hunt like chimpanzees. They don't stalk strangers in enemy territory in gangs. So will they pass the simple tolerance test?

Kikongo and Tatango are a grown male and a juvenile. Two chimps of this age wouldn't even be in the same room together. Or the male would be at the front, staring ferociously at the food, and the juvenile would be cowering in the back corner.

However, there is a twist: Bonobos are scared of doors. Between the rooms are doors that the keepers pull open. We need to move the bonobos in and out because that is the protocol for the experiment. Both bonobos must enter the room together, and then we present them with food on either side of the plank. The chimps did it every time without a hitch, for a peanut. But every time Jacques opens the door, despite the mountain of bananas in the room, Kikongo runs down the corridor, shrieking. Tatango doesn't particularly want to come in either.

"Who's afraid of a door?" Brian throws up his hands. This could be a world first. You can have pluviophobia, the fear of being rained on, or peladophobia, the fear of bald people, but there is no medical term for the fear of doors.

"Kikongo, Tatango, Kikongo, Tatango."

My voice is hoarse. We throw chunks of banana into the enclosure. Tatango walks in, sits down, and chews on one. After running up and down the corridor, Kikongo bolts through the door into the testing room, screaming his head off. Jacques closes the door and Kikongo clings to the bars as though he'll never see freedom again.

"Calm him down," says Brian.

"Why don't *you* calm him down?"

"You know why. They don't trust me."

In another startling twist, bonobos are wary of men. Except for the full-grown males, most of the bonobos at Lola treat Brian as though he is a steaming pile of dog turds. Females won't come near him. Infants turn away and refuse his greetings. Brian, who has always been a favorite of chimps, is a little hurt.

The bonobos don't have any beef with me. So instead of "helping out," I am running the experiments. Because Brian doesn't speak French, I have to talk to the keepers. Which means that while Brian fires instructions to me, I have to translate them into polite flowery French, then Brian demands an answer and I have to gently request a response and run the experiment at the same time.

This new Brian is a stranger to me. For the past twelve months, he has done a fair impression of a New Age Prince Charming. He flew me to Paris for romantic walks along the Seine. I have rings and necklaces from Tiffany. He opens doors, pulls out chairs, and makes sure I never walk beside a gutter. He gives me his dessert. I've never picked up a check or paid a bill. He writes me awful but heartfelt poetry and calls me beautiful or a similar adjective around three hundred times a day.

But suddenly Brian has turned into an obsessive-compulsive dictator, prone to explode at the slightest breach of protocol. I know I should apologize meekly and try to concentrate.

"This is the stupidest experiment I've ever heard of," I say instead. "It's not even working."

Brian is concentrating his chimpanzee mind powers on the bonobos, so he doesn't hear me.

"Kikongo!" I call. "Come here, Kikongo!"

Kikongo runs over to me and hurls himself against the bars, waggling his penis as though it's a cute furry pet that needs affection. I grit my teeth and give it a quick pat.

We're supposed to wait until the two bonobos are equidistant from each other and the plank, but Kikongo has the attention span of a fruit fly. He starts running in circles around the testing room, making himself dizzy by looking at the ceiling.

"This is impossible. Let's just give them the food."

We load the long red plank with bananas on each end and push it toward them. And then we get the first break we have had all day. Kikongo sidles up to Tatango, a pipsqueak only as big as Tatango's knee, and they eat out of the same dish. Side by side they sit, eating food from the same pile. From Brian's face you would think he had just seen the Messiah.

"They're sharing food," he whispers. "A grown male and a juvenile. This is incredible. We can barely get the chimps to sit at the plank, much less sit in each other's laps."

Tatango gets up and walks over to the other side of the plank and eats the bananas. Kikongo gets up and follows him, apparently not wanting to eat alone. Brian beams. This is clearly what he has been waiting for. I try to feel something for him, pleasure or celebration. All I feel is hungry.

I wonder if Brian wishes he could share this moment with someone who cares. Someone who would take his hand and bask in mutual triumph. I wonder if I can fake it. I can't.

"Does this mean we're finished?"

It might be my imagination, but I think I see a little sadness in his smile. "It means we just got started."

AT LUNCH, we meet Christelle and Tony, who have arrived from Brazzaville. They manage a sanctuary for orphan gorillas on the other side of the Congo River.

Christelle hasn't had a lot of sleep. She has been nursing a baby gorilla whose parents were shot by poachers. The baby died yesterday.

"Gorillas and bonobos are the same," Christelle says. "They just die. They see their mothers killed and they give up."

Tony is British and looks like he is about to die himself. His face is pale, and he's sweating profusely. The skin underneath his eyes is yellow, rimmed with red.

Claudine frowns.

"You have malaria."

It isn't a question.

"We think so," says Christelle. "He's been sick for two days."

"You don't play with that here," Claudine warns them. "You should take the medicine."

I'm fascinated. I've seen malaria before, but nothing like this. I can feel the ache in Tony's bones by the way he lies. He can't lift his arms or move his legs. Sweat dribbles down his face and he can't keep his eyes open. His tongue lolls out of his mouth, and the edges of his lips are caked with paste. Claudine rests a cool hand on his forehead.

"I don't want you dead in my house."

This stumps me. "Dead?" I ask. "From malaria?"

I knew this could happen, but I thought it happened after months of illness. To very poor people in backwater villages.

"Cerebral malaria," Claudine says. "It can kill you in four days."

I grip the arms of my chair. Malaria is a parasite that lives in the saliva of the anopheles mosquito. When the mosquito bites, the parasites travel through the bloodstream and hide in the liver, where they reproduce prolifically. Then the parasites flood back into the bloodstream and infect red blood cells, which carry oxygen around the body. The red blood cells burst, spreading the parasites through the vessels to infect and reproduce again.

Malaria is the developing world's worst nightmare. It infects almost half a billion people each year and kills one person every fifteen seconds. Falciparum malaria is a particularly virulent strain that causes 90 percent of malaria-related deaths. It destroys so many red blood cells so quickly that they choke up the vessels of major organs. But if it gets into your brain, you are totally screwed. It then becomes cerebral malaria. The parasite disappears into the deep vascular beds of the brain, causing havoc, quickly followed by seizure, coma, and death.

"We had a woman staying here," Claudine says. "She went home and three weeks later she thought she had a cold. Six days later she was dead. Another woman, same thing. But it was six months later when it killed her."

The problem with falciparum is that everyone thinks malaria comes with shivering and sweating. But the symptoms can be as subtle as a headache or nausea and may not appear until a year after you get bitten.

"My son Thomas," Claudine says. "He always gets a sore throat."

I look at Brian and wait for him to signal that we should pack our bags and get the hell out of here. Four days? I mean, we're on prophylaxis, but they are about as effective as a condom. Do we really want to gamble with that 1 percent?

If I were about to get hit by a car, I want to believe Brian wouldn't just stand there. If he didn't throw himself in front of it, I hope he would at least try to push me out of the way. So if he finds out we are in a country where malaria can kill you in four days, shouldn't he, out of basic chivalry, suggest we leave?

Brian sips his Coke, and it's perfectly clear that if a car were barreling toward me at full speed, I would be roadkill.

This is so not part of the deal. When he asked me to marry him in the Blue Mountains near Sydney, the word "protect" was clearly stated. It was raining, and he insisted on finding a waterfall. I found him one, wondering why you would need to look at falling water when tons of it was already pouring from the sky. I turned around, and there was Brian kneeling in a puddle, mud soaking into his pants.

"Will you marry me?"

It was hard to hear over the falls. "Huh?"

"Will you marry me?"

This had to be a joke. "No."

"What?"

"No!"

"Why not?"

"You can't be serious. If this is a serious proposal, where's my ring?"

Out came an emerald-green box with silver trimming. Inside, resting on a velvet cushion, was the first diamond anyone had given me.

"I love you. I don't want to be apart anymore. I'll protect and cherish you forever. Please, marry me."

I couldn't take my eyes off the diamond. I always thought they were for rich, wrinkly old women. But now that I had one in front of me, I changed my mind. Brian said something.

"Huh?"

"I said, *will you marry me?*"

"Yes! Oh, yes!"

PROTECT AND CHERISH ME, my ass, I think as I look at Tony, hardly able to hold his head up. Christelle brings him the medicine, three small pills. He takes one.

Is it foolish to marry someone who puts you in peril? It always looks good in the movies, when James Bond and the Bond girl are suspended over a pool of sharks. After all, danger is supposed to be the ultimate aphrodisiac. But the unspoken agreement is that Bond is going to get them both out of it. Preferably swinging on cables and shooting some bad guys on the way out.

How is Brian going to save me from falciparum malaria? Or will he just smooth back my hair, as Christelle is smoothing Tony's, then close his eyes and pray the drugs will work?

Chapter 9

Chimpanzees eat like Americans. They can down a pile of bananas in a New York minute. There is no eye contact. Very little conversation. It's more refueling a car than sharing a meal, and afterward the dining area looks like a bomb went off.

Bonobos eat like the French. No one is happy unless lunch takes three hours. There is a lot of talking in between courses (will you have a bite of pineapple with your mango? Oh no, please, you first). Peels are folded back delicately; seeds are carefully removed. The meal is all about the company, and afterward, everyone lounges about in a food coma, grooming and staring at the sky.

We tested twenty bonobos in the food-sharing test and they all passed. Sometimes there was a little sex before or after, or a playful romp. No hissy fits. No dominance displays. A baby bonobo could even nibble food out of a grown male's mouth.

Unlike with the chimps, Brian doesn't have to mix and match to try to find a tolerant pair. Everyone is tolerant. So Brian is now ready to test the next step—the bonobos are tolerant, but will they cooperate?

SEMENDWA LOUNGES IN HER HAMMOCK, one leg draped over the side and one hand lazily trailing the air like she's Cleopatra cruising the

Nile. Isiro watches me suspiciously. She comes right up against the bars and stares fiercely, daring me to put a foot out of line. All she needs is a black leather trench coat and a pistol.

"Okay, girls. Semendwa, come down from the hammock."

Semendwa peers over the edge at me and raises her eyebrows ever so slightly. Her bewitching eyes ask, "Why should I?"

"Come on, Semendwa, you're making scientific history here. You have to come down from the hammock."

She looks at me without moving. I stand on my tiptoes and offer her a banana. Instead of eating it, she takes it, sniffs it curiously, then moves the tip toward her vagina like a dildo. Then she drops it on the floor. How rude.

After I beg her for ten long minutes, she eventually comes down, presumably for a change of scenery. She majestically thrusts out her clitoris and looks at me demandingly.

In the wild, when young females become awkward adolescents, they wander away from their family group to find a new community. With my obviously immature swelling underneath my shorts and my skinny, presumably prepubescent limbs, that is probably what Semendwa takes me for—an immigrating female. I'm making the right noises, begging and pleading with her, and now she is making it clear who is in charge by having me wait while at the same time showing me there are no hard feelings by offering me her clitoris.

It's an impressive clitoris. Her swelling is as large as my head, a salmon-colored organ about to burst. A fold starts at her anus and splits the swelling like a peach, tapering to a clitoris the size and thickness of my little finger. No wonder bonobos have sex all the time. If my clitoris announced itself like that, I'd have more sex too.

Semendwa throws me a powerful beckoning stare. She is no Kikongo, anxiously thrusting the air with his man tool. She is bona fide bonobo nobility, and I'd better pay homage if I want to get anything done. I hold my hand out flat. She rubs her clitoris over it back and forth very fast, her head thrown back, her eyes squeezed shut, as though she is concentrating hard on an important thought.

Afterward, I wipe my hand on my shorts and wish desperately for a Wet One.

"Okay," says Brian, ignoring the boundaries I'm crossing in the name of science. Most of the bonobos are used to him now, as long as he follows the protocol for low-ranking bonobo males and stays on the periphery. Neither Semendwa nor Isiro acknowledges his existence.

He hands me an end of a rope that is threaded through the wooden plank piled high with food on both ends.

"On the count of three, throw them the ropes. One, two, three."

We each throw our end of the rope about a foot inside the enclosure toward the bonobos. Isiro looks at her end like it's a piece of dirt under her fingernails. Semendwa takes the end Brian has thrown and pulls it gently.

"Isiro, come on, you have to pull at the same time."

Isiro ignores me. Semendwa slowly unthreads the rope and pulls it into the room. She winds it around herself, feather-boa style.

"That's a bust," calls Brian. "Let's get the rope back for trial two."

Brian gives me a banana to offer to Semendwa.

"Semendwa. Give me the rope."

Semendwa unwinds the rope, then coils it around her waist and fluffs it up like a tutu. She is clearly infatuated with its tangerine color, its sinewy texture. She pushes her face against it and inhales deeply.

Brian has tragedy written all over his face. For the last ten years there was one thing that made him special—he thinks like a chimpanzee. He can look into their eyes and get a feeling for what they will do, what they want. Chimps aren't afraid of doors. They will sell their soul for a grape. If they take something from you, they will trade it for something better.

Bonobos are genetically so close to chimps that most people can't tell them apart, but Brian doesn't understand them. Everything they do is completely bizarre. And even though Brian prides himself on being one of the few people who think bonobos are different, he still thought he could work with bonobos the same way he works with chimps.

He knows bonobos aren't stupid. He knows the test is possible because he has already done everything at Ngamba Island. If the Ngamba Island chimps were as tolerant as bonobos, there is no telling what they could have done. Bonobos should be able to do this test. It should be easy for them. Instead, the whole experiment is about to fall apart because Semendwa loves the rope more than she loves bananas.

As Brian's faith in himself collapses, his arms hang limply by his sides and his head hangs low.

I put my arm around him and give him a quick hug. I look at Semendwa and the rope. She is hugging and grooming it, smoothing back the orange fibers and kissing them.

"Don't worry, babe, we'll find a way to do it."

Brian shrugs as though it doesn't matter but he is clearly in a world of pain.

"Let's go eat lunch."

"IT WAS A MIRACLE, this place."

Every lunch Claudine tells us a story. A leopard at the zoo that would place a paw on each of her shoulders and nuzzle her hair. A trip to the Mountains of the Moon to talk to Dian Fossey about whether she should leave the gorillas for the photographer she was in love with.

I find Claudine's stories enchanting. Her voice is unhurried and musical. The magic is in the space between her notes. Her pauses and sighs. Her fluttering hands.

Brian is too depressed by the failure of his experiment to listen.

"At the time, I knew almost everyone in Kinshasa."

When word got around that Claudine was taking care of Mikeno, more baby bonobos found their way to her. Some were given up by well-meaning owners who didn't know keeping a bonobo was illegal. Others were dumped on her doorstep by officials who had confiscated a bonobo but didn't know what to do with it.

During the war of 1998, every expatriate in their right mind fled the country. But Claudine couldn't. She had twelve baby bonobos in her garage.

"Are you insane?" asked Jo Thompson, a bonobo researcher forced to flee her field site in the Lukuru reserve. "Do you think they'll stay this size forever? These bonobos are going to be huge. Then what are you going to do with them? Put them in Kinshasa Zoo and let them starve with the other animals?"

"I'm not sure what I'm doing," Claudine said quietly. "But I will never put them in the zoo. I will find somewhere for them. Somewhere they can always see the sky."

Claudine was good friends with the director of TASOK, the American School of Kinshasa. Since everyone had left the country, there weren't many students. Next to TASOK was a thirty-acre forest surrounded by a fence. The director gave Claudine permission to keep the bonobos in the forest. So every day, Claudine drove twelve bonobos to the American school in her SUV. Most of the time they stayed in the forest, except Mikeno, who was obsessed with basketball. Whenever the local kids were playing he would jump the fence, steal the ball, and dribble up and down the court.

It wasn't a permanent solution. For eight years, Claudine kept the bonobos at TASOK. Once, when Kinshasa was under fire, Claudine had to run into the forest, bullets whizzing past her head, until she stumbled on Mikeno lying facedown in the dirt in combat position.

When the war ended in 2002, people began to return and the American school started enrollments.

"I knew I had to find somewhere else. I found money with WSPA. One of their people, Gary Richardson, was an old friend of mine. I found a place twice and changed my mind, because of the political situation. But then I found somewhere perfect. It was the garden of the presidential palace. Mobutu loved nature; he had a forest filled with many animals. This forest was over seventy-five acres, right in the middle of Kinshasa. On the weekends people would come to take picnics there.

"I had everything organized; Gary was arriving in two days. The electric fence was on its way, on a barge from South Africa. Then President Kabila changed his mind. Just *comme ça*, he said no.

"The next morning I woke up full of despair. I made my coffee and stared into it. What was I going to do? Gary was coming, the fence was on a barge, and I had twelve bonobos with nowhere to live. WSPA would pull out; I would lose my funding. Then what?

"That morning the mother of Mimi came over."

The woman who raised the bonobo Mimi as a daughter for fifteen years was a good friend of Claudine's.

"*Mais, ma chère,*" she said when she saw Claudine's face, "I've never seen you like this."

Claudine told her the problem. At the end, Mimi's mother paused thoughtfully.

"But what about Petit Chutes?" she said.

"Never heard of it."

"The owner just got out of prison. Grab your keys. Let's go."

PETIT CHUTES, or Little Falls, begins in the Crystal Mountains and turns into the Lukaya River. Just south of Kinshasa, the river flows over several cascades and forms a lake in the river valley. The sandy shores of the river are a popular picnic spot for those wanting a respite from the heat and dust of the city.

The forest behind Petit Chutes belonged to Mobutu's senior administrator, called Le Chef. He was imprisoned almost immediately by Kabila Senior, who thought after all those years in Mobutu's pocket, Le Chef must have some secrets worth sharing.

"I'll sell it to you," Le Chef said when Claudine told him her story. "I have nothing. I must start again. I'll take two hundred thousand dollars."

It was a pittance for so much land. But to Claudine, it may as well have been $200 million.

"I have not one penny," she told him.

He grew misty-eyed. "Mobutu loved animals," he said. "He was a wonderful conservationist. I helped him make Salonga National Park because he wanted to protect the wildlife."

His eyes snapped back into focus.

"Take it. Have it for your bonobos. You can pay me in a year."

"So GARY ARRIVED. We put up the fence. And when we brought the bonobos here for the first time, Mama Henriette had Maya on her back.

"'Oh,' she said. 'It's Lola.'

"I had never heard this word before.

"'But, Madame,' she said, 'Lola is paradise. It's the sky. It's heaven.'

"And I smiled at her.

"'Yes, it is. Lola ya Bonobo.'"

I AM READY to give a standing ovation. I have tears in my eyes. Brian pushes food around his plate. Claudine is not used to this sullen silence after her miracle story.

"And, Brian," she says tactfully, "how is the research?"

"Well," he says, scraping his fork on the edge of his plate, "bonobos aren't very food-motivated. I think they can do the test but they're not interested in food."

Claudine pauses thoughtfully.

"You know, some nuns came here and asked me which food the bonobos loved most. I said green apples. They brought a whole box and threw them into the enclosure. Oh la la, there was a lot of sex. The nuns were blushing. I don't think they had ever seen such things."

It's worth a shot.

APPLES DON'T GROW IN CONGO, so we have to get them flown in from South Africa. They cost $2 each, the daily salary for a Congolese person. The cost of a box of thirty could feed a Congolese family for two months. I pull six out of the refrigerator.

To me, this doesn't make any sense. I hate apples. Besides being sour, they are a bad-luck fruit. They got Adam and Eve into trouble.

They killed Snow White. At Lola, the bonobos get mangoes, papayas, bananas, sugarcane, a red bush fruit called *tondelo,* and a bizarre fruit with a purple shell and sweet white flesh called mangosteen. Why would they even look at apples when they had the good stuff?

I line up the apples. They *are* particularly good-looking, as you would hope for the price. Their skin is the color of a fern, beaded with moisture. I cut one and it falls apart in two crisp white halves. The seeds are polished cedar. The flesh smells like summer.

Semendwa and Isiro are in the testing room. Isiro glares at me and Semendwa peers over the edge of her hammock.

I put my bag down and pull out an apple. Semendwa lifts her head and says, "Huh."

Isiro tries to squeeze her long body through the bars so she can steal the whole bag.

I waggle the apple in front of them, pushing it under my nose and sniffing as though I'm going to gobble it up right in front of them. They drop the cool act and start chorusing in high, excited squeaks. They look at each other, look at the apple, look at me.

And then I am treated to a legendary bonobo experience.

Semendwa climbs down from her hammock. She is hurrying, making her full hips sway and her breasts swing. Isiro sprawls on her back, legs open wide, hands thrown above her head in abandon.

Semendwa climbs on top of her and pins her arms with her hands. Isiro wraps her thighs around Semendwa's waist and Semendwa begins to thrust her giant clitoris back and forth against Isiro's clitoris faster and faster. Semendwa stares into Isiro's eyes, her pendulous swelling gathering momentum.

Isiro opens her mouth, squeezes her eyes shut, and shrieks. Her hips grind in time with Semendwa's. Semendwa utters breathy, panting cries.

Suddenly Semendwa arches her back, which pushes her loins deep into Isiro's. She throws back her head. Isiro clenches her thighs. Then they both shudder uncontrollably for four seconds—the exact length of my own orgasms.

The apple I'm holding drops from my hand and hits the ground at the same time as my jaw. I turn and look at Brian. He has a guilty look on his face, like I've caught him watching porn.

Isiro reaches through the bars and picks up the apple. She takes a bite, then Semendwa takes it from her and takes a bite. They munch away nonchalantly, as though they have not just had wild, hot sex right in front of us.

It takes twenty minutes for us to recover and for them to politely finish the apple, like friends smoking spliffs in front of the TV. Avoiding each other's eyes, Brian and I load up the red plank with apple pieces on either side. Semendwa turns her vagina toward Isiro, who touches her clitoris lovingly.

We throw the ropes into the enclosure. Isiro and Semendwa each pull their end of the rope and the long red plank inches slowly toward them, shrieking over the floor tiles and resting against the bars of their room with a thud. Isiro and Semendwa sit at the same end of the plank biting into apple pieces with satisfying crunches.

"Well," I say finally. "I'll have what they're having."

Chapter 10

On the steps in front of our house, I see a coiled shadow. In the moonlight I can just make out the absurdly large diamond shape of its head.

Gaboon vipers are the dragons of sub-Saharan Africa. Two horns perch between the nostrils, and beneath the pale eyes two brown triangles point outward. They have the longest fangs and spew the most venom of any poisonous snake. If these fangs find you, the initial symptoms are intense pain and blistering around the bite. Your tongue and eyelids swell, you go into convulsions, and you may defecate or urinate uncontrollably before you lose consciousness. You start to hemorrhage in your lungs, intestines, and urinary tract. Eventually, the venom erodes the muscles around the heart and you die of a heart attack.

And here one is, obscured in darkness on the front porch. I know I should scream for my fiancé, that in such situations, it is supposed to be he who leaps to my defense, brandishing a sword or a gun or *something,* and throws me out of harm's way, thereby saving my life.

"Alan!" I cry. "Alan!"

Alan cleans our house. He is small for a Congolese man because he was poisoned by his stepmother while he was growing up. His mother died when he was five and his father remarried. In small villages, where resources are tight and families are large, joining two families together usually ends up more *Cinderella* than *Brady Bunch*. There are thousands of children who are abandoned once their parents have remarried, or, if they are unlucky, their stepparent goes even further and murders them. Alan's stepmother put small amounts of poison she obtained from a witch doctor in Alan's porridge every morning. So Alan ran away from home and ended up at Lola, where he found himself with a new group of hairy orphans.

Alan loves the bonobos, especially the nursery, and carefully cuts up their food and prepares their milk each morning. He sleeps in a small shed near our house so he can save money on rent.

After hearing my cries, he arrives in seconds.

"It's a snake! Right there! A Gaboon viper."

Alan runs to his shack and returns with a shovel, and while I stand on the outdoor sofa, my hands over my mouth in horror, he decapitates it. The body whips around wildly and I have an outrageous fear that it will grow seven new heads and kill us all. After ten minutes, the thrashing subsides.

"*Merci*, Alan."

"*Merci*, madam."

He picks it up by its tail and goes back to his hut to cook and eat it. I sit on the outside sofa and stare at the smattering of blood on the steps.

WE HAVE BEEN HERE for two weeks. We were supposed to leave with Richard but Brian keeps changing our plane tickets.

The Ngamba chimps were so incredible that the results of the cooperation experiments were published in *Science*, one of the best academic journals. The chimps starred in documentaries by the BBC and National Geographic.

But all you had to do to make their cooperation fall apart was put the food in the middle of the plank. With the food in the middle, one chimp ended up hogging the food and the other chimp would refuse to play the game.

Now that we have figured out that apples are the magic fruit, the bonobos, who have never seen the test before, have conquered so many cooperation trials that we start trying to make them fail. We put the food in the middle. We mix up the pairs. Nothing works. Young ones, old ones, decrepit ones—they all pull the rope together. The only bonobo who didn't cooperate was Maya, who was actually in labor, but we didn't know until she gave birth to a healthy baby boy a few hours later.

Brian, his faith in himself restored, walks around beaming.

"*Bonjour!*" he cries to each of the keepers as they arrive at Lola in the morning.

"*Bonjour!*" they chorus, waving their hands wildly.

I'm exhausted. The experiments are so detail-oriented. Precise. Meticulous. Everything about them goes against my sloppy nature. It takes all my powers of concentration not to screw up.

We get up at six A.M. and we don't stop until fourteen hours later. Cut the apple, load the plank, stop Semendwa from stealing the rope. Again. Again. Change bonobos. Change buildings. Enter the data. We even skip Papa Jean's delicious three-course lunches and grab a quick sandwich so we don't lose time.

The building is sweltering hot with 100 percent humidity. The first day I thought I would faint but now I'm kind of numb. It is as though my blood has thinned so I can bear the heat, but it takes me a week to recover from each sudden movement.

I want to go home.

But Brian has another test. Tolerance is not necessarily voluntary. It can be controlled by your emotions, and like all emotions, you feel it before you can think about it.

If tolerance makes bonobos more cooperative than chimpanzees, then maybe this is a difference in emotions rather than intelligence. If the emotions of chimps are significantly different than those of bonobos, it could clear up a lot of issues, such as why chimps kill each other and bonobos don't. And if we can find out how the emotional lives of chimps and bonobos are similar to and different from our own, then it could tell us what makes humans unique.

One of the most basic emotional tests is to see how someone reacts to new objects. Psychologists do this test with children to predict whether children will be introverted or extroverted as adults, or whether they will be prone to temper tantrums or anxiety attacks. But no one has ever used this test to compare chimpanzees and bonobos to humans.

I want to kill myself just thinking about it.

Brian pokes his head out of the house.

"Hey, Skippy. Can you make me a cup of tea?"

"Alan just killed a Gaboon viper."

I'm not sure what I was expecting. A show of bravado. A blustering assurance that he would have done the same if he had seen it first.

"Eeek!" squeals Brian, and runs back inside the house.

Chapter 11

I pick up a red plastic porcupine the size of a tennis ball and move it right to left across the table.

"Left to right!" Brian hisses. "You were supposed to move it left to right."

I move it left to right.

"Not now, you've already moved it. You're going to fuck up the coding."

It's too late anyway. Kikongo whoops at the porcupine and runs all the way to the back of the room. He approaches a few steps forward, then runs away, shrieking alarm calls, looking around wildly for someone to back him up against the freaky red spiky thing with eyeballs. The concrete acts like a megaphone and Kikongo's cries bounce off the walls, rising in volume and pitch. My ears hurt. I have a splitting headache.

Brian yells something.

"What?"

"The coconut! Don't forget, now it's the coconut!"

I put the porcupine back into a bag of tricks beside the table. Kikongo approaches cautiously, wondering where it went. He raises his arms repeatedly in a solo version of the wave.

"Kikongo!" I call. "Kikongo!"

I offer him a peanut to resume his position in the middle of the table. He approaches distrustfully and takes the peanut. Then I accidentally pull out the police car instead of the coconut. We bought the car in Germany, so it is white and green, with POLIZEI on the side. Kikongo's eyes become large with wonder. He backs away, all the while keeping his eyes on the toy.

I pick up the remote control. I flick the switch. The police car lights up and the siren sounds, and it speeds from the right side of the table to the left.

Kikongo totally freaks out. He Spider-Man-leaps from the floor thirteen feet into the air into his sleeping hammock, which hangs from the ceiling. He screams at the police car, cowering in the burlap sack. He pops up, then ducks, as though the police car is going to shoot supersonic rays at him. He is shrieking so loud that the bonobos come out of the forest and look inside the building to find out what the hell is going on.

Mama Henriette, who used to be Kikongo's substitute mother, is supposed to be helping us with the test. Instead, she is asleep on the floor, although how she can possibly sleep through the racket is beyond me.

The Mamas have a serious attitude problem. We are doubling their salaries, but you would think we were Portuguese slavers. Every time I ask one of them to help in one of the experiments, they look at me as though I've told them to clean a toilet. During the test, they stare morbidly into space or lie down on the floor and go to sleep. In their eyes, I see the reflection of my own thoughts, that these tests are the stupidest thing they have ever seen, that we are crazy, and that no amount of money is worth the physical exertion when it is 100 degrees in the shade.

"Explain the test to them," Brian says, convinced that if they understand the big picture, they will suddenly find participating irresistible. I try to explain the significance of the emotional reactivity test in French, and they roll their eyes and yawn.

"Try and get her to pay attention," Brian entreats, while Mama

Henriette sprawls on the floor, arm over her eyes as though she is imagining she is on a beach in Barbados. But what should I say? We have been testing for six hours in the stifling heat, and lying on the floor and visualizing Barbados is a smart and definitely more appealing option.

I hide everything in the bag. Kikongo goes to the door of the building and sticks his penis through the bars, waving it wildly at the bonobos outside munching on papaya and manioc leaves, begging for a bonobo handshake.

Isiro approaches. She is frowning. Obviously all the yelling is disturbing the peace of her Tuesday afternoon. She yanks Kikongo's penis hard. He shrieks, then shuts up.

Instead of coming back to do the test, Kikongo launches into a running imitation of farm animals. He leaps like a frog. He squats on his haunches and waddles like a duck. Then he gets up on all fours and starts swaying side to side like a hypnotized cow.

"You were supposed to take out the coconut, not the car. How many times do I have to tell you to look at the coding sheets before you take out the objects?"

Brian is talking to me like I'm redefining stupid. I've had it.

"I'm sick of this. I've done nothing but work my ass off for three weeks, and all you can do is criticize. I've never done an experiment before. I have no idea what I'm doing. I'm tired and I want to go home and these bonobos are totally *weird* and none of your experiments are ever going to work."

For emphasis, I throw the red plastic porcupine down as hard as I can. It bounces into the room with Kikongo, who looks at it for a few long minutes, then starts rubbing his penis on the spikes. I run out of the building, all the way back to the house, go into the bathroom, and lock the door.

When I was going all schmoopie for Brian at the source of the Nile, I didn't know the cost of falling in love with a man and his dream. A dream is all-consuming. Nothing exists outside it. There is no other reality. He is a man obsessed or in love. He barely sleeps.

I know he loves me. But if I left him, he would still have his dream. If he lost his dream, he would be nothing.

And the worst thing is, I have no dream. There is nothing I particularly want to do or be. I don't have visions of saving famine children or homeless animals. I'm not cut out for missionary work or heart surgery.

Brian is trying to make ape orphanages in Africa an alternative to cognitive work at biomedical laboratories. What the fuck have I done lately?

I have no home. Our stuff is in Germany, but our furniture is made out of cardboard boxes. Between the two of us, we hardly own anything. I have no family in Germany and no friends. So really, the only thing I have is this dream that is not even mine.

I lie down on the bathroom floor, which smells faintly of disinfectant.

The door handle twitches like a cartoon ghost trying to get in. I hear a deep sigh on the other side.

"Skippy, let me in."

"No."

"Let me in or I'll pick the lock."

Damn it. I could hurl my full body weight against the door to stop him but it would compromise the dramatic artistry of my posture. Using my toes to switch the lock, I unlock the door. Brian takes in the scene and asks the obvious.

"What are you doing on the floor?"

I don't answer.

He kneels beside me and smooths the lank hair from my forehead. "Are you okay? Do you miss home?"

It's not even the beginning of what's wrong with me but I nod and start to cry. Not pretty crying but throaty, unapologetic howls. The bonobos probably think I'm a werewolf. Brian curls his arm under my neck and pulls me to a sitting position.

"I know this isn't easy for you but it's not forever. If you want, we'll go back to Australia. I'll quit academia. I'll—I'll be a plumber."

I snort at this unlikely scenario. Brian has mysophobia—a fear of germs. He opens doors with his shirtsleeves and pushes ATM buttons with his knuckles so he doesn't get other people's bacteria on his fingertips that might spread to another part of his body. I can hardly see him unclogging a toilet, arm deep in someone else's shit.

"You're my whole world. I'll do anything to make you happy. We'll sort it out. Everything will be okay."

He holds me patiently until I'm cried out. He gently takes off my clothes and puts me in the shower. The warm water feels good on my body. It cleans out my tear ducts; the steam opens my lungs. Afterward, Brian wraps me in a lemon towel. He smells good, like a feather blanket or a cup of hot chocolate. He sounds like the ocean where I grew up. He feels like home.

Until now, I've had only one foot in this relationship. Sure, we're engaged, but I haven't really committed. I haven't even bought the dress. It's time to either jump in or pull out.

I always imagined doing something worthwhile with my life. But I got adventure confused with substance. I thought if I went amazing places and did interesting things, that would be enough. But that's just a spectator sport. Every time I got bored, I packed up and ran around until I found the next interesting thing. I never stuck around long enough to build anything meaningful.

I sigh. I know someone I can talk to. He'll know what to do.

I SIT BY THE LAKE, looking for him. Mimi sits dead center in the food patch. She is Zen calm. There is an invisible circle around her, and all the food within the circle is hers. If one of the little boy bonobos reaches for so much as an orange pip, she simply looks at him. They turn to stone, then slowly, as though tiptoeing past a sleeping beast, they back away into the safe zone.

Mimi rarely interferes in a fight but she might stand up and turn her Medusa eyes to the offending party, at which point her police force, led by Isiro, swiftly deals the punishment. Mimi never actively defends anyone but she allows bonobos to hide behind her tiny frame.

This is enough to protect them, since no one, but no one, charges Mimi.

There are so few female-dominated societies. Hyenas are one, but female hyenas are as beefed up as the males, and they also have penises. Female black widow spiders eat their mates, but they are four times bigger.

Mimi is half the size of Tatango but she is clearly dominant over everyone. She has complete power without using any force.

Tatango is by the fence, his fingers through the wire, looking grim as always. Everyone has a different story of how Tatango lost his smile. Claudine says it was when he was "corrected" by the Terrible Five. Jacques tells me it was because when he was little, he used to have a best friend called Vivi and they went everywhere together with their arms wrapped around each other. Then Vivi died of a sickness and Tatango never smiled again.

Tatango fascinates me. He is endlessly displaying, but he displays with twigs and squeaks instead of roars. He throws dirt at visitors, but only because he wants you to manicure his fingernails (he can't stand it when they are dirty). He terrorizes the males but hides behind Mimi at the slightest sign of trouble.

Isiro flanks Mimi. Out of the corner of her eye, she sees Kikwit with a juicy piece of sugarcane that she wants. She stares at him, her eyes burning a hole through his head. Kikwit is built like a football player—all muscle and no neck. He could probably pick up Isiro and throw her into the forest, but instead he starts squealing, drops his sugarcane, and rubs his penis over Kikongo.

Semendwa lolls back luxuriously, one hand on her belly. She is so pregnant her full breasts are bursting with milk. She flicks her chin at one of the young girls, who immediately comes over and starts combing through Semendwa's hair. I try to imagine Semendwa as a devoted mother, doting on her young. I can't quite picture it. I think she will be the kind of mother who hires a night nurse and puts her baby in day care.

Then I see him. He sits in his special pose, fist under his chin, elbow on his knee. I sit down in front of him and start talking. The way he looks at me convinces me he understands at least a little of what I'm saying.

There is something in the eyes of a bonobo that you don't see in those of a tiger or a shark. They are human eyes, but not the cautious glimpse of a stranger you pass on a city street, or the pretended interest of a shrink you're paying $300 an hour. Or someone you think you recognize but don't.

The eyes of a bonobo are the eyes of your best friend or a lover or a priest. They see into you. They see nothing else. They invite confession.

I tell Mikeno things I don't tell anyone. How watching my parents' marriage fall apart took away my faith in happy endings. That I'm worried Brian will suddenly wake up and realize I'm not good enough for him, that he could do so much better than me.

Mikeno nods slowly. I'm sitting on a slight hill so I'm holding on to the chain link of the fence for balance. He covers my hand with his.

I don't usually talk to animals, and if I do, I don't expect them to talk back. But sitting here, hypnotized by Mikeno's flickering eyes, I hear a voice in my head.

Don't be afraid.

It could be my subconscious telling me not to fuck up a good thing. It could be God trying to get in touch—I've heard He does this kind of thing to people who have been ignoring Him for years. But as soon as I hear the voice, Mikeno smiles, and I feel calm.

Isiro approaches the fence. She has been watching us. She adores Mikeno. When the keepers moved him to another group, she pined for him so much they had to move him back again. The other females, even the dominant ones, are always presenting themselves to Mikeno for sex. He is the Brad Pitt of bonobos, and the girls are lining up to give themselves to him any way he wants. But Isiro loves him most.

Isiro's eyes are as black as coal. There is no mistaking the look she gives me, the way she snatches his hand from mine. These are universal signals among women. *He's mine.*

She softens. It's not my fault that along with every other female, I've fallen in love with him. She shows me her swelling as if in compensation and takes Mikeno away.

Chapter 12

❧

Six months later, Brian and I are married on a blue summer's day on a beach in Australia.

It is joy and hope and love and light.

It is the perfect end and a perfect beginning.

It is truly the happiest day of my life.

ALL OF A SUDDEN, we are back in Congo. But now we are man and wife.

Chapter 13

❧

While Brian and I were getting married, Congo was preparing for her own big day—her first democratic elections in forty years.

After decades of corruption and bloodshed, Congo's honor is about to be restored. She will be led, a blushing bride, toward the altar of democracy.

Everyone wants the ceremony to go off without a hitch. The rest of the world, particularly Western Europe, is footing a whopping $500 million bill. With more than half of the world's cobalt, a third of the world's diamonds, and 70 percent of the world's coltan, Congo could lift Africa out of poverty and bring peace to the Great Lakes region.

Like groomsmen, whose traditional role was to protect the bride from abduction by a warring clan, seventeen thousand U.N. peacekeepers are in attendance. It's the biggest peacekeeping force in the world, with troops from America, South Africa, Belgium, and Japan.

But who will be the groom?

At the first round of elections in July, thirty-three suitors lined up for Congo's hand. From their ranks, there emerged one clear favorite—Joseph Kabila, Congo's first knight, who has guarded her faithfully for the last five years.

Kabila has a face you want to run your hands over. High, sculpted cheekbones. Bowed, sensuous lips. He has the cool beauty of a marble bust, but instead of a dull gaze, his eyes seem to burn with the weight of his country's burdens. It is hard to imagine him as the son of the thug Kabila Senior, who took over Congo after Mobutu fled the country.

Kabila Junior has the eyes of an angel witnessing the Fall.

His past is a mystery. Rumor has it he was born in a rebel camp in the mountains of eastern Congo, where Kabila Senior was plotting to overthrow Mobutu's government. He may or may not have had a Rwandan mother, and Kabila Senior may or may not be his father.

While still a child, Kabila Junior was smuggled across the border into Tanzania to escape Mobutu's intelligence service. He did not return to Congo until his father launched his full-scale attack on Mobutu in 1996. Kabila Junior led the Kadogo army of children to Kinshasa, winning many battles along the way. When his father set himself up as president, Kabila Junior reportedly went to China and was trained by the military before returning to be his father's chief of staff.

But none of these "facts" have been confirmed. There are no books on Kabila, no papers published on his past. It's as though he is a ghost, conjured from the smoky mountain air.

Kabila Senior was assassinated by his bodyguard in 2001. The guard walked up to the president in the middle of a meeting and shot Kabila three times at point-blank range. Ten days later, his son assumed power. At only twenty-nine years old, he became the youngest president in the world.

Kabila Senior was a corrupt and belligerent tyrant, and many were afraid to hope his son would be any better. But Kabila Junior has done Congo proud. He brought peace to the whole country except the east, bringing together rebels and warlords to form a government of national unity. He created a parliament that drafted and adopted the constitution of the third republic.

And now, like an honorable knight, he is allowing Congo to choose who will rule her.

The people in the east love him. He is their native son and was born in their mountains. He fought against the Rwandans and the

Ugandans, who terrorized the villages and stripped the land of its resources. But Kinshasa, with its nine million people, does not trust him. He speaks Tanzania's languages, English and Swahili, better than he does Congo's tongues, French and Lingala. He went to university in Uganda, and then there are those rumors of his Rwandan mother.

Kabila isn't perfect. Kinshasa's urbanites have watched the standard of living fall and unemployment break record levels, while the political elite postponed the transition so they could enjoy high paychecks and royal benefits. There are rumors of vote rigging and sabotage. *Is he even Congolese?* Kinshasa mutters. *Is this even an election?*

In all fairy tales, there is a villain. In the July 2006 elections, Kabila won 45 percent of the vote, but he needed 50 percent to become the undisputed ruler. So now there is a standoff between Kabila and the next in line—rebel warlord Jean-Pierre Bemba.

Like any good suitor, Bemba is well-connected and filthy rich. He has at least several hundred million dollars. His sister is the wife of Mobutu's son. He even served as Mobutu's personal assistant in the early nineties, which is no doubt where he learned the lifestyle of the rich and infamous.

The man is enormous. He is more than six feet tall, and his massive girth makes him look like a silverback gorilla. After an MBA in a prestigious Brussels university, Bemba grew fat on the profits of his family businesses of wood and coffee, as well as running other endeavors on the side. But Bemba soon realized that money was not worth having without power. In 1998, when Kabila Senior seized the government, Bemba turned in his Armani suits for combat fatigues and started the rebel group the Movement for the Liberation of Congo (MLC).

Armed to the teeth, his reign of terror is vividly remembered by the people in the east. Near a town called Beni, U.N. investigators reported 117 executions; 65 rapes, including the rape of children; 82 kidnappings; and 27 cases of torture. People were made to eat members of their families, and the rebels also ate human flesh. It was rumored that Bemba himself ate an Ituri pygmy.

Backed by several African leaders, Bemba occasionally took time out from menacing Congo to help his buddies. One of them was the president of the Central African Republic, Ange-Félix Patassé, who asked Bemba to bring his rebel group over to suppress a coup attempt in 2002.

What Bemba and his rebel army did in the villages of that country had the International Criminal Court screaming for his head. The allegations included looting villages, torturing and killing innocent civilians, mass-raping women, and, to top it off, "committing outrages upon personal dignity."

THE FINAL ELECTION IS IN OCTOBER 2006, three months away. Who will Congo choose, for better or for worse? The mysterious prince who, despite his five years as president, is still a stranger? Or the fat mercenary whose victims' screams still trail in his wake?

Of course both parties promise to honor the votes cast by the people. They promise to accept defeat gracefully, should it come, and to help their rival build a better, stronger Congo.

Yeah, right.

OUR TRIP TO LOLA was already booked when the international airport of Kinshasa shut down. The first round of elections was relatively peaceful—only a dozen or so dead, with forty polling stations burned down. Which everyone agrees is almost perfect compared with the prospect of another war.

But the day before we arrive, violent clashes between Bemba's and Kabila's men leave twenty-three dead and forty-three wounded. The Republican Guard has moved heavy artillery into the city, including armored personnel carriers with machine guns and tanks with howitzers. The airport is in lockdown and Brian and I can't get in. So we take a little detour.

WHEN THE PORTUGUESE ARRIVED on the coast of West Africa in the early fifteenth century, they expected to find a land full of monsters and people with two heads. Europeans called the waters below Morocco the Sea of Darkness, and beyond that it was rumored that ships would be swallowed by boiling waters or destroyed by flames falling from the sky.

When the Portuguese explorer Diogo Cão ventured even farther south than the Sea of Darkness into the Sea of Obscurity, he found a kingdom that defied description. The blue-green waters of the ocean turned a muddy brown, and fish as big as children leaped into the sailors' starving nets.

As Cão pressed on, suddenly the land split to give way to the yawning mouth of the largest river anyone had ever seen. Seven miles wide, the other bank was a faint line on the horizon as golden water spewed into the sea at a rate of a million gallons per second. The pounding flow was so powerful it carved a ravine in the ocean floor that plunged 4,000 feet deep and ran for 100 miles. Strange trees grew their roots into the sea, and the giant river was threaded with sandbanks and streams.

The indigenous people called themselves Bakongo, or "people of Kongo." They were part of a great and mighty kingdom that spread from Angola to the top of DRC.

The Bakongo were no savages. They greeted the Portuguese in a lyrical language rich with flowery metaphors. As they led the Portuguese through their lands to the king, the explorers saw that farmers had cultivated the jungle and grew crops of fruit and vegetables. They also raised livestock such as cows, goats, and pigs. Blacksmiths smelted iron and forged copper. Sculptors, potters, weavers, and artists were busy at work and there were marble columns, obelisks, and intricate designs carved into ivory. Cowrie shells were used as currency, and the king collected taxes for public works. The kingdom was so successful that crime was scarce and the population of three million was growing steadily.

The royal court was on top of a cliff, southeast of the Congo River. The king of Bakongo, Nzinga Nkuwu, sat on an ebony and ivory throne. He held an elaborate court, complete with concubines, advisers, attendants, and even an executioner.

But what most impressed the Portuguese, and what would ultimately become the downfall of the Bakongo, were the slaves. These were prisoners the Bakongo had captured in warfare, convicted criminals, debtors, or children who had been sold as part of a dowry. The Portuguese immediately saw a source of labor for their sugar and coffee plantations in their new colony, Brazil. So the Portuguese began a trade in human lives with the Bakongo ruling class. The slave trade became so profitable and so vicious that some Bakongo even sold members of their own families.

Distressed by the exodus of his people and disillusioned with the Portuguese, the next Bakongo king, Afonso, tried to sever the ties. But it was too late. The trade continued and expanded until other European countries pushed the Portuguese south into Angola and scrambled for the remainder of the Bakongo kingdom.

While Henry Morton Stanley was blasting his way through the Crystal Mountains, building King Leopold's railroad into the interior, Pietro di Brazza, the seventh son of an Italian count, claimed the north bank of Stanley Pool. The pool was actually a wide stretch of the Congo River, and di Brazza would build the capital city of the land he claimed for France. Brazzaville and Stanleyville (now Kinshasa) are the only two capital cities in the world that face off across a river like two gigantic egos.

Both the French and the Belgians named their territories after the Bakongo people, and so the two countries became known as French Congo and Belgian Congo. I still can't get the two sorted out, so Brian simplifies it for me by calling them bonobo Congo (Belgian Congo/Democratic Republic of Congo) and chimpanzee Congo (French Congo/Republic of Congo), because even though there are chimpanzees in both countries, there are bonobos in only one.

When France took over chimpanzee Congo in 1880, it set about ruthlessly enslaving the locals to extract rubber, ivory, and timber. In 1960, the country was given independence but was still heavily dependent on France for aid. During the oil boom of the late seventies and early eighties, massive reserves of oil were found offshore. The

French company Elf set about drilling, and in return for the massive profits, France built schools, supermarkets, and hospitals.

When oil prices crashed in 1985, the dictator of chimpanzee Congo, Denis Sassou-Nguesso, was in the middle of a spending spree and was forced to mortgage Congo's future oil earnings to the French. By 1990, Congo was almost $5 billion in debt. Unfortunately for the French, in the democratic elections of 1992, Sassou was defeated. The elected president, Pascal Lissouba, was less than friendly toward Congo's former colonial ruler and tried to introduce free trade by allowing other foreign companies to drill for oil. In retaliation, France virtually cut off aid to Congo and inflated the Congolese franc by 200 percent. The country descended into civil war as the ex-dictator Sassou tried to get his old job back.

A third of the country was displaced, tens of thousands were killed or injured, and thousands of women were raped. But unlike bonobo Congo, where a hundred men with guns can hijack a diamond mine and force the local population to dig for gems to exchange for guns and ammunition, oil rigs are a little more difficult to seize. Miles offshore, oil rigs pose logistical problems for rebels, who couldn't operate the technology even if they got there.

Without a government, there was no oil, and if there was no oil, there was no money. The elite quickly decided it was worth putting aside their differences. The French president, Jacques Chirac, supplied Sassou with arms and aid, and Sassou toppled the democratically elected government and regained control in 1997. His opposition settled for lucrative places in his government, and it was business as usual. Democracy was put on the back burner until a rigged election in 2002, where Sassou won by a landslide because there was no opposition party.

In 2006, chimpanzee Congo pumped out 265,000 barrels of oil per day, more barrels per person than Iraq. Oil provides 90 percent of chimpanzee Congo's foreign exchange earnings, 40 percent of its GDP, and 70 percent of its government's revenues.

.   .   .

THE PLANE TO POINTE-NOIRE, the Republic of the Congo's oil nerve center, is half business class. More than half the flight is full of fat oil barons wearing Armani suits and gold Rolex watches. Air France has a direct flight from Paris to Pointe-Noire that can cost up to $6,000 in economy class. The food is magnificent, and the earplugs, earphones, and eye masks are packaged in deep-blue satin pouches. Even the leg room is twice as spacious as a normal flight.

Brian and I are the only people on the flight not heading into Pointe-Noire to roll around in oil money like pigs in mud. We, with our unwashed hair, tracksuits, and baseball caps, look like backpackers who ran out of cash six months ago. But Brian's head is held high, because just like the Blues Brothers, we are on a Mission from God. Or at least Brian's god, who is Science, hallowed be His name.

Chapter 14

When we arrive at the Pointe-Noire airport, the luxury plane tips us out unceremoniously onto broken tarmac that leads into a dirt cowshed. The immigration policy is scrawled on the wall in chalk, and dust tinkles on the corrugated iron roof.

The customs officials sit at old-school desks punctured by termites and a couple of bullets. We line up for an hour while the officials scrutinize the passports of everyone on the plane. Another official eyes us with suspicion and asks what we are doing here.

Finally, we are allowed blinking into the new sun that has just risen over the grubby parking lot. The people who watch us emerge are not the laughing Ugandans or the smooth-operating Tanzanians. They are harder. More hostile. Oil money has made them expectant, then bitter. They see money dripping from oil barons and don't understand why they aren't getting richer.

In truth, it is the people who are keeping the country poor. When your economy is based on oil, economic theory says you need about 25 barrels of oil per person each year to see any kind of advantage. Chimpanzee Congo, with its 24.7 barrels of oil per person, is right on the cusp. They aren't poverty-stricken Nigeria, which, despite its millions of barrels of oil, has so many people that there are only 6 barrels of oil per head. But they aren't Kuwait either, whose 300 barrels per head keep the desert sultans in gold and diamonds.

The Pointe-Noire oil boom in the eighties led to massive construction projects in the city. Now it is slowly falling apart. Concrete cancer eats away at the buildings, and the roads are pockmarked with potholes. In the parking lot, children hurl themselves at us, demanding money. A woman kicks me in the back.

"White witch," she hisses. "I have put a spell on you."

We get into an SUV and drive forty minutes out of the city. The crumbling buildings give way to small villages and the occasional resort. Suddenly the air turns to salt, and we are driving along the same sea that the Portuguese sailed past in wonder almost four centuries ago.

About a mile before the road runs out, there is a dirt track that leads us back inland. The houses disappear. The coastal thickets turn into a savanna with oases of forest. When the wind blows, the golden strands of grass ripple like mermaids' hair, and brightly colored sunbirds somersault after long-legged crickets.

It is precisely the beauty of the landscape that leaves me so unprepared for the savagery of screams floating down from a nearby hill.

As WE PULL UP AT OLETI, the biggest chimpanzee sanctuary in the world, this is what we see:

Chimps are running everywhere. Keepers run after them yelling. The chimps yell back and run even faster.

A chimp tears through a clothesline and ends up with a shirt on his face. He waves his arms blindly in front of him, then crashes into the monkey enclosure, where Baboo, the killer monkey, goes into a psycho fit.

Another three chimps run from a furious housekeeper chasing them with a broom. One of them is holding a pink plastic shoe.

"Water!" one of the keepers yells. "Get some water!"

But there is no water. The nearest well is a twenty-minute drive away. So the keepers chase the chimps around with empty cups, but no one, including the chimps, thinks for a second there is any water in them.

A chimp pole-dances around the stalk of the satellite dish, apparently enjoying the dizzy sensation. There are chimps on the roof of the car, inside the laundry chewing on soap, running in circles around the mango tree. It's kindergarten on methamphetamines.

"At least it's not on fire," I say hopefully. On our last visit, the sanctuary caught fire twice and the staff manager was almost killed in a car crash.

Brian hides his face in his hands.

Maria, the new manager, sees us. She walks calmly through the pandemonium, a cup of coffee in her hand, as though she is on her way to the library. Her long hair is braided into a rope that hangs over one shoulder. She has the body of a swimsuit model. Brian and I look at each other and wonder the same thing. What the hell is she doing here?

Maria is the third manager in six months. The last few have gone nuts trying to manage 140 chimpanzees in the middle of nowhere. As a result, the sanctuary is a disaster. There is no water and no electricity. The whole place is infested with rats.

All the chimps do is plan jailbreaks with brilliant ingenuity. The electric fence has ten thousand volts running through it, enough to knock a grown man flat on his back. To the chimps, it is nothing more than a psychological barrier. They have figured out that green sticks conduct electricity and hold one end to the wire and the other to the ground, thereby short-circuiting the whole system and shutting down the electricity. They routinely check the electric current using a twig, listening for breaks in the snapping that indicate the current is accidentally off. They use long branches to pole-vault over the top and heavy logs to lever and snap the wires altogether.

The fences have been built higher and then reinforced. The wires have been thickened, the electric current increased. The keepers monitor every move. But at least once a day, someone busts out. And usually takes twenty friends with them.

The bonobos at Lola are equally talented. When Tatango uses a log to climb over the fence, he breaks it afterward, to destroy evidence at the scene of the crime. Max, the gay fashionista, climbs a palm tree, wraps two palm fronds together, and swans gracefully across this makeshift tightrope over the fence.

But the difference is that bonobos don't want to get out. They know they can get over the fence, but they are happy enough sitting down for their three-hour lunches and grooming each other. Even if they do get out, Mikeno runs around trying to find someone with a basketball, Tatango jumps into another enclosure to have sex with the females, and Max heads straight for the kitchen so he can drink five gallons of soap and amuse himself by burping bubbles for days.

Chimps, on the other hand, are a bunch of frat boys on spring break. They want to make a party out of it. They bust into the food rooms, streak the keepers, rip washing off the lines, and smash windows to get to sodas and beer in the refrigerator.

BRIAN AND I HAVE TAKEN OUT BETS on how long Maria will last. She is Spanish, so her French is bad and her English is worse. She has been in the jungle for twelve months, so she is probably crazy.

Brian says six months. I'm not sure. There is something about her that is strong and fluid at the same time.

It depends on how long she can go without water to wash that long, beautiful hair.

THE MORNING AFTER WE ARRIVE, I wake up with cockroaches crawling on my face. Brian finds packages of cockroach eggs in our bed. I freak out for a bit, then go into the bathroom. The truck that drives to the well for our water never gets back before ten A.M. So before that, I'm left with the dregs at the bottom of the barrel, which is brown and smells like something died in it.

I decide against washing my face and pull out some bread for breakfast. Because there is no electricity except for a few hours at night on the generator, there is a swamp at the bottom of the fridge where strange creatures evolve from the scum.

While I am spreading jam on my baguette, a rat jumps onto the sofa, shits on it, then jumps off again.

It's not even seven A.M.

BRIAN AND I SIT on the front porch of the house, in full view of Baboo, the killer monkey. Baboo is the most feared primate at the sanctuary, which is ridiculous because he is a putty-nosed monkey and his face looks like a bird pooped on it. A dozen adult male chimps can escape and the keepers will fearlessly go after them until they are back inside. If Baboo gets out, everyone runs home. He once ripped out the jugular of a Swiss volunteer. The guy came in to pet the female monkey, who is as sweet as can be, and Baboo lurked in the shadows until he had a clear shot, then vaulted onto the volunteer and sank his teeth into his neck. The manager had to sew up the jugular and squeeze it shut with his fingers for the forty-minute car ride into Pointe-Noire.

Despite Baboo's evil eye, the porch is the nicest place to sit. We are up on a hill, and the breeze ripples in from the savanna, cooling us down for the rest of the day. The yelling juvenile chimps are behind us, and all we can see is the faint outline of the forest, where the adult chimps live.

But Baboo has these psychotic fits where he hypnotizes you by swinging his head back and forth. Then, when you have been lured into an odd kind of calm, he leaps through the air like a bat, all four limbs outstretched. He flies toward you impossibly fast so you're a deer in the headlights, fixed with his manic grin and demented eyes. Just when you think you're a goner, he slams into the wire mesh of his cage, which you have forgotten is there to protect you, and slides downward, teeth bared and fingernails raking the chicken wire, his eyes holding the promise of a future attack.

He repeats this performance twenty times while I distractedly chew on my baguette. Brian explains his global tactics while I try to pay attention.

Now that we know bonobos are more cooperative than chimps and we know that tolerance is what allows this to happen, we want to know why. Why are chimps less tolerant than bonobos? Do they learn to be intolerant because they fight and kill each other? Or do they fight and kill each other because they are born intolerant? As the media love to ask, is it nature or nurture? Or is it an interaction, a little bit of both?

The intolerance of the chimps is not intellectual. They don't say to themselves, "It's not fair you get more food. Therefore, I should become upset." According to basic economic theory, given how much chimps love food, even a measly piece of banana is better than nothing and worth cooperating for. But like humans who reject money when they think an offer is unfair, if one chimp tries to steal more food than his or her share, the other chimp can't bear it. Their emotions overcome them and they refuse to cooperate, even though this means no one gets anything.

So now we are going to take a close look at the emotional lives of chimps and compare them to those of bonobos. In the basic emotional test we did last year with Kikongo and the red porcupine, we compared bonobos and chimpanzees to children. We found that both bonobos and kids are much more wary of new objects. This seems strange to me because my two-year-old niece, Escha, is so curious about new people and new toys. But she is still shy compared to a two-year-old chimp. Escha might hesitate a moment before picking up a toy she has never seen before, while chimps are fearless. As soon as they see something new, they will jump on it like it's a Christmas present.

The clear emotional difference between chimps and bonobos indicates that this is a phenomenon worth pursuing. The way you respond to a new object is unconscious and involuntary. You are either scared, wary, excited, or blasé, or a mixture of everything. But how do you measure emotions?

There is a left and right side of your brain. When you are negatively aroused, which includes emotions like fear, anger, and stress, the right side of your brain becomes active. As blood rushes in to feed the right hemisphere, it generates enough heat to increase the temperature of your right ear canal. Your hands get cold because in response to stress, all the blood rushes from your outer limbs to your heart. If you are positively aroused, which includes emotions like joy and contentment, it is the left side that is active and the left ear canal that heats up.

We are going to confront chimps with someone they are least likely to cooperate with—a stranger. Chimpanzees have a very strong sense of "us versus them," and when two groups meet in the wild, it is never friendly.

In the 1970s, Jane Goodall reported that a group of chimpanzees at Gombe had divided into two groups—the Kahama group and the Kasekela group. One by one, the Kasekela group killed members of the Kahama group until it was obliterated. At first, no one believed this was natural. But over the years, lethal intergroup aggression has been seen at almost every field site across Africa.

We will play the Oleti chimps the call of a stranger—a recording of a chimp from the Leipzig zoo called Patrick. Chimps recognize each other's voices, so they will know they haven't heard Patrick before. Knowing that an encounter with Patrick might lead to someone being killed, the chimps should have a physiological response when they hear his voice. Their hands should get cold. Their right-ear temperature should go up. To show that the fear of strangers isn't something they learn from experience, we will do the test with one- and two-year-old chimps who have just been orphaned. They have probably never seen an intergroup encounter so they have not been taught to be afraid of strangers.

In comparison, if two strange bonobo groups meet, they are more likely to have sex and groom each other for half an hour. If there is aggression, everyone seems to come out relatively unscathed. No one gets killed. So the right-ear temperatures of the bonobos shouldn't do anything.

We will also confront the chimps with a stranger visually. Tetsuro Matsuzawa, who runs the chimp research group in Japan, has shown that chimps recognize each other from photographs. So we will show chimps photographs of chimps they know and photographs of strangers in Leipzig and monitor which photo they touch or look at. Then we will do the same for bonobos.

IT STARTS OFF PLEASANTLY ENOUGH. We are in the night building for the juveniles. There are three small rooms that connect into a main room with doors. In the far back room, we set up a pet pack, the kind that is used to crate a dog. We put speakers in the pet pack, then wire them to a laptop.

I ask the keeper Amandine to bring in the first subject. She brings in Celia, a seven-year-old chimp with a freckled face. I show Celia a single peanut, and she breaks away from Amandine, runs into the testing room, closes the door behind her, and crouches, her eyes laser-beamed on the wine bottle full of peanuts behind me.

Unlike Kikongo and every other bonobo, there is no dancing, no spinning, no cartwheels. She wants the food, and she is ready to do just about anything to get it. I use the single peanut to get her exactly where I need her, and then we begin the test.

I sit outside with the laptop. Brian gives the signal and I play the call of Patrick in Leipzig. Brian shakes the pet pack. New chimps are often brought into the sanctuary in the pet packs, and we want Celia to think Patrick is inside. Celia leaps to the window and tries to peer inside the pet pack. Brian shakes it, and I play the scream again. Celia leaps around the room, clearly agitated. Amandine goes in and Celia clings to her.

Amandine takes Celia's measurements. Brian writes them down.

"Did it work?" I ask. "Did her right ear go up?"

Brian raises his eyebrows. "Perfect result."

Six more chimps follow. Each of them is finished in eighteen minutes. A trial with a bonobo takes about an hour. There is no waiting for the bonobo to leapfrog around the room or try to steal the rope. There is no penis touching or clitoris rubbing before participation in the test. All the chimps care about is getting that one delicious morsel of peanut goodness. They'll do whatever it takes.

I'm starting to wish we worked with chimps all the time when things begin to get ugly. Celia, upset that the peanut party is over, busts out of her enclosure and walks right into the testing room. I slowly move to protect the video camera. She looks around, then steals our damn peanuts. She takes the bottle right up to the top of a eucalyptus tree and eats every single one of them, waving the empty bottle around like a drunk.

Soon after, Litu escapes and runs over the roof of our building, completely freaking out another chimp in the testing room. Another three chimps break out and we have to stop testing.

Mr. Nyani, the liaison between the sanctuary and the government, drops in for a visit. Chimps are running around everywhere. Our peanuts are gone. I am shielding the camera with my body.

"*Bonjour,* Monsieur Nyani," I say politely in French. "My name is Vanessa, and this is my husband, Brian. We have come to study the chimps at Oleti."

"Please tell Mr. Nyani that I am honored to make his acquaintance," Brian adds while I translate. "I have heard he is a very important person."

Mr. Nyani breaks into a big smile and, ignoring me completely, says to Brian in French, "Yes, of course. I have seen you walking around here with your wife."

Brian nods and smiles while I translate.

"Me," says Mr. Nyani, "I leave my wife at home."

"Oh," says Brian.

"Because if I take her with me, how can I find another wife?"

Brian laughs as if this is the funniest thing he has ever heard. Mr. Nyani's smile becomes strained.

"I don't understand why you don't leave your wife at home. How are you to find a wife among our beautiful Congolese women if your wife is always with you? It is the right of a man to take another wife.

I advise you to leave *her*"—he indicates me with by pointing with his lips—"at home the next time."

I look over at Amandine, her profile outlined by the sun. How could I not have noticed what a gorgeous creature she is? Her work clothes and the chimp shit confused me, but there is nothing confusing about her cheekbones and those precisely curved lips.

Brian is smiling idiotically. I want to hit him.

"Thank you very much for your advice," I say curtly on Brian's behalf. "But I am very happy with my wife and there is no other woman for me. Have a good morning."

THERE IS NO PAPA JEAN to cook us three-course meals. At lunch Brian yells at me for not scrubbing the tomatoes with detergent before I made the salad.

"Why don't you get Amandine to wash them?" I yell back.

"Amandine? What's she got to do with anything?"

"That would be perfect, wouldn't it, you asshole? She can cook and translate and run your stupid experiments while I stay at home next time. Maybe you can have a whole little Congolese family here!"

"What? Wait—"

I cut him off by slamming the door and run down the hill.

WHEN I GET DOWN TO THE BOTTOM, I stop. I don't usually come down here. These chimps aren't the little guys we are testing at the top, the ones Amandine can lead into the testing room by the hand and coax into doing anything she wants. The adult chimps are altogether different creatures.

Simba is about my weight, 120 pounds, and a little shorter at five foot three. But while I can barely do a push up, Simba could probably throw a car across the room. His arms are as thick as my thigh, and his thighs are as thick as tree trunks. When he stands, he is nothing but muscle. His long arms are roped with brawn.

Simba, more than any other chimp at Oleti, is an escape artist. He will try to pick a lock with anything, a piece of straw, an oily rag.

The keepers love his keen intelligence as much as his sweet and gentle nature.

A few years ago, Simba escaped from his enclosure and took two chimpanzees with him. They came across a group of women on the way to the market. Most of the women dropped everything and ran, but one woman clutched her basket of fruit and stood her ground.

The chimps tore out her throat and ripped open her stomach. She was pregnant, and when the keepers found her, her fetus lay beside her in the dirt.

This was not the first time chimpanzees have killed people. Brian's first research was on nine chimpanzee attacks and three deaths in rural villages in Uganda. "Killer" chimpanzees abducted six children from the village, who were later found eviscerated, with the occasional foot or arm missing. A nine-month-old baby had her face gnawed off.

Just like people, chimps have a darker side to their nature. At Ngogo, in Kibale National Park in Uganda, a group of male chimps beat a young male to death. They took turns kicking, punching, and slashing him with their teeth. When he tried to run away, they broke his leg by twisting it and pulling the bone out of the socket. Nearby another male chimp was found with his throat slashed, penis ripped off, and testicles sixty-five feet away from his body.

Many animals kill members of their own kind. A male deer might mortally wound a rival. Even rabbits fight to the death over territory. But a group of bunnies will not go into enemy territory to hunt down another bunny. They don't form a gang and hold down the victim and punch and kick him and break his legs and rip off his testicles and scream in cruel triumph. They don't drink his blood and tear off his fingernails. It takes a certain amount of intelligence to get the bone-chilling satisfaction of causing so much pain to someone else. It requires sophisticated emotions that resemble hatred and jealousy and spite.

Chimpanzee warfare has been seen in zoos, sanctuaries, labs, and the wild. It is becoming increasingly clear that to chimps, the "us versus them" concept is very powerful and not something they can always control.

Chimpanzees are not evil. They are capable of kindness, love, and grief. In fact, they are very similar to us. Chimpanzee violence occurs in the same context as human violence: over females, enemy males, and territory. In hunter-gatherer societies, where people live off the land like chimpanzees, the homicide rate is about the same.

Unfortunately, in most states in America, you can order a baby chimp for $50,000 over the Internet and have it delivered to your door. What the sellers don't tell you is what the cute little chimp the size of a cat will eventually turn into.

In 1967, the NASCAR racer St. James Davis rescued a baby chimp from poachers in Tanzania. He called the chimp Moe and brought him back to LaDonna, his girlfriend in California.

St. James and LaDonna got married, and since cancer left LaDonna infertile, they raised Moe as a surrogate child. He slept in their bed, watched cowboys and Indians on television, and learned to use a toilet. As Moe grew older, he began destroying the house, so he had to be confined in a ten-by-twelve-foot cage in the backyard. Trouble started. He mauled a police officer and bit the top off a woman's finger. The authorities confiscated him, and Moe ended up in an animal sanctuary in California for exotic pets who had worn out their welcome.

On Moe's thirty-ninth birthday, the Davises brought him a big raspberry cake with blue icing. As LaDonna cut the cake, she saw a teenage chimp had escaped from his cage. The teenager was one of two Hollywood chimps who had been surrendered by their trainer when they grew too big and aggressive to perform.

As the chimp prowled toward her, LaDonna made a big mistake—she made eye contact. The chimp slammed into her and bit off her thumb. As her husband pushed her out of harm's way under the table, the second Hollywood chimp appeared and joined in the attack on St. James.

They bit off his nose and nearly every one of his fingers. They gouged out his eye. They ripped flesh from his buttocks and left foot. They tore off his testicles.

The sanctuary managers came running when they heard LaDonna's screams and shot both chimps in the head.

St. James was nearly dead. After weeks in a coma and dozens of surgeries, his face is grotesque. There are two slits in his face where his nose should be and his mouth is a lipless, twisted line. A glass eye sits in an artificial socket.

The medical bills total over a million dollars and the Davises are locked in legal battles that will drag on for years.

Chimpanzee breeders will tell you that this kind of violence is freakish behavior, that with love and affection, chimpanzees can be tamed, and people who are injured by chimps must have done something wrong. But the darker nature of chimpanzees cannot be bred out and is not something that goes away when they are raised as a dog or a surrogate child.

SIMBA HAS THE CALMEST EYES. They are orange, flecked with brown. He reaches out his hand toward me, palm down. He wants me to groom him. I know why people think chimps make good pets. If Simba was the size of the five-year-old chimps we see on television, then those liquid eyes, his outstretched hand, would make him irresistible.

But the chimps on television and in magazine advertisements are never fully grown. Before they turn seven, they are stronger than the world's strongest man. In order to perform, say, on a movie set, where every minute of disobedience is worth thousands of dollars, the chimp actors have to be controlled, and the "smile" of chimps on television, with lips stretched back over their teeth, is often a grin of fear.

Sarah Baeckler worked for a year at Amazing Animal Productions in San Bernardino, California. The chimps had been photographed with Natalie Portman, Arnold Schwarzenegger, Adrien Brody, and Dakota Fanning. They starred in movies and television shows, making thousands of dollars for Amazing Animal Productions. Baeckler saw trainers punching baby chimps in the face, kicking them in the head, and beating them with a hammer. Other trainers beat their chimps with baseball bats, electrocute them, and pull out their teeth so it won't hurt when they bite. The common theory with animal trainers is that chimps are tough and they don't feel it.

By the time chimps are ten, they are no longer cute. They cannot be controlled, even with electrocution. Their emotions take over. They are given to occasional tantrums, the ferocity of which can rip a human to pieces. They have the strength and teeth of a tiger, but unlike a tiger, they can open doors and pick locks and deceive with uncanny intelligence. And it is at about this age that they end up in roadside zoos, like Chubbs from *Planet of the Apes,* who was found living in a pile of garbage and his own shit at a zoo in Amarillo, Texas. Or Donna, who worked for Animal Kingdom Talent Services until she was twelve years old. She was walked into a cage at a biomedical facility, and was locked in for nineteen years. She was anesthetized 172 times for HIV and other experiments, including bone marrow biopsies. She occasionally went into shock from the pain and was constantly mutilating herself.

The problem is larger than the individual chimps in the pet trade and entertainment industry who are suffering. How can any conservation organization turn up in Africa and condemn hunters for killing chimps and selling babies as pets when the hunters and the villagers can point to movies like *Speed Racer* and photos of Hollywood stars hugging baby chimps? If we, in America, can keep chimpanzees as pets, why can't they? And if we can dress up chimpanzees in our clothes, laugh at them, and ridicule them, why should Ugandans or Tanzanians or the Congolese treat chimpanzees with any more respect?

Quaking, I take Simba's hand between mine. His hands are as large as a wrestler's and I can barely wrap both hands around one. He has cool and leathery skin, like a man who works outdoors. Otherwise everything is the same—our fingernails, our thumbs, the creases on our knuckles, and the life lines on our palms.

He could tighten his grip, yank me toward the bars, and kill me with a flash of those long, curved canines.

But instead, he sighs, and those orange-flecked eyes close at the solace of my touch. It's not his fault he is locked up like a criminal. You wouldn't blame a tiger for biting, even though he purrs. Simba was just doing what came naturally.

In the wild there is no punishment for such a crime.

Chapter 15

❧

$\mathcal{E}$very morning at Oleti, as soon as Brian wakes up, he checks BBC News to see if Kinshasa is safe. It clearly isn't. The two grooms should be in a campaigning frenzy, but both are afraid they will be assassinated. So they have locked themselves in their homes while their armies roam the streets. There are occasional skirmishes and the reports are confusing. Five dead. A hundred and twenty dead. Two hundred dead.

Kabila's troops shot a shoulder-fired missile at Bemba's helicopter, which now sits in a mangled lump of metal on his front lawn. Bemba is screaming from his rooftop that the electoral process is a fraud. No doubt he will change his mind if he wins, but at the moment he is laying the groundwork for a full-scale rebellion.

The European Commission is begging Kabila and Bemba to proceed peacefully. MONUC (the United Nations Mission in DR Congo) is using every persuasive power it can. Kofi Annan is on the phone to Kabila; European diplomats are over at Bemba's house. It is still two months until the election, which is long enough to start a war. You can cut the air in Kinshasa with a knife.

The Congolese are desperate for peace. In the first round of elections, more than twenty-five million people registered to vote—almost half the population. More than eighteen million lined up for hours at fifty thousand polling stations. Some of them walked for days. Many of the polling stations had no roads. They came despite death threats and rumors that the elections are a fraud. They came despite the quickly spreading news that polling stations have been attacked by fire, others taken by force.

I read the news over Brian's shoulder, feeling confused. Part of me wants to yell that of course we are not going to bloody Kinshasa, we are going home as soon as we are done testing the chimps. I think about the news articles I read about aid workers killed in Afghanistan, journalists killed in Cambodia. I shook my head and thought, Well, you turn up in those countries—what do you expect?

But another part of me is ashamed of myself. I used to be fearless. Where is the girl who skidded over a thinning glacier to get a perfect shot of penguins? Who drove a Land Cruiser through rebel territory in Ethiopia to find the watering hole of a bunch of zebras? I know it was just the stupidity of youth and that as I barrel toward thirty, a little self-preservation will get me to my fortieth birthday, but I miss my old spirit of adventure.

Mikeno, the Brad Pitt of bonobos, will be sitting in his Rodin's posture, waiting. I told him we'd be back. Can I forget him, like everyone has forgotten bonobos?

I can't make up my mind. Brian keeps reading the news and calling every American embassy, consul, and representative to ask whether Kinshasa is safe. They all tell him the same thing, that he is nuts to even think about going there, and he should get his ass back home before war crosses the Congo River and we get royally fucked.

It looks hopeless.

And then Debby arrives.

BESIDES INTRODUCING CHIMP GIRLS like me to their future husbands, Debby is a veteran around the sanctuary junket. After making Ngamba one of the best-run sanctuaries in Africa, Debby handed it over to the Ugandans. She now shares herself around and has come to help Maria fix the disaster that is Oleti.

Maria has barely had time to speak to us since we arrived. I've seen her hold a baby gorilla infested with lice, patiently feeding him milk while parasites crawl over her naked arms. I've seen her mud-wrestle a young chimp to the ground so she could take his heart rate. I've seen her calmly stick a needle in an adult male chimp twice her size.

But she is still a mystery. She keeps to herself in her house. Her office light is on from dawn to eleven at night. I see it flickering from our bedroom window, its silver phosphorescence as constant as a star.

She and Debby will either get on like a house on fire, or they'll kill each other.

"DEBBY, THERE'S NO WATER!" I cry in the way of greeting when I wrap my arms around her for a big hug. Debby's steel blue eyes flick over the sandy soil.

"There'll be water."

My eyes widen in wonder.

"How will you make the water come, Debby?"

"Like we do in Australia. We'll drill for it."

"Debby, there are rats everywhere."

"We'll get cats."

"And cockroaches."

"Bug spray."

"Debby, we want to go to Lola but they're killing people in Kinshasa."

She squares her shoulders. "I've never seen bonobos. I'll come with you."

Debby has driven through Burundi during the genocide with orphan chimps in the trunk of her car. She has been thrown onto the tarmac while soldiers held an AK-47 to her temple. She is like the Terminator with boobs. If anyone can get us into Kinshasa, she can.

NOW THAT DEBBY IS ON BOARD, Brian steamrolls into action. He figures if we can get out of Kinshasa before the final elections on October 29, we should be safe. It's already the twelfth of September. Before leaving Oleti, we need to squash three weeks of testing into four days. I go to the head keeper and tell him we need to run through seventy chimps by Friday.

The ear temperatures of the chimps are showing a definite pattern. When they hear the scream of a strange chimp, their hands get colder. Their right-ear temperature goes up. They are definitely aroused. Even babies as young as a year old who have never been attacked by another chimp are aroused when they hear the call of a stranger.

When we showed the chimps photographs, the males didn't have a preference, but the female chimps didn't like to look at strange males. Female chimps can be seriously injured by strange males, not to mention have their babies killed, so I understand why they get scared when they *hear* a strange chimp—they don't know it's just a recording. But a picture? They know the photograph represents someone, but like us, they know the difference between a photograph and a real chimp. And they still avoid looking at or touching the photographs of strangers.

We have so many chimps to test that Brian and I are too exhausted to yell at each other. We test for eight hours a day and collapse on the porch. Baboo shakes his head at us, as if we will pay for our folly.

On the fourth day, our bags are packed, our tickets are booked, and we are ready to go.

Chapter 16

❧

*I*t's a bad sign when your flight is completely empty. It usually means no one else is stupid enough to go where you're going.

"Wow," says Brian, patting his armrest. "A 727. This baby is older than I am."

I can't imagine this is a good thing for a plane. We arrive at the Kinshasa airport in broad daylight. It's the same mustard yellow as when Muhammad Ali touched down to fight his Rumble in the Jungle in 1974. The whole place is a plane graveyard, and as we taxi down the runway, we pass the stripped carcasses of Russian Antonovs and other 727s that didn't have such a smooth landing.

We walk out onto the tarmac only to be accosted by a leggy blond air hostess wearing blue eye shadow.

"*Messieurs, mesdames,* we are not stopping here. Please get back on board."

"We flew Hewa Bora," I tell her.

She frowns.

"Are you not going to Belgium? Are you not looking for the Air Brussels flight?"

"No. This is our stop."

"Oh," she says, lost for words. She looks at the doors to immigration, which are locked. "All right. Good-bye then."

And she hurries away, as though she might catch the disease we are carrying.

FOR THE FIRST TIME, there is no line at immigration. No mass of people on either side, shouting and jostling, waving placards and passports. The man behind the counter stares at the ceiling of his cubicle, tapping his pen on the table. I gather he has not been very busy lately.

"*Passports, s'il vous plaît.*"

He flicks through my passport and Brian's. He sees the blue Democratic Republic of Congo visa with its lion's head and stamps us. When he gets to Debby's, he flicks through it twice.

"Visa, madam?"

Debby has crossed so many borders illegally that she thinks of visas as optional, like a spare toothbrush or mouthwash. Brian begged her to get a visa before we left, but she brushed him off with "No worries" and proceeded to travel without one.

"We have a letter waiting for us," says Debby. Claudine, who has done her fair share of border running in her time, has organized a protocol man, who is nowhere in sight. The immigration official starts berating us.

"You cannot come here without a visa. With no visa, you must go back."

This is not going well. Without a protocol man, we'll be up for about $1,000 in bribes.

At that moment, Claudine's protocol man comes running through the baggage area, sweating and waving a letter. The immigration man screams at him, furious his bribe is escaping.

"Make sure you have a visa next time!" he rails.

"See?" says Debby as we grab our bags off the carousel. "No worries."

THE FIRST THING I NOTICE ABOUT LOLA is the dead calm. The place is empty. There are no visitors staying at the guesthouses. No volunteers from Europe. No visiting ambassadors or dignitaries. Gradually, word spreads that we have arrived. Jacques presses my hands in his own with a shy smile. Papa Jean comes out of the kitchen, waving his spatula and beaming. The Mamas with attitude, Henriette, Yvonne, Micheline, and Esperance, look surprised, as though they can't believe we have come back.

As we sit on the patio, a car pulls up and a brown girl with freckles on her nose bounds up the steps. A sash is tied diagonally from her shoulder to her waist, and inside, African-style, is a tiny wrinkled baby.

Claudine follows closely behind, wearing caramel lipstick that sets off her dazzling white shirt and freshly washed hair.

"We must look a mess," she says. "We haven't slept at all."

The brown, freckled girl is Fanny, Claudine's daughter. They look nothing alike. Claudine's red waves and smooth curves remind me of a river. Fanny, with her wild mess of curls, long limbs, and black eyes, is more like a wire trap.

Fanny reminds me of someone. I try to think of whom.

I assume the baby is hers but when we look inside the pouch, the crown of black hair belongs to a baby bonobo. His hands wave tiny fingers around, reaching for something to clutch.

"It's Mimi's baby. She practically threw him over the fence."

When apes are taken from their mothers at a young age and don't grow up around other apes, they usually reject their own newborns. It's not Mimi's fault. She was raised by a human family so she never got to see how she was supposed to raise a bonobo. But Claudine, mother of five, is exasperated.

"She was horrified that something so messy came out of her body. *Quelle idée!*"

"It's my fault the baby's sick," Fanny says, distraught. "Maman was away and he came down with a fever so I took him to the doctor, who gave him honey in the milk, and now he has the most dreadful diarrhea. And cramps, *mon Dieu,* he is in a lot of pain."

I can't stop looking at Fanny. She is not beautiful. She has a sharp, angular face; her eyes are too big; her nose is too thin. But when her eyes catch the light, or her tight-sprung curls sweep her shoulders, she is more than beautiful. She is mesmerizing.

I realize whom she reminds me of—Isiro.

"We call him Elombe, which means 'little warrior' in Lingala."

We stand around the baby and coo, sure that now that Claudine is here, he will get better. We congratulate her on the birth of such an adorable baby boy.

I'M A LITTLE NERVOUS that Claudine and Debby will hate each other. People tend to take after whomever they spend the most time with, which is why some people end up looking like their spouses and others end up looking like their dogs.

Chimp people are as rough as guts and as tough as nails. At the slightest disagreement they're ready to get bloody but after a couple of punches they can make up and get on with it.

Bonobo people are more subtle. They are always pleasant but it is difficult to know what they are thinking. If you were their least-favorite person, you would never know it, because peace in the group must be maintained at all costs. But if you rack up enough infringements, bonobos will slowly gather their alliances and *chicka chicka boom*! You've been taught a lesson you won't recover from for a while.

More to the point, chimp people, in all their carrying on about chimpanzee conservation, forget to mention there is a sister species that unfortunately also gets called a "chimpanzee." Bonobos are as closely related to humans as chimps and are more in danger of extinction. But even at great ape conferences, bonobos are completely left off the map. Of all the conservation money that pours in to save chimpanzees, bonobos barely see a penny.

As I anxiously make the introductions, I am feeling a bit like a bonobo myself. These are two of the people I admire most, and I want to dispense bonobo handshakes to make sure everyone gets along. I needn't have worried. Claudine is a gracious hostess and Debby is the perfect guest. And they have something important in common. They are both sending their orphans back to the wild.

Every sanctuary in Africa has the same problem—they are almost full. Deforestation, new logging, and mining contracts build roads into habitat, and with the road come people, and with people come hunters who harvest the forest. All sanctuaries have seen a steady increase in orphans in the last decade.

Release is every sanctuary's dream. To send the orphans they have cared for back to the forests they came from. They will replenish the falling wild populations and there will be more room at the sanctuary for the orphans who continue to arrive.

There are plenty of scientists and conservationists who think every ape in a sanctuary should be shot in the head. They argue the cost of running the sanctuaries should fund national parks and protect thousands of apes instead of a few dozen. They are afraid sanctuaries monopolize grant money that should be used to conserve apes in the wild. And they are worried sanctuary animals may carry diseases from their human caretakers that could wipe out wild populations.

But the biggest threat to apes isn't disease, it's the bushmeat trade. Hunting has caused a decline in ape populations in 96 percent of protected areas. In the twenty African countries torn apart by civil war since 1960, marauding soldiers disrupt harvesting and agriculture, which sends the local population into the forest, hunting for bushmeat. Sometimes the soldiers give the locals bullets and hold their families for ransom until they come back with dinner.

Sanctuaries are often the only place the indigenous people see apes as anything but prey. Lola alone reaches up to thirty thousand people each year through education programs.

In terms of conservation, the sanctuary apes come from all over the country, which means they are genetically diverse enough to reproduce. But in order to have a successful release program, there have to be a few test runs. If sanctuaries wait until apes are almost extinct in the wild before they release their apes, one mistake could wipe out the future. They need to find a method that works.

HELP Congo is not far from Oleti, and in 1996, they began releasing orphan chimpanzees into Conkouati-Douli National Park. In a series of meticulous studies, they reported that among the thirty-seven release chimps, the survival rate was 62 percent. By 2004, four females had given birth to five infants—the measure of success for any reintroduction program.

Debby and Claudine are determined to follow in HELP's footsteps in strict accordance with the International Union for Conservation of Nature guidelines. Debby is going to release the chimps onto several islands, like HELP Congo. The chimps will get used to foraging on their own and living without people. Eventually, when she has found somewhere safe, she will release them into the wild.

Claudine has been looking for her release site for years. She has sailed up and down the treacherous waters of the Congo. She has journeyed overland through rebel territory in a truck. At first she was looking for an island, like HELP, but the waters of the Congo River flood during the wet season, and most of the islands she found were underwater by Christmas. She found sites and rejected them; the people were too aggressive, or bonobos were still on the menu. Then, finally, she found it.

As the Congo River sweeps upward in a rainbow toward the interior, part of it breaks off and flows steadily for several hundred miles before dividing into dozens of smaller tributaries. The main river is called the Lopori and before it splits, it passes a town called Basankusu. About twenty minutes by canoe past Basankusu, the Lopori River splits into two. And nestled between the split lie almost fifty thousand acres of pristine forest, an area three times the size of Manhattan. This is the forest of the Pô.

The Ilonga Pô settled in the area more than a hundred years ago. Ilonga was a man from Lisala, a town two hundred miles to the northeast. He was traveling with his sons in search of food and provisions. Most likely they had come downriver to fish, but judging from their distance from home, they weren't having much luck.

Tired from the journey, they camped next to an old tree trunk.

They stayed longer than they expected. In fact, they stayed so long that locals passing by started to call the stranger Pô, which means "rotten tree trunk" in the local language.

Ilonga Pô, as he became known, never left. There were a couple of skirmishes with the local Mongo tribe, but the Pô kicked them out and have lived there ever since. Mainly fishermen, the Pô no longer rely on hunting for their diet. The forest is a perfect bonobo habitat but no one has seen one for more than twenty years.

Claudine fell in love with the Pô instantly. They are a gentle, sweet people and didn't demand that she build them an airport and send everyone to Paris like some of the other tribes she has met. Claudine promises the Pô that if they agree to become bonobo guardians, the bonobos will, in turn, become theirs. Bonobos will provide material for their schools and medicine for their clinic. Bonobos will employ their men and educate their women and children.

Other projects are aggressive about conservation. In the Central African Republic, the World Wildlife Fund hired ex-military to train park rangers. In Salonga National Park, the eco guards are armed with Kalashnikovs.

The Pô do not want guns. They have seen too much of war.

"Let us defend the bonobos," says the chief, who wears a necklace of leopard teeth. "No one enters or leaves this forest without us knowing it."

Claudine agrees. No guns.

Mimi's baby cries, and Fanny coos and runs off with Claudine to find Crispin, the vet. Brian and I take Debby to see the bonobos.

Mikeno is sitting where I left him, his chin on his fist like Rodin's thinker. He squeals in greeting and holds out his hand.

Semendwa has had her baby. Elikia is a pretty little girl, with her mother's wide eyes and rosebud mouth. She is crawling all over Tatango. She wiggles her tiny fingers into his ears, pulls down on the corners of his mouth. She wants him to smile. He stares stoically heavenward without even a smirk.

Apparently not concerned that her baby is a hairsbreadth away from the sharp canines of an adult male, Semendwa's eyes have narrowed to laser beams and are honing in on the green necklace Debby gave me. The beads are tightly rolled paper, made by a women's group next to Ngamba Island.

I want that necklace. Semendwa's eyes speak clearly. When the bonobos want something, they do something called "peering." They get right up in your face and stare at what they want as though sheer willpower is enough to transfer ownership.

Semendwa pushes her face against the fence and peers at my necklace. There are a good three feet between us but I step backward. Semendwa, like any beautiful, vain woman, covets just about anything she doesn't have. When it comes to acts of petty theft, the girl's got talent. She has stolen dozens of cameras and keys, the shoes from people's feet, watches from their wrists. Once I saw her steal glasses right off a man's face.

"No," I say, feeling safe with the distance. "Mine."

Semendwa picks up a handful of dirt and throws it. It lands all over my chest, spattering me and my necklace with mud. In a flash, Isiro is right beside Semendwa and they both glare at me as though I've violated some code of the secret sisterhood. Isiro looks like she is going to pull out a police siren and stick it on her head.

"Nice to see you girls again too."

Mimi is peeling a mango. Maniema has graduated from the nursery and he sits with Kikongo at Mimi's feet, peering timidly. I wonder if Mimi is worried about her baby that she threw over the fence. She doesn't look worried. She seems to be thoroughly enjoying her mango. It is the first mango of the season, smooth, fat, and golden. Juice dribbles down her fingers.

The boys sit on their haunches begging but the empress doesn't deign to look at them. She gazes into the distance, thoughtfully chewing as though she has important matters of state on her mind. But every now and then she lets a piece fall from her mouth, leaving Kikongo and Maniema to dive for it.

"They have such small heads," Debby keeps saying. "What happened to their heads?"

"That's nothing," says Brian. "You have to see this."

Night is falling, and we walk toward the building. The bonobos follow us. Jacques is at the entrance.

"*Allez!*" he cries, and all the bonobos chirp back that they are ready and waiting.

At Oleti, Ngamba, and every other chimp sanctuary, when it is time to go into the building at night, the big male chimps come first, pounding through the long mesh tunnel, displaying and shouting. Next come the young males, in order of rank. Then come the females, and then the young females. The big males have already gone in and claimed their sleeping spots and most of the food. The females creep around them and try to avoid getting into trouble for trespassing. Sometimes, to avoid being beaten up as part of a display, they prefer to sleep in the forest.

When Jacques opens the door, there is no yelling, no pushing or shoving. Instead, Mimi takes her sweet-ass time coming through the tunnel. She steps into the night building and starts gathering up all the straw. She makes just about the biggest nest imaginable, right by the door. She could hide an elephant in it and no one would know. She climbs inside and nestles down. She permits the entry of Semendwa, Isiro, and the other ladies, who climb into the comfortable hammocks. Tatango and Mikeno come in and either climb into a hammock or start collecting straw. Then the young girls come in and they all get ready for bed.

Five minutes later the teenage males and the little boys creep down the tunnel. Kikwit, Kikongo, Maniema, and everyone else wait in the tunnel as night falls.

Mimi closes her eyes like a sleeping dragon. Kikwit, the footballer, takes a few steps toward Mimi. She opens one eye. Kikwit retreats. The boys lurk in the tunnel, waiting, waiting, until again, Mimi's eyes close. This time, Kikongo, who is gutsier and smaller than the rest, tiptoes through the entrance and past her. You can feel the tension of the other boys as they watch Kikongo run the gauntlet.

Kikongo tiptoes one little inch at a time. He is nearly in. He can see the hammock he wants, right next to Isiro in the first room on the left.

Mimi's hand shoots out like a trip wire and her long bony fingers clutch Kikongo's ankle. Kikongo screams. Kikwit screams. The little boys scream as Kikongo wriggles out of Mimi's grasp and they all sprint far back into the tunnel.

And there the boys stay, in the tunnel, until long into the night, when, exhausted, they can creep past Mimi, find a few scraps of straw, lie down on the ground, and go to sleep.

Brian turns to Debby proudly, as though he has orchestrated the whole thing himself.

"Wow," says Debby, shaking her head. "Weird."

THREE DAYS LATER, Mimi's baby dies. The diarrhea was deadly for a bonobo only a few weeks old. Fanny's face is tear-streaked. Claudine has dark circles under her eyes.

"Well," she says sadly, "at least now we can sleep."

I had no idea bonobos were so fragile. I thought they were tough, like baby chimps. I thought that inside the sanctuary, with Claudine, they would be safe.

I couldn't have been more wrong.

Chapter 17

Claudine's car pulls up at eleven A.M. She jumps out looking flustered.

"There has been shooting in Kinshasa. It took me all morning to get here. We must go."

Debby has already gone back to start rebuilding Oleti. Skimishes in the city led to the cancellation of her flight back to Pointe-Noire and she had to hire a boat and cross the Congo River into Brazzaville.

Two of Bemba's television stations have been set on fire. In retaliation, Bemba supporters are burning tires in the street. This morning, someone fired a gun and the whole city is in hysterics. Everyone is on their mobile phone, jamming the network. Traffic has been backed up for hours. Claudine is careful not to alarm us.

"It was just one shot. The rest is *radio trottoir*," Claudine says. *Pavement radio,* or the word on the street. "But better to be safe than sorry, *oui?*"

We pack hurriedly, not knowing whether we will be back.

CLAUDINE'S HOUSE IS IN MA CAMPAGNE, a suburb in the airy hills of Kinshasa. The houses are surrounded by high white walls, some of them topped with barbed wire and shattered glass.

Waiting at home is Fanny, watching Nigerian soap operas, and Claudine's husband, Victor.

"Voilà," says Claudine, half-mocking, half-fond. "My pasha."

Victor does indeed look like Turkish nobility. Half-Rwandan, half-Italian, he has a regal profile and a certain air of command. It is obvious where Fanny gets her dark curls and feline grace.

Victor is in the transport business—he is the man who knows how to get things from A to B in a country three times the size of France swarming with rebels and with only 1,300 miles of roads (of which barely half are usable). He is a blockade runner of sorts. A modern-day Rhett Butler. He lounges on the sofa smoking a cigar, one hand on his magnificent belly.

"You think this is trouble?" His gravelly voice booms throughout the house in stereo. "You should have been here during the *pillages*."

In 1997, as Mobutu's star was waning, the unpaid military revolted and led thousands of people through Kinshasa.

"There were mobs, masses of them; they were looting and burning everything in sight. They came right up to the house; they were banging on the gates."

"What did you do?" I ask. Victor gives me a broad smile.

"What can you do? I opened the gates! I said, 'Welcome, my friends, you can take anything you want! Feel free, help yourselves.'"

I couldn't imagine letting everyone in the neighborhood take all my things. "You didn't even try to stop them?"

"There was a man a few houses down. He climbed onto his roof and he was screaming that if they didn't leave him alone, he would open fire. The mob kept pressing in; they kicked and beat at his gates. So this man, he opened fire. Directly into the crowd. But there were thousands of people, more than you can imagine. And when he opened fire, they were angry. They became furious. And eventually, you know…" Victor shakes his head. "You have to run out of bullets."

Fanny tells me that when her father opened up the gates and spoke courteously in Lingala, the mob brought chairs for the family to sit on. So Victor, Claudine, Fanny, and her younger brother, Thomas, sat on their dining chairs on the lawn while robbers looted their house.

"And they took everything," Claudine adds ruefully. "You cannot imagine. They even took the copper wiring from the electric circuits."

WE STAY AT THE HOUSE FOR SEVERAL DAYS, watching Nigerian soap operas with Fanny and talking about her future. She has just finished her law degree and has no idea what she wants to do except that it doesn't involve being a lawyer. Fanny has the same problem as all talented twentysomethings—her choices are so varied and dazzling that she is paralyzed. Should she return to Congo and try to save the rain forest, or should she marry the Parisian rock star she's dating? Brian helps her surf through environmental programs on the Internet while I talk to her about the pros and cons of being a permanent groupie.

The hallways are plastered with photos of Claudine's fifty years in Congo. Claudine as a young woman gazing out over the Mountains of the Moon. Claudine with Victor swanning around Kinshasa. Claudine being hugged by a leopard. Claudine and her children and grandchildren.

As beautiful as she is now, Claudine in her younger years was a vision. Her hair was the bloody red of the inside of a pomegranate and it tumbled down her shoulders in thick barrel curls. Her hourglass curves, her arched eyebrows, and her carefully painted lips gave her the glamour of a silver-screen goddess.

Fanny tells me her mother is always freshly washed and perfumed. She is never without makeup; her hair is never a mess. Now that I think about it, I have never seen Claudine without at least mascara and a bronze dusting of eye shadow, even at the breakfast table.

"*Ma chère,*" Claudine says gently to Fanny when she turns up to said breakfast table in a tank top and shorts, "I hope your *amour* never sees you like that. You have to make a little effort. To show him you care."

I sit next to my *amour* looking as I always do in the morning—

like I just crawled out of a laundry basket. My hair and teeth aren't brushed. I'm wearing tracksuit pants sagging in the ass and an old T-shirt with AUSTRALIA printed on it in optimistic colors. Suddenly I have a vision, accompanied by music, where Claudine takes me in hand, like Eliza Doolittle, and turns me into a fair lady. But secretly I know I'm too lazy. And these trackies are *so* comfortable.

At night we listen to Victor's stories about trekking up-country through Congo and look at his photos of pulling trucks across the river on tree trunks. There is one photo of two canoes strapped together and an SUV on top.

"I had to drive it onto the pirogues while they were in the water," Victor says, laughing. "You can imagine what would have happened if I had missed."

Claudine has her ear to the ground, listening for potential trouble. Bemba's campaign rally at the stadium ended in a clash with police that left six dead. Kabila's bodyguard shot the vice president's bodyguard. A Belgian plane crashed near Mama Henriette's house. A billboard of Kabila has been peppered with bullets. Potshots, really. No one has cast the first stone. Or fired the first bazooka.

Bemba's and Kabila's men slink around the city and the truce between them is uneasy. Having each displayed their potential for destruction, they are content to cooperate, for now. After a few days, Claudine deems it safe to go back to the sanctuary.

"*En fait,* if anything happens, you will probably be safer there. We may all come and join you."

WHATEVER IS GOING ON IN THE CITY, life at the sanctuary is enchanted. Brian is calmer this trip, despite the tests taking twice as long as with the chimps because the bonobos won't participate until they do cartwheels around the room and make you touch their genitals.

"Mama Yvonne!" I call from the path leading into the forest nursery to warn the Mamas I am coming and that they should call off their savage little charges. I burst through the forest to the Brigitte Bardot playground. The four Mamas see me and smile.

I've been working hard at winning them over. I make sure I sit with them at least once a day and try to get to know them as individuals rather than a coven. I've learned many interesting things. For instance, the big-bosomed Mama Henriette is a choir soloist. She is so well known that people used to come from all over Kinshasa to hear her. Twenty years ago, her voice was so lovely that her pastor fell in love with her and they have been married ever since.

Mama Yvonne, the Amazon, is a single mother with three children. She used to be a ballerina, which seems obvious when I pay attention to the graceful way she moves her long, hard limbs. She is a rigid classicist with a disdain for anything modern. She has an ear for music, and when she stopped dancing, she took up the violin. Mobutu used to have her orchestra play for his official functions.

Mama Esperance is without doubt the most beautiful creature I have ever seen. She has languorous eyes that catch the light. I would die for her supermodel figure, which makes anything she wears look like haute couture. Every day at least twenty young men risk electrocution to push their phone numbers through the fence around the nursery. Mama Esperance turns up her dainty nose and lets the baby bonobos tear the paper to shreds. She may be just nineteen, but she is not stupid. Her boyfriend is none other than the spiritual adviser to President Joseph Kabila.

Mama Micheline is still an unknown entity since she doesn't speak French. But I know she has more grandchildren than teeth, and given the life expectancy in Congo, it's a miracle she is still alive.

The more I hang out with the Mamas, the more they loosen up. They even give me a nickname—something they do for all new bonobos.

"Vaneh?"

Mama Yvonne grasps my hand as a bonobo falls from the sky onto my head. The bonobo wraps her arms around my hair and clasps her hands over my eyes.

"Malou!" Mama Yvonne pulls the bonobo off me and Malou runs away cackling. Another four bonobos simultaneously appear, climbing up my legs, swinging from my hands, slapping me to get my attention. It is hard to be mad at all that cuteness. Yvonne patiently pulls them off me.

"Mama Yvonne, your little baby is a retard."

"Who?"

"Kikwit."

Mama Esperance rolls her eyes and laughs.

"Kikwit is *zoba*." Which roughly translates to "dumbass."

Kikwit is the football player with no neck. I personally love him and want to hug him all the time but Brian is nervous about those meat-locker hands. We have been trying to take his temperature for the emotion study, but he refuses to let anyone stick the thermometer in his ear.

"Kikwit is *zoba*!" repeats Mama Henriette for emphasis, and starts regaling me with Kikwit stories. Apparently when he was little, he used to pee and poop where he was eating, which, as far as potty training goes, was fine when he was two, but not when he was five. All the bonobos except Kikwit would climb off their Mama to do their business at a polite distance. Even bitty babies who had just arrived were toilet trained quicker than Kikwit.

"I guess he didn't want to leave his food," Mama Esperance adds thoughtfully.

But what Kikwit lacks in brainpower he makes up for in sweetness. He is so sweet that one day he hugged a visitor and didn't let go. When the visitor left the sanctuary, Kikwit went with him. He got all the way home and probably would have hugged that visitor till he died except the visitor brought him back to the sanctuary and got someone to remove him.

"What a dumbass." Mama Henriette shakes her head while Mama Micheline cackles. "Hey, Yvonne, do you remember that time he got lost?"

Mama Yvonne tightens her lips, irritated that she has to hear this story yet again. The Mamas think of their bonobos as their children. They are proud when they are smart and a little bit sad when they are stupid. The Mamas are constantly tormenting one another. Mama Henriette turns to me.

"He disappeared one day at the American school. Three days we were looking for him—three days! We searched the forest, we looked in the classrooms, the food storage, everywhere. Then, on the third day, we see crows circling a mango tree and we thought, that's weird, why would crows circle a mango tree? So one of the keepers climbs the tree and sees Kikwit, right at the very top, covered in leaves. Can you believe it? For three days, he just sat in a tree and covered himself with leaves. I mean, what the hell is that?"

"At least he didn't get beaten up by a bunch of girls," Mama Yvonne shoots back, unable to stand it any longer. She is referring to Tatango, Mama Henriette's baby.

"Ha! Tata is chief!"

"*Mimi* is chief! Tata got his ass kicked like a big sissy la-la."

It goes on for a while, Mama Esperance and Mama Micheline howling in laughter until finally Mama Yvonne swipes the air with her hand and follows me down the hill.

When Kikwit sees Mama Yvonne walk into the building, he starts squealing. He holds on to the bars of the enclosure and wails, jumping up and down and waggling his penis in excitement. When Yvonne enters his room, he flies through the air and wraps his arms around her neck. She almost collapses beneath his weight, but she croons to him softly, "Kikwit, you dummy, you sweet little dummy," and he melts into her arms.

We play the call of a strange bonobo, and Mama Yvonne takes Kikwit's ear temperature. She calls out the numbers and Brian adds them up and frowns. He expected the right-ear temperature of bonobos to go up less than that of chimps, but so far, the bonobos' right-ear temperature hasn't gone up at all. Because bonobos are so nervous around new objects, he thought they would be at least a little apprehensive when he rattled the pet pack and played the strange bonobo call. But it turns out to be the opposite. Some of the bonobos cautiously approached the pet pack, while most of the chimps did not. If anything, the bonobos' *left*-ear temperature went up, the side of the brain responsible for *positive* emotions. Brian double-checks the calculations. Either the thermometer is broken, or when it comes to emotional responses, their brains are wired completely differently.

MAX IS IN THE TESTING ROOM. He is the perfect male model, his luxurious hair fans out in all directions. He shakes his locks when he sees me.

Yes, his eyes tell me, his eyebrows raised at a devilish slant. *I am gorgeous.*

I offer him a piece of apple the size of a pea. He daintily takes it from me and spends five minutes eating it. He shakes his hair again and gives me his own version of Derek Zoolander's Blue Steel: one shoulder slightly forward, lips puckered, cheeks sucked in, and eyes squinted just a little, as though a wind is blowing in his direction.

"Max," I say, "have you ever wondered if there was more to life than being really really ridiculously good-looking?"

He takes a deep breath and exhales sharply. I am frustrating him with such a stupid question.

I present him with a photo of Tatango and a photo of Joey, a bonobo in Leipzig. Max stares at the photos thoughtfully, then touches Tatango. After a moment, he touches Joey.

"Touches Tata first," I say for the camera. Brian makes a note.

Then I show Max a photo of two chimpanzees, one in Leipzig, one in Oleti. Max looks at the chimps and freaks out.

"Eeeeeeeeeeeeeek."

It's a high, rasping sound, the sound only Max can make, and only when he has just seen something disgusting.

"Eeeeeeeeeeeeeek."

Max refuses to touch the photos, goes to the back of the room, and stares at me in outrage. He spent time next to chimps for several months before he came to Lola. Apparently his memories are not happy ones.

"Come on, Max, it's just a photo. It's not even a real chimp."

After twenty minutes of pleading and cajoling, it becomes clear that Max will no longer be participating. Since the tests are voluntary, we give up and let him out to the forest. As he walks past me to get to the door, he narrows his eyes at me. I have played a dirty trick on him and he doesn't appreciate it.

Next is Isiro, who walks in and starts checking the locks. This is typical of her, and we have to factor an extra ten minutes into every test because she absolutely will not do anything until she has double-checked all the locks. It's not that she wants to get out and run amok. Isiro is smart enough to break out every day if she wants to. She is just confirming we are doing our job properly. That we are following the health and safety protocol and not getting sloppy. She rattles each one and tries to pick a couple with a piece of straw. Only when she is satisfied that we have locked each and every padlock will she settle down to do the test.

She doesn't react to the chimp photos as Max did, but she spends less time on them than on the bonobo photos. When she gets to Mikeno's photo, she tries to pull it between the bars into the room with her. I wrestle it from her.

"Isiro, you can't have Mikeno's photo. He's just outside, for Christ's sake. Give it back!"

The next subject is Kikongo. He is growing on me. If all the bonobos at Lola have their assigned roles—Mimi the empress, Isiro the police, Kikwit the one who will not be toilet trained—then Kikongo is the class clown. He taps the floor with his feet while he eats. He opens his mouth as wide as he can, then tries to touch his chin with his tongue. He is a break-dancer when he lies on his back on the floor and spins himself round in circles. He is Gene Kelly when he leapfrogs in the air, kicking his heels together. He is Animal from *The Muppets* when he shakes his head until I think his brain will rattle itself into a concussion. If the keepers sing, he will dance, wiggling his bottom and clapping his hands in time. Kikongo is the *Saturday Night Live* show that never ends.

After doing his little dance, running around in circles and making himself dizzy, he finally settles down to do the test.

Everything progresses smoothly until he sees the photo of a baby girl bonobo called Louisa from the Leipzig Zoo. He lifts her picture up to his face and kisses it, his tongue slobbering all over her pouty lips. I remember doing this to a poster of Michael Jackson when I was eight. He rubs his genitals on her face. Which I did not do to my Michel Jackson poster.

When Kikongo puts Louisa's picture on the floor and starts tracing the outline of her face with the tip of his penis, I can't stand it anymore.

"Do you think we should turn off the camera?"

"It's a result. He likes the strange bonobo."

"This isn't a result. This is soft porn. We should take the picture away before it's covered in jissom."

"Not until the trial is up."

Kikongo shrieks when I try to take away Louisa's photo. He clasps it to his chest and runs to the very back of the room. He looks frantically at us, the bad people who want to take his precious Louisa away. He puts the photo on the floor and humps it. Brian and I are too stunned to move.

And they call this science.

CLAUDINE WARNS US not to test on Sundays, but Brian can't imagine a day where he doesn't get any data, so he ignores her.

Lola has twenty thousand visitors a year, most of them schoolchildren who have never seen a bonobo. Lola, with its beautiful lakes and picnic areas, is the only place they will see bonobos in something resembling a natural habitat.

During the week buses drop school groups at the gates to tour the sanctuary. They have already been visited by Pierrot, the education officer, at their school, where he showed them videos and slides of bonobos and talked about what they could to do to protect the bonobos in Congo. The education programs are so successful that several orphans were surrendered because schoolchildren had gone home and told someone in their neighborhood with a bonobo that it was illegal and they should take them to Lola.

Usually, hundreds of families visit on Sundays, but not this Sunday. This Sunday, the place is swarming with U.N. peacekeepers and military personnel killing time until the final elections on October 15. Helicopters have been flying over the sanctuary all day.

During World War II, when the Allies were bombing the shit out of Germany, there was a group of bonobos in a cage next to the chimps in Munich's Hellabrunn Zoo. During a particularly brutal bombing, every one of the bonobos died of fright. The chimps were fine.

So you can imagine what low-flying helicopters are doing to the nerves of the Lola bonobos. They can tell the difference between aircrafts, and they know the U.N. helicopters are sure as hell not the Air France flight 866 to Paris. On top of that, most of the bonobos were orphaned after the war. Rebels and soldiers were supposed to be demobilized and assimilated back into society, but with no money and no jobs, many of them used their guns and ammunition to feed themselves. So men in uniform were the last thing many of the bonobos saw before their mothers were murdered.

Some peacekeepers storm into the testing room and demand to know what we are doing here. Every bonobo except for Kikongo has melted silently into the forest, and the soldiers are determined to see one.

"I'm sorry," Brian says. "This area is closed to visitors."

"What are you doing here, then?"

The U.N. has recently been rocked by scandal. There are more than 150 cases of sexual misconduct by their peacekeepers, including some paying $1 for sex with girls as young as twelve. Pornographic tapes were found in a French peacekeeper's bedroom that were sold throughout Congo. A couple of Russians exchanged sex with young girls for jars of mayonnaise and jam. According to a rebel leader, all the U.N. will be famous for in Kisangani is running after little girls. I would have thought any peacekeepers worth their salt would be desperate to redeem themselves, but apparently not.

Brian finally gets them to leave and Kikongo is almost calm when we hear a heavily accented shout.

"Kikko! Kikko, *mon cher*!"

Kikongo starts squealing. He climbs the wall and sticks his head out, going crazy while someone talks to him on the other side. I go outside to see what's going on. A rotund Indian man in his midforties holds Kikongo's hand with such gentleness, I swallow my irritated comments. Jacques greets the man warmly.

"This is Kikongo's father," he says to me.

No one knows what Kikongo's father does, but his trips to Saudi Arabia smack of diamond dealing. He bought Kikongo from a wildlife trader and brought the bonobo to his Kinshasa home. Kikongo was more beloved than a child, but when his father saw Lola, he knew Kikongo belonged with the other bonobos. Kikongo's father sends a bus full of flowers for Claudine's birthday and always leaves a heavy wad of cash.

"I've brought a month's supply of food," he says. "If the elections go bad, I don't want Kikko or anyone else to run out."

Brian concedes that Claudine is right and testing on Sundays is, in fact, impossible. We give up and break for lunch.

At the swimming pool, near enclosure one, some Belgian peacekeepers surround Claudine. Their hips are cocked and their stance is aggressive.

"We are here protecting the country. We shouldn't have to pay to come in."

"You are my compatriots," says Claudine, genuinely hurt. "This is not government property, this is my sanctuary."

They are stubbornly silent.

"I don't get paid a salary. All the money for the entrance fees goes to protect bonobos. Don't you want to help the wildlife in Congo?"

A few shrugs. Claudine draws herself upward, her hair crackling in the midday sun.

"Then, *messieurs,* you are not welcome here."

What strikes me about these men is their proprietary manner. They act as though the uncertainty in the run-up to the election gives them some kind of ownership of Congo. That Congo is up for grabs.

When Joseph Conrad saw how Europeans behaved in Congo in 1890, he described them as "reckless without hardihood, greedy without audacity, and cruel without courage…To tear treasure out of the bowels of the land was their desire, with no more moral purpose at the back of it than there is in burglars breaking into a safe." More than a hundred years later, not much has changed.

The men storm away. Claudine shakes her head sadly.

"They are paid five thousand dollars a month to be here," she tells us. "Plus a bonus for being in a dangerous country. The entry fee for non-Congolese is five dollars. It is not so much, *non?*"

Just as the U.N. force is leaving, a North Korean general pulls up his black Mercedes next to the swimming pool. Claudine rolls her eyes at us as if to say, "Here we go again."

"*Excuse-moi,* Monsieur General, but you can't park next to the swimming pool."

"Of course I can," he snaps.

"But there is a parking lot outside."

"This is where I park."

"This is my home. You either move your car or leave."

I am amazed at how tranquil Claudine is. I have never heard her raise her voice or say anything rude. She is as calm as a Hindu cow. If this were my sanctuary, I would have already lost my temper fifty times before lunch. Brian, being from Atlanta, would have pulled out a gun and shot someone.

Eventually, the Korean general throws the keys to his driver.

"I'll move the car. But I'm not paying to get in."

Claudine sighs and walks with us to lunch.

Chapter 18

❦

Mikeno lies with his head in Isiro's lap. He closes his eyes against the dappled sun through the palm trees. Blue dragonflies dive through the water lilies. Occasionally there is a splash as a fish swallows an unlucky bug from the water's surface. The bonobos lie among the scattered remnants of brunch, the peels of pink grapefruit, mangoes, and sugarcane.

Isiro combs through Mikeno's hair, raking her fingernails gently over his scalp. Occasionally, he grasps her hand. She pulls it away playfully, and when he catches it, he kisses her fingertips.

Whatever she is doing to his head must feel good, because he gets an erection. The corner of her mouth twitches as she bends her long body over his face and nibbles on his ear. He murmurs in her ear. She lies back, and he positions himself between her legs. She wraps her arms around his shoulders and her ballet thighs around his waist.

They stare into each other's eyes and make love face to face. He shuts his eyes and throws his head back when he comes, and she cries out, high and triumphant.

Afterward, they collapse against each other, a warm breeze blowing across the midday sun. Jacques and I watch them from across the pond.

We are a little embarrassed by the passionate sex scene, so we talk about politics. Jacques, being from the east, says he will vote for Kabila.

"Do you think there will be another war?" I ask him.

"We are tired of war. There is nothing left in it for us."

Isiro curls up in the crook of Mikeno's arm and falls asleep.

"By the way," Jacques says casually, "a friend of mine is coming tomorrow. He was in the east, during the war, like me. Do you want to say hello?"

"Sure. Bring him round after work."

MUGWAGU HAS A MOON-SHAPED FACE and a soft voice. Almost immediately, I notice his gentle eyes, his bright smile. He is so different from Jacques. There is none of the *bapfuye buhagazi*, the "walking dead," about him. What makes his smile so light and childlike, while Jacques is still so haunted?

His story begins where Jacques's left off: Kabila Senior had installed himself on Congo's throne and kicked out the Rwandans and Ugandans who put him in power.

With Hutu extremists who had led the genocide still arming themselves in the mountains of eastern Congo, Rwanda wanted a government that was sympathetic to their interests. They thought they had found a puppet in Kabila. They were wrong.

> *When the war started, we were in Uvira. I was studying to be a doctor. My parents worked for Lebanese traders, and my mother ran the shop while my father went back and forth from Tanzania to trade.*
>
> *We heard the war was coming so we left for Bukavu because we thought it would be safer. Bukavu is an important town. We didn't think the government would let the rebels hold on to it for long.*

The war began on August 2, 1998, with a rebellion made up of Mobutu supporters, disillusioned Kabila followers, and unpaid soldiers. Rwanda sent in troops, and together with the rebels, they announced they were in charge of Goma, Bukavu, Uvira, and other eastern towns.

Rwanda expected an easy victory. They were using the same strategy they had used to overthrow Mobutu—take the capital and you have won. The rebels flew to Kitona on the coast on August 4 to broadcast their intention to overthrow the government. The Rwandan army secured the eastern borders and moved south and north, capturing diamond and gold mines along the way. They captured the seaports of Boma and Matadi as well as power plants along the Congo River.

Barely two weeks after the war began, Rwandan troops marched on Kinshasa. They surrounded the capital, cut off the electricity and running water, then began choking the city to death.

Out of nowhere, Kabila, who had the diplomatic finesse of a sledgehammer, suddenly turned on his political charm and managed to recruit Angola and Zimbabwe to his side. He promised them vast concessions—Zimbabwe was after diamonds, and Angola wanted oil. In exchange, they broke the Rwandan stranglehold on the city.

Uganda jumped in to help Rwanda and, while they were at it, headed straight for the diamond mines of Kasai and the copper mines of Katanga. They looted minerals, timber, and livestock. The brother of Uganda's president took over areas of Congo and started an airline company to smuggle diamonds. Jean-Pierre Bemba, the suitor who would later ask for Congo's hand, came with his rebel group and seized coffee plantations, banks, mines, and factories.

Kabila Senior handed out concessions like cigarettes in return for military help. He recruited Namibia, Chad, Eritrea, and Sudan. Soon there were so many troops in Congo from so many different countries that no one could keep up with who they were and who they were supposed to be fighting.

THEN IN 2000, a Congolese mineral shot to prominence in the international market and changed everything. This mineral was more desirable than diamonds, more plentiful than copper, more solid than gold. First discovered in the nineteenth century, coltan in its raw form looks like black mud. "Coltan" is short for "columbite-tantalite," an ore with two rare metals: niobium and tantalum.

Tantalum is used in capacitors to conduct electrical charges in high-tech electronic equipment. The information-technology boom of the late 1990s meant everyone wanted a laptop and a mobile phone, which turned coltan into the decade's hottest mineral. Because coltan is extremely rare, found in only a handful of countries, in 2000, the price of raw coltan ore jumped from $30 per pound to $380 per pound in a few months.

In the riverbeds and vast forests of Congo, a massive belt of coltan runs from Bunia to Goma, Kindu, and Bukavu—right through Mugwagu's hometown. Unfortunately for these cities, the world's largest supply of coltan was literally beneath their feet. It attracted rebel forces like wasps. Coltan, along with other minerals such as diamond and copper, is an easy target. Any general and a small army can take control of a mine and terrorize the local population into working for them.

To defend themselves from the swarm of rebel invaders, local communities formed resistance groups. They called themselves the Mai Mai, and they rallied in defense of Kabila and the towns and villages under attack. Often up against soldiers with superior firepower, the Mai Mai used witchcraft to inspire confidence in themselves. Their name comes from the Swahili word for water, because they claimed the holy water they carried with them could deflect bullets.

But what started as a noble movement quickly degenerated into groups of marauding young men who raided villages, raped women, and also began financing themselves by trading in coltan and other minerals.

The Mai Mai became so powerful that they held up the Lusaka Peace Accord in 1999. In 2001, the U.N. estimated there were up to thirty thousand Mai Mai still terrorizing the eastern province.

The rebels were supposed to be Rwandans, but it was hard to know if they were Rwandans or not. When we got to Bukavu, the Mai Mai were already killing people. These Mai Mai were from the north of Kivu. They were supposed to be helping the government; they said they came to fight the rebels and protect us, but really it was us who needed protection from them.

They slit the throat of my neighbor, Patrice Mukeni. They killed Mutcherdira and Erica Kalous, girls I knew in high school. They said they needed sacrifices for their witchcraft, to protect them from their enemies.

They fired their arrows at me and wounded me all over. Then they stormed into our house and cut me; here on my head you can still see the scar.

My parents watched. What could they do? My mother cried. She told them to kill her but to leave me alone. The Mai Mai said, no, because I was their son, I must know where to find their enemies.

They raped women in our village but really they were interested in the men and the children. They wanted to force them into combat. My mother threw herself at them, and they beat her. But in the end, they left us alone.

The missionary who took care of my wounds told me I had to go, that I was a target for the Mai Mai now and my whole family was in danger. So we left. I had three pairs of pants and two shirts. We left for Tanzania—it was the only thing we could do.

Congo was already in a refugee crisis. After the genocide, 1.2 million Rwandan refugees flooded across the Congo border in four days. By 2003, 3.4 million Congolese had fled their homes, but they never crossed the country's border, which made them hard to track and even harder to help.

In the eastern province of South Kivu, around Mugwagu's hometown of Uvira, fighting between rebel groups and the Mai Mai caused thousands to cross Lake Tanganyika into Tanzania. The camps overflowed.

The U.N. took us to a camp called Kanzibusi. There were so many people, you couldn't count them. When we arrived at the camp, a co-

ordinator gave us a tent number. We shared the tent with another family. There were twenty-seven of us. It was so squashed, we had to sleep side by side, paired by size. If you were short, you slept next to someone tall, to use less space. There were no mattresses, nothing but a thin blanket to sleep on.

We lived like dogs. For six months, nothing to eat but beans. A cup of beans a day for each family. A cup and a half of rice. A little oil. Sometimes tomatoes. Salt once a week. But how do you cook beans when you have nothing to cook them in? A missionary gave me a small bowl full of milk. When the milk was gone, the bowl helped a lot. A bowl is a treasure when you live in a tent.

There were bad people who stole the food that was meant for us. They got in with the U.N., stole money and food, so we had almost nothing.

No one knows much about the military operations inside the camps, but it was fairly easy for rebel leaders to get elected into positions of power by their supporters, then use access to food or medicine to reward or punish people.

The Hutu extremists who started the genocide had been regrouping and rearming in camps along the eastern border for years. Now other groups were using the same tactic. If you weren't on their side, you and your family were more likely to starve.

The worst part about the camp was that it was filthy. There were fifty toilets, which were just holes in the ground. Each toilet had to service ten tents, which could be up to three hundred people. If there was someone inside, you had to wait and wait. And the toilets were 300 feet away from our tent, so the stench was terrible.

Every day, people died, especially those who had already walked a long way. Typhoid, yellow fever, malaria…the doctors didn't come every day, maybe once a month. There was a health clinic but most of the sick went untreated.

My sister nearly died of asthma but my father phoned a friend in Tanzania who brought the medicine she needed.

There are certain things you need to feel human. Enough to eat, a place to sleep, somewhere to go to the toilet. We had none of these.

There was not enough water, not enough food, and not enough medical supplies. As of 2006, the Congo death toll was hovering around five million, most of them from disease and malnutrition rather than bullets. Almost half of the deaths were children under the age of five. In Mobia and Kalemie in Katanga Province, 75 percent of children born during the war died before their second birthday.

The war choked the Congo River, which is the arterial network, the lifeblood of trade. There were so many rapes that women were afraid to work in the fields, so there were no crops to harvest. In the camps, diseases such as malaria, diarrhea, and pneumonia spread like wildfire, diseases you could treat for as little as $3 a person.

Then Mugwagu does something that surprises me. He smiles.

But then I fell in love.

To get water, there was always a long line at the well. The water was not safe to drink, and a lot of people got sick, but we ate ginger or garlic to try to kill the germs. One day I saw a girl lining up with everyone else. She was beautiful. From then on, I went to the same well, just to see her. I found out her name was Leticia, and she was fourteen.

It was a long time before I could talk to her. When I finally gathered my courage, I asked if we could be friends. She said no. I reminded her of one of her brothers who died. I told her that whatever this was, this place we were in, whatever we were going through, we could get through it together.

She worked so hard to help her family. She took special care of her grandfather, who had a bullet in his leg. It was easy to fall in love with her. I wanted to sing all the time.

But then, six months after we arrived, my father arranged for me to escape the camp. I had an uncle in Kinshasa I could stay with. My mother, my sisters, my brother, my father, they stayed in the camp. They sent me because they needed me to be the man for my family. They need me to find a way to help them. Even now, I have this burden. I know I have to save them.

Leticia cried. She said, you're leaving, you're going to forget me. She cried and cried and cried. But I didn't forget her. In all the awful things that happened, she was something beautiful. I thought about her on the plane on the way to Kinshasa; I called my sister to ask after her.

Soon after I left, Leticia went to stay with her aunt in Butembo. Before she left, she went to see my mother. They both cried. I think my mother knows I love her.

Now I'm studying hematology. In five years I want to be a doctor. I want my family to be with me in Kinshasa, and most of all, I want to marry Leticia. There is no girl in Kinshasa more lovely than she is.

I told my brother to get her aunt's phone number. When he does, I'm going to call her. I'm going to call her as soon as I can.

I'm astonished at Mugwagu. He doesn't look upset in the slightest. He looks upbeat, happy, and in love.

I feel like I've been kicked in the stomach. When I first heard about the Congo war, I thought of it as *over there*. One of those crazy places where people ate each other and engaged in savage tribal warfare. I wanted to find out what happened to my father, but I was looking for the abstract, umbrella themes like death and destruction that I could find in any war from the War of the Roses to World War I. I didn't think the Congo war had anything to do with me.

Almost everyone who writes about Congo, from Henry Morton Stanley to cowboy journalists who jump in a canoe and sail down the Congo River, still thinks of it as a darkness, the same darkness that the Portuguese traders feared in the seventeenth century.

"Why are Africans so bad at running Africa?" muses Timothy Butcher, who followed Stanley's journey in 2006 and describes Congo as a "country with more of a past than a future."

Delfi Messinger, an American vet who spent a decade in Kinshasa, urges us to reflect "on the fate of a people trapped in a quagmire of politics, poverty, and ignorance."

Even Michela Wrong, the award-winning author of *In the Footsteps of Mr. Kurtz,* laments the apathy of Kinshasa, the unwillingness of people to take their destiny into their own hands.

But the people I have met tell a different story. There is no apathy in Mama Henriette's singing or Mama Esperance's laughter. No ignorance in Jacques's bitter acceptance of the entirety of his loss. And then there is Mugwagu, who was stripped of what makes him human and still had the courage to fall in love.

If, from a bird's eye, the Congolese seem passive, confused, and helpless, who is responsible?

Congo is not some isolated backwater in the middle of nowhere. We live in a global economy. Congo, perhaps more than any other country in Africa, is wired into the arterial network that sends money, minerals, and everything else that our first-world living requires into our countries, our homes, our mobile phones.

When Rwanda's coltan exports exploded to $20 million a month, when diamond exports jumped from 166 carats a year to 30,500 carats, who bought them, knowing that Rwanda has neither coltan nor diamonds?

When gold became Uganda's second-highest export at $81 million in 1997, who praised Uganda for its growing economy, knowing full well Uganda has no gold?

TWINSBURG, OHIO, is a small town near the Great Lakes. There, near Highway 480, there is a coltan-processing plant called Trinitech. On the company's Web site, you can see a photo of their smiling staff. I wonder if the dumpling Asian lady on the right or the man in the polo shirt on the left knows their coltan was bought from warlords and rebels who enslaved the local population to haul ton after ton of ore from their own land, only to watch it get shipped over the border to Rwanda.

Together with a Dutch company, Trinitech set up a laboratory in Rwanda to analyze the quality of the coltan coming out of Congo. The Rwandan president, Paul Kagame, had an entire section of his ministry—"the Congo desk"—set up just to deal with the minerals they stole. Trinitech's local representative was Kagame's brother-in-law. Of course, Trinitech claims it never knew where the coltan came from, but since there is no coltan in Rwanda, where did they think it was coming from—Canada?

TRINITECH IS ONLY ONE COMPANY AMONG MANY. The U.N. lists twenty-six countries in Africa, Asia, Europe, and North America that are involved in the exploitation of natural resources in Congo, including multinationals, banks, and small-scale traders.

Coltan from Congo was brought to China, Kazakhstan, Germany, and the United States. Metalor Technologies in Switzerland bought a large chunk of the $60 million of Congolese gold exported from Uganda. Anglo American traded gold with rebel groups. Companies in Belgium and the Netherlands bought mineral concessions from the government. Jean Boulle, cofounder of American Mineral Fields, let rebels use his private Learjet. Bechtel Corporation paid for NASA satellite studies and infrared maps of the mineral potential of Congo for the rebel government and helped Kabila deal with ethnic uprisings.

Anvil Mining Limited, an Australian company, backed government forces who massacred more than a hundred people in the town of Kilwa. Anvil supplied the vehicles and aircraft to the soldiers to suppress a rebel uprising that threatened the company's mine, which yields the highest grade of copper and silver in the world. The soldiers used Anvil vehicles to carry rebels and ordinary civilians to their torture and execution. I am immeasurably saddened by this. Like Brian, like anyone, I want to think my country is the land of the free and the

Malou wraps her arms around Brian's head.

Brian throws Malou in the air as high as he can.

Mwanda kissing and grooming Lomela's foot

The Mamas, left to right:
Yvonne, Henriette, Esperance

Mimi, the Empress,
has something to say.

Mama Yvonne and
one of the nursery terrors

The assistant vet,
Anne Marie, and Lomela

Kata arrives at the
sanctuary in her
wooden crate.

Semendwa reclining
like a painting of Venus

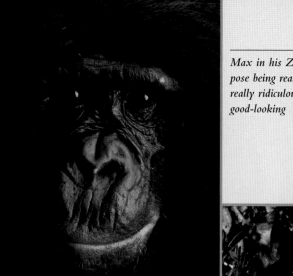

Max in his Zoolander pose being really, really ridiculously good-looking

Isiro ballet-leaps from the log.

Seeing how bonobos react to new objects. Vanessa presents the red porcupine to Mama Henriette and Kikongo in the night building.

Mikeno, otherwise known as Rodin's The Thinker

"She is too sad to live." Claudine cradles Kata in her arms.

Jacques collects Maniema, who has just busted out of the nursery.

*Tatango in an amorous kiss
with one of the females*

*Tatango in a magnificent,
angry charge*

*After being charged by Tatango, Kikwit runs down to the lake and is so upset,
he starts hitting his own reflection in the water.*

Masisi sips on warm tea with honey and lemon to help her recover from the flu.

Two females g-g rubbing.

Lounging around on Sunday afternoon

A young male bonobo blowing raspberries rolls off the log into the water.

Taking the ear temperature of Lodja, with the red lips and long eyelashes, who won't stop laughing

home of the brave. But there is nothing honorable or brave about how any of us acted in Congo.

IGNORANCE IS NOT AN EXCUSE FOREVER. I've had six cell phones and three laptops in three years. I never stared hard at my marvelous machines and asked where their organs came from. I fueled the war. I funded it. The second Congo war, with more dead than any other war since World War II, is on my hands.

Chapter 19

"We shouldn't be here."

Brian is lying on the couch reading a book by candlelight because the electricity has gone out again.

"We can't learn anything from bonobos. They aren't anything like us. We have the torture-and-kill gene and they don't."

Brian raises an eyebrow. "Have you been reading Richard Dawkins?"

"We're chimpanzees. We might be capable of love but the rest of us is this *awfulness*. Congo isn't a freak accident. It happens all the time, all around the world. Everything we need to know is back over on the other side of the river at Oleti. We should just pack up and leave."

"But what about our cooperation experiments? And the emotional reactivity studies?"

"They don't matter!" I burst out impatiently. "None of your stupid experiments matter. You're chasing some esoteric gibberish that will never mean anything except to you and a couple of other scientists. Five million people just died here. What are your ropes and temperatures going to do for them?"

I half expect him to get angry but he doesn't. He gets up and pulls me onto his lap.

"But, Skippy," he says gently, "that's exactly what we're doing. Congo is falling apart because no one is cooperating. Don't you think it would help if we could figure out what makes cooperation work and what doesn't?"

Brian scribbles his master plan on a piece of paper.

"Look. From their ear temperatures, we can see that chimps have an involuntary negative reaction if they hear the voice of a stranger. Their emotions are so strong that the right side of their brain actually heats up. To chimps, the 'us versus them' concept is very powerful, so powerful that they sometimes try to kill whoever is part of 'them.'

"At Yerkes, if we divided a group of chimps, six months later, we couldn't put them back together—it would cause a war. You remember the Stanford prison experiment?"

The Stanford prison experiment has been in the news lately because of the Abu Ghraib scandal.

In 1971, the navy asked a Stanford professor called Philip Zimbardo to run an experiment to explain the abuse of prisoners by guards in navy ships. Were prison guards naturally sadistic people? Or were they turned nasty by their job? Zimbardo took twenty-four white, middle-class Stanford undergraduates and told half of them that they were prisoners and the other half that they were guards. Then he threw them into a simulated prison in the Stanford basement and watched what happened.

Without any prompting or instructing, the guards became sadistic and cruel. They made the prisoners clean toilets by hand and defecate in a bucket in their cells. They locked the prisoners in solitary confinement and sprayed them with a fire extinguisher. They humiliated the prisoners by making them strip naked and simulate homosexual sex. Everyone was so absorbed in their roles that the experiment had to be stopped after only six days. Both prisoners and guards suffered trauma for months afterward.

In 2004, rumors of abuse by guards began to leak from Abu Ghraib prison in Iraq. Guards sodomized the prisoners with batons, urinated on them, dragged them by their penises across the floor, and burned them with phosphoric acid. The military claimed it was the work of a few "bad apples" but further investigations found that the condoning of torture went right up the chain of military command.

"When it comes to 'us versus them,'" says Brian, "we behave a lot like chimps, but our concept of who is part of 'us' is more fluid. The Hutus versus the Tutsis, North versus South, even UNC basketball versus Duke. Humans do terrible things to people we think of as 'them' and cooperate more easily with people who are like us. Bonobos don't have the same response. Somewhere during their evolution, they gained an ability to see every strange bonobo as 'us.'"

"But we don't have it," I interrupt. "And that's the whole point."

"We do have it. Martin Luther King. Gandhi. Shit, even U2. Their message struck the hearts of millions of people because we recognize that to live peacefully and cooperate, we need to be one people."

Outside, the bonobos settle down for the night. They call to each other as they climb into their hammocks and gather up their beds of straw. Their voices are like sonar, crawling over the contours of darkness, searching for the hidden shore. As if in response, the generator roars to life, flooding us all with a hungry golden light.

Chapter 20

༄

*I*t is a gorgeous day. The sunlight sparkles on the river and we can hear the women singing on the other side while they pick their crops. Claudine's daughter Fanny and I lounge on the porch talking about her rock star.

"I wish you could see his music video," she tells me. "It's on MTV, like, *all* the time."

Fanny fascinates me. Her mind is a whip; it's always coiling around thoughts and snapping at the air. I want to know what she is going to do with all her intelligence, all her beauty. I can't imagine her boxed up in some Parisian apartment, smoking cigarettes and acting artistic. She talks about living in Kinshasa, getting into the government and writing policy. But what to do about the rock star in Paris?

Dump him, I implore her silently. *He can't be good enough for you.*

Suddenly, Papa Jean runs past us. I have never seen Papa Jean run. As *le grand cuisinier,* he has his assistant, Alan, run everywhere for him.

"Papa Jean, what's going on?" Fanny calls out in Lingala.

"It's Mikeno," he says. "He's collapsed."

People appear from everywhere.

"Not Mikeno, not Mikeno," chants Jacques as he flies toward the forest. The vet, Crispin, the Mamas, the keepers, everyone runs past us like a flock of birds.

As though called, we join the flight. Down the hill, along the river, past the bungalows where the keepers sleep, past the hollowed-out shed, past the cool room where the food is kept.

We arrive at the enclosure. Mikeno is sprawled on the ground, facedown, his arms crossed in front, his forehead resting on his arms. Bonobos around him are going crazy. They make a vocalization I have never heard before. It is half-yelp, half-scream. It echoes into the bushes and circles above our heads. The bonobos surround him. They pull back his eyelids. They shake him gently. They touch his mouth.

There is a confusion of voices.

"I saw him fall," says Jacques, distraught. "He was fine all morning, then he fell down, right here."

"We must move him."

"He is breathing. We have to get him out."

Claudine and Brian walk toward us. Brian is wound as tight as a spring. He obviously wants to sprint but he won't go faster than Claudine, who could be on a garden stroll. She looks into the enclosure.

"He is dead," she says calmly.

Then she turns and walks away.

The bonobos are wilder than I have ever seen them. They shriek and keen with their teeth bared. No one can go into the enclosure, not even the Mamas. The keepers take long poles and start pushing the bonobos away so they can retrieve the body.

Most of the bonobos scream and retreat. But four bonobos will not leave Mikeno. Lomami, the young male with the mutilated hand, holds on to Mikeno's foot, and Isiro hangs on to a fistful of his chest hair. She bends over his face and blows into his mouth.

Everyone goes silent.

The keepers start whispering in Lingala. Fanny translates for me.

"They say she is trying to give him breath."

Isiro lingers over Mikeno's face. She bends close as if there is a secret she wants him to hear.

The keepers open the door to the enclosure. The four bonobos start screaming, and it is an ungodly howl. They clutch at the poles and push the keepers backward.

When I talk to people about what makes us human, some people say it's our tears. Because we are the only ones who weep, only we can feel true sorrow.

When I hear this, I remember Isiro's face, her anguished eyes as she cried for Mikeno, how she screamed at the keepers with her teeth bared and pushed at the poles. How she dashed back to his body and dug her fingers into his chest as if the strength of her grip could bring him back.

There is sorrow without tears. Of course there is.

The keepers finally manage to fight Isiro and the other bonobos back into the bushes.

"Now!" Jacques rushes with another keeper into the enclosure. They pick up Mikeno and drag him out. Isiro rushes forward and hurls herself against the fence. If she feels the electric shock, she doesn't show it.

Crispin checks Mikeno's vitals and nods sadly.

The keepers hoist the body onto their shoulders and we form a funeral procession behind them.

Isiro sits behind the fence, watching them take away the one she loves most. Her whole body is shaking.

WE FOLLOW THE BODY. Slowly, solemnly. The Mamas begin to wail. Papa Jean is beside himself, wringing his hands and pacing. Jacques obviously feels the burden of death weighing heavily on him. He knows sooner or later he will have to face questions he doesn't have the answers to. Like an absentminded guardian angel, he will have to explain why the death happened on his watch.

I walk back with Fanny to find her mom.

"If it just could have been any other bonobo," she keeps saying. "Any bonobo except Mikeno."

"She was very quiet," I say. "Do you think she's in shock?"

Fanny shakes her head.

"She's always calm in a crisis. The worse it is, the calmer she gets."

It is a terrible calm. Claudine stands on our front steps, watching them carry the body of the first bonobo she held in her arms. Mikeno, who brought comfort to a woman whose daughter was killed. Mikeno, who played basketball with the local children and stole sodas from the fridge. Mikeno, who would sit with his fist under his chin and listen when you most needed a friend.

"Claudine," I say, hugging her, "I'm so sorry."

She is motionless. Her eyes are as dry as the wind.

I don't know what is holding her upright. Surely she should be sobbing like everyone else. I have known him for only a year and I want to crumple to the floor.

She walks toward the vet block, where she will watch Crispin cut open the body she so loves. She will watch him close the eyes and peel back the skin, cut open the rib cage, and take out the heart.

"I have lost my prince," she says softly to no one. And I start to cry. Because the set of her shoulders, the way she does not drop her chin, the light on her hair—it is enough to break anyone's heart.

Chapter 21

❧

*I*siro doesn't eat for a week. I visit her enclosure every afternoon. Some days she doesn't appear. Some days she gives me a long look, gets up, and walks away. But every now and again she walks over and sits in front of me by the fence. She slides her fingers through the wire and I touch them with mine.

She stares at the blue sky and blinks.

"I know," I whisper. "I miss him too."

CLAUDINE LOSES HERSELF in the hunt for what killed Mikeno. She sends samples of his brain, liver, and heart to a specialist in France. She makes Jacques recount what happened over and over. He saw Mikeno in the morning. He was fine. At three in the afternoon, he came out of the forest to eat. He stood up on two legs, then collapsed.

During the autopsy, Crispin finds a contusion on Mikeno's brain, possibly caused by concussion. If Mikeno fell out of a tree and hit his head on the ground, his brain may have stretched and torn in his skull, causing a hemorrhage that would later lead to death.

It's the closest they can come to an answer. Claudine buries herself in work.

. . .

BRIAN AND I KEEP TESTING. I am more helpful, less difficult. I don't feel the urge to throw a tantrum when the tests take a little longer or sabotage the experiments when I'm hungry for lunch. Quietly, I start reading Brian's research. I read Richard's research and other papers I sneak off Brian's desktop. I begin to understand the theories behind aggression and cooperation.

At the same time, I read about Congo. Until now, I have read only *King Leopold's Ghost* by Adam Hochschild, which is brilliantly written and reads like a thriller. But beyond Hochschild, I was having difficulty. Brian brought a whole stack of books with titles like *The African Stakes of the Congo War* and *The Democratic Republic of Congo: Economic Dimensions of War and Peace*. The academic writing put me to sleep and I couldn't get any of the rebel groups straight.

Suddenly I'm interested enough to plow through them. I read by lamplight until Brian starts to make fun of me and call me his "little academic." If there is anything I don't understand, I ask Jacques. He draws me maps of Congo and marks out towns in the east. "This is Goma, big city, full of Lebanese, very dirty." He summarizes the various rebel groups, "All you need to know is that Rwandans are pigs." His explanations are a little biased but I get the point.

Meanwhile, Brian starts to visit the nursery. I go every day because I enjoy sitting with the Mamas and playing with the babies. But Brian never comes with me because as a scientist, playing with little bonobos is beneath his dignity. He's not interested in their cuteness, he's interested in their *minds*.

So the Mamas and I are surprised one afternoon to see him walk up the nursery path with a bonobo wrapped around his head.

"Bra!" the Mamas chorus.

"Who's this little monster?" he asks, pulling the bonobo off his head and tickling her in his arms.

"Malou."

In October 2006, an airport official at an X-ray machine at Charles de Gaulle airport in Paris noticed something the size and shape of a small child stuffed into someone's hand luggage. He detained the owner, who was in transit to Russia, and unzipped the bag. The creature inside was so wasted with dehydration, the official presumed it was dead. It looked so human, it could have been a child, but the official concluded it was a chimpanzee.

When they finally figured out it was a bonobo, the Paris zoo wanted to keep it. Only a handful of zoos in Europe have bonobos and they are a prized exhibit. Claudine heard about it and got on the phone to the French ambassador, who got on the phone to French president Jacques Chirac, who told the airport authorities to send Malou back to Congo, where she belonged.

She was almost dead on arrival. She had fallen into a fire somewhere along her journey and was covered in burns. She was so dehydrated she could barely move and so malnourished every strand of her hair had fallen out.

"We thought she was going to die," says Mama Henriette. "But she made it back. Malou, la Parisienne."

On cue, the Mamas start to sing,

> Oh, Malou, you went to Paris
> What presents
> Did you bring back for us?
> A zebra from the zoo?
> Some jewels from the marquis?
> Oh, Malou, our Malou from Congo

As if aware that this is her sound track, Malou grasps Brian's hands, runs, and launches herself into the air.

"You want to helicopter?" he says. He grasps both her hands and swings her around in a large circle. Malou laughs, a raspy sound that comes from deep in her stomach. When he stops, she staggers until she falls on her bottom, looking at the sky. As soon as her head clears, she runs straight for Brian, grapples up his arm, wraps her legs around his neck and her arms around his forehead.

Brian bends over so she falls forward into his arms, then tickles her until she is in wheezing fits.

The funny thing about bonobos is they choose you. I've played with dozens of orphan chimps and they seem to like one person as much as another as long as you like tickling and don't mind a few slaps. But bonobos are very discerning. You're either in or you're out, and it is rarely anything in between. Malou picks Brian in a second. She hangs around his neck and giggles flirtatiously in his arms. She curls her fingers into his hair and kisses him all over his face.

It's a little sickening.

What's more, once she figures out that I am Brian's woman, I—whom she has never had a problem with before—am instantly on her shit list. If I stand within twenty feet of Brian, she leaps from the trees and kicks me in the head. She bites me, bungee jumps from my shoulders by my hair, and leaves bruises from my waist (which is as far as she can reach) down to my ankles.

It's maddening, because Malou is the international celebrity and everyone loves her. She *is* beautiful; once a bald alien, she is now covered in lush hair and has exotic almond eyes. She loves the attention and whenever film crews or photographers turn up, it's camera time.

"Over here, Malou!"

"Turn this way, Malou!"

And doesn't she play it up, the little trollop. She peers through her lashes and smiles becomingly. Out of a medley of sixty bonobos, without an audition, she consistently ends up the star in everything from *National Geographic* to the publicity shots for Claudine's new book.

The Mamas sing her song at least once a day and she is the darling of everyone in the nursery. Brian will not hear a word spoken against her, and whenever he hears her name, he goes soggy.

"Brian loves Malou more than me," I joke to the Mamas.

"Vaneh is jealous!" they hoot. "Brian will run off with Malou, and Vaneh will be alone!"

"Married, Malou, married," I hiss furiously, tapping my wedding ring. In response, she kicks me in the shins, then runs up to Brian, who scoops her in his arms and croons her name lovingly. She squints her eyes at me in triumph.

And Brian—who has never had a favorite chimp, who makes it his scientific duty never to get attached, who likes all apes equally *for their minds*—falls in love. He visits the nursery every day, and as soon as he arrives, Malou flings herself into his arms to show the trauma of being apart from her man.

We sit in the nursery with the Mamas and talk about the elections. Over and over they ask me, "Who should we vote for, Vaneh?"

"Kabila!"

"Why?"

" 'Cause he's hot!"

And they collapse in laughter and screech that I'm going to leave Brian for Congo's interim president and have caramel babies.

We hear nothing about the elections from Kinshasa. It's as though the world is holding still for a little while so we can heal from Mikeno's death and prepare to begin again.

Chapter 22

I poke Kikwit in the balls and he laughs. I poke him harder and he collapses on the floor, giggling. I can feel Brian's impatience behind me.

"Is that really necessary?"

"Do you want him to do the experiment or not?"

"Yes, but do you have to molest him?"

"Don't you even speak to me. I had Malou all over my breakfast this morning."

Malou has started to run down from the nursery every day looking for Brian. As soon as she sees him, a huge grin spreads over her face as she flings herself on his lap and hides under his T-shirt from whichever Mama has to come down from the nursery to find her. This morning as she left, she kicked over my tea and stole my toast.

"Are you jealous?"

"I'm bruised. She's been beating me up ever since she fell in love with you. I can't go into the nursery without her bungee jumping off my hair. Soon I'll be bald, and wouldn't that be perfect for the two of you?"

There is a loud babble of voices outside. We turn around and Crispin walks into the vet room with a pet pack. I walk off to find out what's going on.

"Hey," Brian says. "Where are you going?"

"Back in a minute!"

The eyes in the pet pack are frightened orbs surrounded by a halo of black hair.

"Oh, *mignon,*" I croon.

Behind me, Crispin and the Mamas are having a heated discussion. All four of them are yelling. I don't pay much attention; the staff are always yelling. At first, I thought everyone was going to start punching one another, but since then, I've learned it's pretty much standard volume. I put my finger in the pet pack and the bonobo reaches out an emaciated hand. Then he flinches and pulls away, as though I have threatened to hit him.

"Who's going to be his mom?" I ask.

"Actually," says Crispin hesitantly, "we are going to try a new technique. We are going to keep him in quarantine."

This is highly unusual. As soon as a new baby arrives, it is plastered onto the bosom of one of the Mamas. If necessary, the Mama is isolated with the baby, but the baby is never isolated by itself.

"I want to make sure the baby is healthy. We will keep him here for a few days to run some tests."

I understand why Crispin is worried. At Ngamba Island, the new chimps go through a month of quarantine. The genetic makeup of chimps, humans, and bonobos are so similar that we can give each other all sorts of diseases. Monkey virus. Ebola. Marburg.

But a new chimp, like Baluku, was always plastered to someone, like me. The orphans are so traumatized when they come in, they need a warm body to cling to. Anyone can see the baby bonobo is scared shitless. He has already pooped the pet pack and he is trembling.

I find Brian loitering outside, kicking his heels.

"Bunny," I say sweetly. He is instantly suspicious. "There's this baby bonobo in there with no one to look after him."

"Why aren't the Mamas looking after him?"

"They're scared of catching something. They want to put him in quarantine."

"That's a great idea. You have no idea what he's got. He could have SIV, HIV, Ebola—anything."

"But he's scared and lonely. Can't I look after him in the house? I've done this before with Baluku—I know what I'm doing."

"What about the experiments? We haven't finished Kikwit."

"Brian, this is the life of a bonobo we're talking about. Don't you think that's more important?"

The look on his face tells me he clearly doesn't.

"Where are you going to sleep?"

"Since you're so mean and heartless, I'll sleep with him on the couch. Please, baby, pleeeeeeease. He's all alone. He needs his mom and she's dead and he probably saw them cut up her body and eat it right in front of him—"

"I get it, I get it." He sighs. "Let's talk to Crispin. It's his decision. He's in charge since Claudine's in town today, so it's his call."

CRISPIN IS PREPARING the various injections for the new bonobo, whom he has named Bolombe.

"Crispin, we want to ask about the baby."

"Not we," Brian mutters under his breath.

"I'm worried about him without a Mama. Do you think I can look after him? I don't mind."

Crispin searches my face. Then he looks at Brian. He senses an imminent divorce and wants to get involved about as much as Brian wants me sleeping on the couch with a disease-ridden bonobo.

"I think," he says slowly, "that it is best we leave Bolombe to rest here calmly. Then I will take blood and serum and do the tests. When the results come back in a few days, he will be free to go with a Mama."

We walk outside.

"You sabotaged me," I hiss.

"I did not. You're crazy. You're going to leave Kinshasa with your face falling off."

"Pfff. Whatever."

We actually knew someone who came back from South Africa with a rare flesh-eating disease. He had to be hospitalized for months, and it did, in fact, eat up a lot of his face. Brian is just using this as leverage for his argument.

It's almost lunchtime, so we pack up the experiment and head up the hill.

"Bolombe!" says Papa Jean. "That is my hometown."

Claudine and the staff name the bonobos at Lola after towns and villages in Congo. Most people who visit Lola have a connection to a village with the same name as a bonobo—Kikwit, Tatango, Isiro. It reminds them that bonobos are their national treasure, scattered throughout the forests at Congo's heart.

"He's so small and skinny," I lament. "And those evil poachers killed his whole family. I hope something terrible happens to them."

"You know," says Papa Jean carefully, "I used to see elephants all the time outside my bedroom window. They would walk by, hundreds of them. But we were poor and had no guns to hunt them.

"When I was nineteen, I stood on the banks of the river with my whole village and we watched poachers kill thirty elephants while they were bathing. Females, males, babies—they killed all of them. The poachers took the ivory and left us the meat. We had a big feast. We were so happy; we hadn't eaten meat for so long.

"We lost so much over the years. We didn't eat one grain of sugar. We had no soap to wash our pants."

Then he comes to his punch line, for spoiled white kids who have never been hungry or suffered the indignity of being unclean.

"For soap, for sugar, for a little bit of bread, you would kill a bonobo too."

I VISIT BOLOMBE after the keepers have gone home. He is in a cage by himself, next to the other babies in their night cages. A pile of food sits next to him untouched. His arms are wrapped around his knees and his head is buried between them. He rocks. Back and forth, back and forth. His eyes are squeezed shut and he rocks like a child who is sorry for something that is not his fault. He rocks like someone who will tear himself open if he stops. He rocks like someone who has nothing left.

"Hey," I say softly as I approach. He lifts his head weakly and makes a small sound. I want to open his cage door, gather him in my arms, and kiss him fiercely. But I know if I do that, I won't be able to let him go.

I think through turning up at the house with Bolombe's poo-stained body plastered to mine. Not only would Brian be furious, but it would be disrespectful to Crispin. Crazy white people occasionally turn up and run around the sanctuary, bossing the keepers around, thinking they know best and disobeying the rules.

Instead, I reach my hand through the squares of the night box. He stops rocking and clenches his whole body. I gently stroke his back and sing a French lullaby my mother used to sing to me. He goes limp. His hair is long and soft, encrusted with what might be small pieces of excrement or his mother's blood. Underneath I can feel the ridges of his backbone. There is so little flesh on him.

A mother dead and an infant orphaned. It is not such a huge tragedy. But in the night box next to Bolombe, there are six more orphans with dead mothers. Then, beyond them, another twenty orphans with dead mothers. Then in enclosures two and three, thirty more bonobos with dead mothers. And then there are those who never made it, the ones who died of starvation, thirst, and fright on the Congo River. Those who live scattered in people's homes, tied up with ropes around their necks beside market stalls, smuggled in planes to Europe, the United States, and the Middle East.

It is a cumulative tragedy, the same tragedy that blights the entire country. With so many dead bodies, how do you begin to rebuild? How do you trust enough to hope? And how do you hold on to life when it no longer seems worth living?

I haven't put on any repellent and the mosquitoes are eating me alive. The light has vanished and my legs are hurting from standing for so long. I've been stroking him for hours and I think he has finally fallen asleep. I try to sneak away, but as soon as my hand leaves his back, he yelps.

Bolombe would have been the little prince of his tribe. Unlike baby chimps, who are at the bottom of the hierarchy and likely to be killed by males, baby bonobos are almost the alphas.

I discovered this one morning when I was trying to take a photo of Semendwa and her baby, Elikia. Normally Semendwa loves the camera, but there was something about the long lens pointed toward her newborn that made her nervous. She gave me plenty of warnings but I didn't listen.

When the shutter made the first click, I heard a scream and saw a flash, and before I knew it I was knocked flat on my back. Semendwa was screaming and in a second, Isiro, Mimi, and the other females were bashing at the fence. They shot their hands through the spaces between the electrified wires, clawing at me. Their teeth were bared and their lips were curled in snarls. Never since I was surrounded by wild chimps in the forest have I been so afraid. If the fence hadn't been there, I would have lost a limb.

Most mothers defend their young, but rarely will five unrelated females flock to help them. And it's not just when the babies are in danger. When we try to figure out who is dominant, we put food between two individuals and see who gets it. You could put a grape within twenty feet of Elikia and if she so much as glances at it, even Tatango will run the other way. Baby bonobos can take the food right out of someone's mouth.

Bolombe would have gotten the best fruit, the juiciest leaves. He would have crawled over the sleeping males and pulled their ears and their hair. He would have climbed into the arms of his mother every night and gone to sleep with the gentle contentment of one who is loved.

As I walk away, he whimpers. Then he starts to wail. His voice is shaking, and in the pitch of it is all the longing and sorrow of being utterly alone.

As I walk outside, I look up at the swollen moon and I'm crying.

. . .

I WAKE UP AT SIX and run down to Bolombe. I've brought him slices of green apple.

"Hello, cherub."

He blinks off sleep and sits up, rubbing his eyes. I hand him some apple. He takes it in his skeletal hands and squeaks. He gnaws on it with his molars because most of his front teeth have rotted out from whatever his captors fed him.

I stroke him while he eats, until Brian yells from the house that it's time for me to tickle Kikwit's balls.

CLAUDINE ARRIVES AT ELEVEN A.M., and we emerge from testing Kikwit to find her ripping Crispin's head off. Her French is machine-gun fast and I can't understand a word she is saying. I have never seen her so angry. Her blue eyes are sharp and narrow, and sparks are practically crackling from her hair. She storms over to Bolombe's night box, takes him out, and cradles his head against her chest. He whimpers and clings to her so hard his knuckles turn white.

"*Mon Dieu,*" she fumes to no one in particular. "These Mamas with their ideas. If they don't want to catch disease from bonobos, they should go work with chickens."

"I'm sorry," I say, shooting an *I told you so* look at Brian. "I wanted to take him but I didn't know what to do."

"It is the Mamas who must care for them. That is their work here."

Anne Marie, the assistant vet, takes Bolombe gently from Claudine.

"Take him to see the other babies. He must know that there is hope, that there are others like him who have survived."

AT LUNCHTIME I find Anne Marie with Bolombe outside the nursery enclosure. The other babies stare at him curiously. Malou cocks her head, as though she recognizes herself in that tiny wasted frame.

"Vaneh, can you hold him for a few minutes? I need to get some medicine."

I take him in my arms and stroke his hair. In the daylight I can see the true extent of his emaciation. His skin hangs slackly on his bones. His fingers are claws. He is limp against me, as though he doesn't even have the strength to hold up his head. But behind his eyes, there is a sweetness. This bonobo will not grow to be a Tatango. He will be more like Kikwit.

He will not drink any water or milk, but when I peel an orange, he nibbles on a juicy segment. Then I feed him some white berries that grow in the forest. He eats them one by one, making little peeping sounds.

Then he falls asleep against my chest, listening to my heartbeat.

CLAUDINE CHECKS ON HIM every half an hour. He wakes up but keeps his eyes closed.

"*Mon coeur.* You do not want to see any more of the world or what we have done to you."

I hand him back to Anne Marie reluctantly to finish the temperature studies. At the end of the day, he goes back into his night box with its bed of soft straw and enough food to feed an army.

"What can we do?" I ask Claudine. "What does he need? I'll do anything."

"See if you can get him to drink something, anything, Fanta, water, milk, red cordial. Just try to make him drink."

SO MORNING AND NIGHT I carry cups of anything I can find in the kitchen. Cherry soda, orange juice, peach juice, sugared water. He chirps when he sees me and my cup, wondering what I will serve to him in his silver spoon.

Brian has giardia, or we think he does because his farts smell like rotten eggs and his poop is bright yellow. I'm happy because it means we can't test and I can spend more time with Bolombe. Brian feels neglected and is suspicious Bolombe gave him the disease.

I think he is getting better—Bolombe, not Brian. Brian is a typical male and refuses to take antibiotics until all of his fluids are in the toilet bowl. I think Bolombe is growing strong. He is still a furry skeleton, but his blood results are back from the lab and they are normal. He has taken medicine for worms, amoebas, and bacterial infections.

Crispin says he will be fine, but Crispin always says everything will be fine. Claudine says nothing, just sits with him, coaxing small amounts of liquid into his mouth.

So I bring platters of food, pieces of mangoes thinly sliced, oranges peeled and broken into segments, apple cubes with pale green skin clinging to one side, the glassy white berries, sweet sugar bananas usually reserved for our lunch, bright orange papaya, and trapezoid pineapple bits. I arrange them on the plate with care, as though it will influence how much he eats. I run up and down from the house, fetching various liquids. I stay for hours by his cage, stroking his hair, humming lullabies.

He is getting stronger. He can sit up on his own. He can even crawl around a little. Today he called out to Malou, and she squealed at him, offering her curled pink clitoris. When he goes into the nursery, they'll become friends. Maybe with a new BFF (best friend forever), Malou will wean herself off Brian and stop beating me up.

I put Bolombe to bed. As he closes his eyes, I catch something in them. It is so fast, it could be the reflection of the light from outside. He turns over, away from me, but I think about his eyes for a long time. A small flicker and then nothing.

Soon his chest is rising and falling in a quick flutter. He must have a high metabolism, because he breathes as though he has run a long way.

Tomorrow, I think, I will make him fresh lemonade. I will squeeze the lemons and dissolve a spoonful of sugar in a little hot water. Then I will fill the cup with cool water. He'll drink that. No little boy can resist lemonade.

WHEN I RUN DOWN TO THE ENCLOSURE at six in the morning, carrying the lemonade, Jacques is sweeping the floor. When he sees me he stands in the doorway, blocking my way.

"The baby is dead."

I think I have misunderstood his French, although there isn't much room for confusion with "*Le bébé est mort.*"

"What? No. It can't be. He was fine. He was—"

I push past Jacques and run to Bolombe's cage, which is covered with a blanket. I tell myself Jacques is wrong, that he is just sleeping deeply and that if I stroke him gently, he will wake up. I lift the sheet, and there is no confusing sleep with death.

Death is not peaceful. It isn't a blessing. Death is having the life ripped out of your throat. Bolombe is contorted into a horrible shape. His back is arched, and his left hand is plunged deep into the straw, as though he is in the middle of a convulsion. He looks frozen in excruciating pain, as though he died during torture. His mouth is open, and his lips are already desiccated. His eyes are wide open and now, only now, do I recognize what I saw in them last night.

He had given up.

He wanted to die.

I can't bring myself to touch him.

I run to the house. Brian is weakly standing, making a cup of tea.

"He's dead." I'm crying so hard I can barely talk. "He's dead and it's my fault. No, it's your fault. You told me I couldn't take him. If I'd taken him he wouldn't have been so scared the first night. He needed someone to hold on to. He needed me and I didn't do what was right. He should have been sleeping on my chest last night. I would have known something was wrong."

I hit Brian in the chest with both fists, and I am bawling, choking on my tears. There is mucus running down my face, pouring from my nose, and I am heaving great wracking sobs. Brian holds my fists, then he wraps his arms tightly around me.

I go slack, and he has to hold me on my feet or I will crumple to the floor and cry myself inside out.

"I'm sorry," he says. "Skippy, I'm so sorry."

"It's all my fault."

"It's not. You did everything you could."

"I didn't do anything. I should have ignored you. I should have picked him up and carried him day and night. I would have taken care of him."

"I know you would have. You would have loved him till his last breath, but no one would let you. I'm sorry, Skippy, I'm so sorry he died."

I'm not sure I believe in a God who makes so much room in the world for suffering, but still I ask in a small voice, "Do you think he's in heaven with his mom?"

Brian crushes me against him and I cry into his heartbeat until I can barely breathe.

Chapter 23

❧

Claudine asks me to walk around the sanctuary with her. She starts working at four in the morning and often doesn't finish until late at night, but whenever she is at Lola she walks around the entire sanctuary to visit everyone.

Lately, she has started dropping by the house to see if I want to come. Fanny has gone back to France. There are no visitors. So we walk, just she and I, around Mobutu's forest.

They emerge from the trees at the sound of her voice. They flock to the edge of the lake and call. They bring their babies to show her and put their hands through the fence so she can stroke their fingers.

I think she needs this, especially now. To see the bonobos who didn't die. We sit at group two, where Kikongo and Maniema jump off their log bridge into the lake. They leap from the log and canonball into the water. They burst to the surface laughing at the splash they have made. They chase each other around the bank before canonballing again.

Usually Isiro has control of the log. She leaps from it like a dancer, spinning herself around, hands folded gracefully in front of her, head thrown back. Mikeno used to watch her. We all did. It was one of the most graceful things I've ever seen.

But Isiro is no ballerina today. She lies on the grass, her face hidden in her arms, while Semendwa gently strokes her hair.

Claudine tells me there was fluid around Bolombe's heart. That the stress of his capture was too much. I always thought hearts were broken, but apparently they drown.

I try not to cry, but I'm a pathetic wreck. I can't believe Bolombe died. I thought bonobos were survivors, like chimps. Baby chimps can go through hell but usually, if they can make it to a sanctuary, they fight and they live. Bolombe was safe. He was fed. He was loved. But it wasn't enough.

"I don't know how you do it," I tell her. "I don't know how you watch them die and keep going."

She smiles at me sadly.

"You know," she says slowly, "people ask me if I am prepared to lose my bonobos when I release them back into the wild. Mikeno was hard to lose. But for the rest, I am ready. I am ready to let them go."

Claudine has more bad news. Her husband, Victor, may have cancer. He is flying to Belgium tomorrow for diagnosis and possibly chemotherapy. He has ordered Claudine, threatened her and begged her, to leave Kinshasa before the elections, but she refuses.

"My children are angry with me. They say, '*Maman*, *Papa* is sick. He may be dying. How can you not come here to be with him?'"

I realize I think of Claudine as something more than human. Like Mother Teresa or Nelson Mandela. These people, they save the world and you assume it is because they are programmed to do it, like Pavarotti was meant to sing and Lance Armstrong was meant to ride a bike. But it isn't that simple. Every day is a choice. A choice that gets harder and harder. Claudine has a husband who needs her, children who get angry with her. She is an ordinary person. It's just that she does extraordinary things.

Claudine turns to Kikongo and Maniema, two wet mud balls wrestling on the grass.

"But how can I go?" she asks softly. "What if the city falls to soldiers and rebels? What if they come in here and shoot them all?"

Any scientific detachment I have crumbles.

"I'm going to help you. Tell me what to do."

The storm clouds have been gathering all day. Every year on October 15, the rainy season begins. Brian is sitting on the porch, watching the setting sun shoot orange and red laser beams between the clouds. I lie on the couch and put my head in his lap. He has just had a shower and he smells like my apple-mint shampoo.

"I want to help the bonobos," I say. "But I don't know how."

We are getting ready to leave. The final elections were supposed to take place today but they have been delayed until October 29. Kinshasa is armed to the teeth. In addition to the seventeen thousand U.N. peacekeepers, the EU has flown in another thousand soldiers.

Brian and I will see how everything unfolds from our apartment in Germany.

"You're already helping bonobos," he says. "With the research."

I pull his wet hair.

"I want to do more than that. I want to help Claudine. But I don't know how much use I'll be. I'm too selfish. I'm not as brave as she is, not as strong."

Brian kisses the top of my head. "Why don't you start doing a little bit? Then you can see what happens."

The rain begins. It's like being at the bottom of a waterfall. Great sheets of water pour from the roof and run down to the river, which swells over the banks. We couldn't talk even if we wanted to. The rain is a thousand drums.

Brian and I watch, mesmerized. We could be the only two people in the world.

Chapter 24

❧

*T*he final election is held two weeks after we leave Congo, on October 29, 2006. The last five years have been straining toward this moment. Everyone expects a massacre. U.N. peacekeepers have their hands on their guns. The presidential candidates' soldiers have their ears pricked for the order to fire. Foreign correspondents press their mouths to their recorders, waiting for first blood.

It doesn't happen. Instead it rains. Water pours from the sky at dawn, turning red dust to rivers of mud flowing over the potholed streets of Kinshasa. Thunder claps overhead like gunfire. Lightning brightens the clouds like missiles. Still no weapon is fired.

The Congolese emerge from their houses and walk the long, waterlogged streets to the polling stations. Some have been walking for days. They cast their ballots and emerge still sopping wet.

Kabila crushes Bemba in a landslide victory. Bemba, predictably, cries fraud. He takes his claim to the Supreme Court, but they uphold the result. In retaliation, Bemba sets the Supreme Court on fire. But this last act is his swan song. Kabila is sworn in as Congo's first democratically elected president in forty years.

It is over. Kabila has won.

. . .

IN OUR APARTMENT IN GERMANY, we watch the ceremony. Kabila is splendid in a dark blue pinstriped suit. He smiles as ten thousand guests, including presidents, kings, and queens, pay their respects. His National Guard marches in perfect formation to the sound of trumpets. Canons fire in salute.

He is no longer his father's son. Now he is truly a king.

IT'S THE SUNDAY BEFORE CHRISTMAS and I'm cleaning the house. I'm in a good mood because I've just spoken to Dominique Morel, the president of Friends of Bonobos, the U.S. charity that supports Lola.

By day, Dominique is in the business of calamity. She works for Catholic Relief Services, and every time the shit goes down, Dominique is there mopping it up. She lived in Kinshasa for eight years during the war and became one of Claudine's best friends. Dominique was in Banda Aceh when the tsunami hit. She was in Pakistan when Bhutto was shot. When I first talked to her on the phone, she was in Afghanistan and I could hear gunfire in the background.

By night, Dominique works for the bonobos. She applies for funding, manages the adoptions, and writes the donor reports. Although she brings in tens of thousands from grants, there are hardly any free donations from the United States. In 2006, only eight Americans sponsored bonobos through the adoption program.

My first job is to revamp the Web site so that people can make donations online instead of sending a check or wiring funds through their bank account. Dominique puts me in touch with Alasdair Davies at the Great Primate Handshake. Another superhero, by day he works at the London museum, and by night he helps primate organizations update their Web sites.

I guess I thought Claudine was a one-woman band, but after talking to Dominique I realize how much Claudine relies on volunteers to handle the accounts, manage the visitors, and keep the donations coming.

As I'm thinking about the Web site, my broom brushes up against an old backpack full of water bottles. It is fraying at the seams and the straps are falling off. Brian used to use the bag as a weight until I gave him barbells for his birthday.

"Babe," I say, walking into the living room, "I'm going to throw this out, okay?"

Brian is in his e-mail vortex, where he is actually inside his in-box and can't hear or see anything else. So it is not until I'm holding the bag above the garbage bin in the kitchen that he turns around and yells so loud, I jump.

"Don't you touch that bag!"

"What? I was just—"

"Get your fucking hands off that bag; it was the last thing my grandmother gave me before she died!"

He says it so fast I can barely understand the words, but I recognize the Tone. I hate the Tone. It usually appears when we're in the middle of a huge fight, and just the sound of it is enough to get my hackles up. The fact that it has appeared suddenly and without warning makes me furious. I storm into the bedroom, sit on the bed, and cook up something scathing to say.

"You shithead," is the best I can do.

No reply from Brian. I stew a little more. I wait for him to apologize. Nothing. I sit on the edge of the bed, getting angrier and angrier, until I have an idea. I storm into the kitchen, grab a hammer and a nail, and walk back into the bedroom. Brian follows me just in time to see me nailing the bag to the wall.

"What are you doing?" The Tone has changed. It's low and dangerous, almost a growl. I know I'm crossing a line, that I'm about to push the nuclear button, and inside I'm a little scared. But I keep going.

"What does it look like I'm doing? I'm nailing your precious bag to the fucking wall. Maybe while we're at it we can get some cow shit from your grandparents' garden and put it on the living room floor."

There is a dark silence. Brian crosses the floor in about a second, picks me up like I weigh nothing, and throws me onto the bed. He pins me down by my shoulders and screams so loudly it fills my whole head.

"How dare you!"

His teeth are bared, and I can see the redness at the back of his throat. His hair is standing on end, blowing him out of proportion. All he needs is a tree trunk to drum on and he would be Simba, the killer chimp.

For the first time, I am afraid of him. Brian's Little League baseball team were state champions and Brian was famous for being a crack shot. I see his arm out of the corner of my eye, his batting arm. It is raised in a fist, and I become aware that he wants to beat the shit out of me.

He screams again, and it's a horrible sound. He tears himself away from me, goes into the kitchen, and throws a chair across the whole length of the apartment. I know he is pretending the chair is me and that he did it to stop himself from doing worse.

"Submit," I hiss at myself. *"Huddle in a small ball and submit."*

Instead, I chase Brian into the living room. He is breathing heavily and staring at the chair. He has thrown it so hard, two of its legs have broken off and there is a hole in the wooden floor.

"Oh, so we're throwing things now?" I taunt him. "Fine." I go into the cupboard, take out the biggest jar I can find, and hurl it across the living room after the chair. It smashes into a million pieces. Each glass shard is no bigger than a dust mote and they bounce off the living room floor and land on my desk, the sofa, the telephone table, the fronds of the Christmas tree.

Brian is looking at me, and in his eyes there is no sorrow or even anger. There is only hatred, as pure and cold as the driven snow. He turns away, goes into the bedroom, and locks the door.

I'm shaking. I survey the room. The broken chair, the hole in the floor, the shards like diamonds everywhere. I pick up my wallet and my jacket and run out the door.

I GET ON THE FIRST TRAIN that pulls in at the station. It is going to Dresden.

Two hours later, I check into a hotel, then catch the tram into the old city center, beside the River Elbe. It's dark and very cold. Next to the Zwinger museum, some fire twirlers in gothic clothing are hurling lit brands into the air. The flames cast orange shadows over the face of a giant statue—Atlas holding the weight of the world.

It's a terrible thing when violence walks into your home. My father beat me once, just once. I was a teenager and he was losing control of me. He dragged me out of bed into the kitchen and hit me until I went limp. Strangely, it didn't hurt. Afterward, nothing was broken. But most cases of domestic violence aren't about doing any damage. They are about gaining control. My father's rage filled the whole room. It was a creature all of its own. Once it happens, you stop feeling safe. I loved my father, but I no longer trusted him.

In the three years I have known Brian, he has never raised a hand against me. If someone had asked, I would have said he wasn't capable of it.

Besides warfare and killing other males, chimpanzees have another unattractive trait they share with us. Richard Wrangham calls it battering.

A male chimpanzee will begin a long, slow assault on females he lives with. He beats them for superficial misdemeanors, but the underlying reason, as in human males, is to display dominance and gain control. Every female chimpanzee is battered. When males reach adolescence, they start to hit, kick, bite, and pummel each female in turn until she acknowledges his authority and submits. The main benefit of battering is that while the female may not feel very amorous after she's had the shit kicked out of her, she is more likely to mate with the male who battered her, days, weeks, or even months later.

The fire twirlers brandish their flames in the night, surprisingly light-footed in their black cloaks and leather boots. Their kohl-rimmed eyes and pale skin are straight from a fairy tale. It starts to snow. My head hurts. My fingers are numb.

I remember what Empress Mimi did when Tatango hit her across the side of her head. She didn't cower or raise her arms to protect herself. She faced him with her teeth bared and screamed like a banshee. Within seconds, Semendwa, Isiro, and three others were right beside her and together they chased Tatango all around the night building. Their collective rage streamed out behind them as poor Tatango ran for his life. At the time I laughed at the miserable look on Tata's face.

Now I feel desolate, because, like Mimi, I will not stand for violence in my home. But unlike Mimi, I have no one to come running to protect me.

It is past midnight. I catch the bus back to the hotel, crawl under the covers, and cry myself to sleep.

Chapter 25

I don't leave him. But I don't forgive him either. Instead I gather my alliances as best I can. I tell my sister in London I may arrive with a suitcase at any second. I tell my mom I might come home, it might be over. I discuss the situation extensively with my girlfriends. And then I wait.

It's hard to live with someone you haven't forgiven. It's like a cavity in my tooth that I can't see but I keep pushing at with my tongue. I'm afraid it will crack but I can't leave it alone.

I'm almost relieved when we go our separate ways for a few months in March. A book I wrote about chasing monkeys in Costa Rica is being published in Australia. I go home for the book tour while Brian goes back to Lola.

At Lola, Brian continues the experiments. While he is there, Claudine is running the first health check. It is still two years before she'll release the bonobos but she isn't taking any chances. She wants to be absolutely sure her bonobos don't have any diseases they might pass on to wild populations. Parasites, tuberculosis, measles, tetanus—you name it, Claudine is testing for it.

In the middle of my book tour, Brian calls me. Even on the wretched phone line, I can hear his voice shaking.

"Lipopo died."

Lipopo was one of our cooperation stars. He was a sweet seven-year-old who liked to hold your hand. Most of the time, he didn't even eat the apple, he just enjoyed the game. Whenever he got a trial right, the keepers cheered and Lipopo clapped his hands and ran a victory lap around the room.

"It was unbelievable; you should have seen Mimi. She wouldn't let them take the body."

"Like Isiro? But Isiro loved Mikeno. Mimi didn't even like Lipopo."

Mimi didn't like any of the little boys. They were the ones who had to lurk in the tunnel until she fell asleep. Lipopo had been in Mimi's group for only a year and they barely spent any time together.

"It was even more than that. She pushed at the poles, like Isiro, and she held on to the body. She just kept grooming his face for hours and trying to keep the flies away. It was as though she was mourning his death but still felt she had to protect him. It was already enough Lipopo was gone, but to see Mimi so upset—everyone was crying.

"The body was in a tight space, near the tunnel. She must have been afraid, all those men with sticks, but she wouldn't let him go. Then Crispin turned up with the dart gun, which looks like a gun, right? The last thing these bonobos saw before their mothers died was a man with a gun. So Crispin comes out with the gun to try and get Mimi to leave the body, but she refused. She wouldn't let Lipopo go."

Ask any scientist and most would agree that what makes us human is altruism—helping an unrelated individual at a cost to yourself. Animals help one another all the time, but only for their own reproductive success. Each night in northern Costa Rica, thousands of vampire bats fly out of a cave in search of food. Vampire bats must drink blood every few nights or they starve to death. When the vampire bats return, those who have been successful regurgitate blood for bats who are hungry. They aren't related, but by sacrificing a little of your meal, the bat you save one night could save you the next. By the same token, if you refuse to give blood to a hungry cave mate, next week you could find yourself on a quick road to starvation.

If some animal story works its way into the media—for example, the dog in Chile who dragged his wounded friend off the highway, or the dolphins who saved a teenage boy from drowning—scientists tend to snort at the gullibility of the public. The dog was hungry, they'll say. He was dragging the other dog off the road so he could eat him. Or the dolphins thought the boy was a toy; they were just tossing him around, accidentally keeping him afloat until they reached the shore.

Even if these esteemed scientists do concede something might be going on, it is so rare, it's almost a freak accident, like lightning hitting someone twice. Only humans, they argue, are altruistic all the time. We give blood. We donate to charity. We help little old ladies across the street. Small acts of kindness toward others who will never repay us. Even babies too young to talk will help a stranger without praise or reward.

Then there are the really heroic acts. The man who jumped on top of a ten-foot crocodile and gouged its eyes out to save an eleven-year-old girl. Or the fireman who dressed up as Spider-Man so he could coax an eight-year-old boy from falling off a building.

As humans, we worship altruism. Gandhi, Nelson Mandela, Wonder Woman—we idolize people who do good for no other reason than they want to help.

Now Mimi has blown everything out of the water. What higher form of altruism could there be than risking your life for someone who isn't related to you? How many humans would throw themselves between a dead body and a gun?

Brian doesn't know how to process the data. He can't publish it. There are too many variables, too many unknowns.

"But I know what I saw. She was prepared to die for him."

He sounds wired, elated, and bitter.

"How the fuck can people think bonobos don't matter?"

There is no answer. Even I used to think bonobos were just funny little chimpanzees. Science ignores them. The media thinks they are boring. The rest of the world doesn't know they exist. By the time anyone realizes they are important, it might be too late.

· · ·

Two MONTHS LATER, we meet back in Leipzig and hit the ground running. The countries stream by: Germany, Kenya, Zanzibar, Japan, America, and Uganda. It's only after we go back to Australia for a wedding that things start to fall apart.

THE WHOLE FLIGHT Brian complained he had a headache. I thought it was altitude. Then he said he felt sick to his stomach. I thought it was the airline food.

As soon as we land, Brian says his throat is raw and his body aches all over. We barely have time to hug my mom and get home before Brian starts shivering. He is shaking so hard he can't walk to the bathroom. I watch him carefully, an awful thought forming in my head.

"How do you feel?"

"I feel cold." His speech is slurred.

I map out our journey, calculate the incubation period.

"Shit."

Mom and I wrap Brian in a blanket and drive to Woden hospital. It's Saturday morning and the emergency ward is full.

"It's going to be a long wait, love," says the nurse.

I look her dead in the eye and speak very quietly. "I think my husband has cerebral malaria."

"Malaria?"

"We were in Uganda two weeks ago in a high-falciparum malarial area. He is on prophalaxis but they're new and no one knows how effective they are." Just in case she doesn't get it, I add, "It can kill you in four days. I think he's had it for two."

As if for effect, Brian goes into the hot-flush stage. He strips down to his T-shirt and collapses sweating on the seat. It's 30 degrees Fahrenheit outside. The nurse looks worried.

In under twenty minutes, Brian bypasses the six-hour queue, the blood-caked collarbones, the little girl who had a near-fatal asthma attack, and all the other crises that apparently don't rate with brain-eating malaria.

The intern's jaw drops.

"I've never treated anyone for that."

I look over her shoulder, absurdly hoping to catch a glimpse of the T.V. doctor House, who will come limping in and save Brian's life with a curmudgeonly prognosis. Instead, the intern butchers Brian's arm drawing blood and sends it up to Infectious Diseases, a special unit of the hospital.

They strap Brian to a bed and hook him up to an I.V. drip and an ECG machine. Then they leave me watching the blue line and the blinking heart that tell me he's still alive. His face has completely drained of blood. His lips are white and flaky, like a mermaid's tail out of water.

I read the book I've brought on malaria cover to cover and then reread it, trying to find out how far along his symptoms are and whether Australia is going to have the right drugs.

Brian drops in and out of consciousness. Which could be the coma phase. Which is followed by death. Cerebral malaria hits hardest the first time you have it. Average time to live when you first get it is 2.8 days. I put my hand on his forehead and tell him, "Please stay awake, baby, you have to stay awake and tell me what's going on."

Two hours later. Then four. Then six. I haven't slept in two days. I doze off in the plastic chair by the hospital bed. Nurses and doctors come and go, taking more blood, more urine samples, more temperatures. They are running every test known to humanity because he is going downhill rapidly and they might not have a second chance to get it right. Spinal meningitis. Hepatitis. Yellow fever. Dengue. The digital heart blinks and blinks.

There is a certain point in our lives when we get acquainted with death. For the first thirty years of my life, it has been a stranger, something that happens to other people. Suddenly it seems death comes rolling in a couple of times a month. A friend from Sydney gets hit by a bus. Three friends of my mother's die from cancer.

Jacques's sister-in-law dies of malaria. Papa Jean's wife. Mimi's baby. Mikeno. Bolombe.

So when I'm crouched over Brian sweating in his hospital bed, I don't automatically think everything will be all right. I don't have the same disbelief on my face as others in the hospital.

Instead, I have this terrible knowledge that Brian could die. Here. Now. Fast.

I hold his hand and press my face into it. I realize I have never played him my favorite song. I start to panic. That's the first thing you do when you fall in love. Favorite books, movies, and songs. What if he never hears it? What if it's too late?

Almost crying in frustration, I fumble for my iPod and put one earphone in his ear and one in mine. I scroll down to Duran Duran's "Come Undone." When the electric synthesizer hums through the part about clinging to the one you love when everything falls apart, I lose it and start bawling into the starched hospital sheets.

I feel a weak hand on my head.

"I'm sorry, Skippy," he whispers. "I'm so sorry."

It's as though he doesn't have enough breath, as though he only ever had a finite number of breaths and now he is running out. The hospital is white noise. I can't see color. Everything is gray and blue and the strange pearl of his face.

In this moment I know that the man in front of me is the man I love most and that if he dies, I will have lost everything. The hollowness of the last few months, the broken trust—all of it means nothing. Because resentment and anger are what you hold on to when you have all the time in the world.

Eight hours later the intern finds me passed out across his chest. She motions for me to stand up, and I do, feeling dizzy. She leads me to the doctor, who is nothing like Dr. House except he is grumpy.

"He doesn't have cerebral malaria."

"What then?" I nearly scream. The doctor is visibly upset. It's HIV. It's Ebola. It's the flesh-eating bacteria.

"He has the flu."

"What?"

"Your husband has the flu."

I put my hand over my mouth to stop whatever is about to come out. I start choking and at first I think I'm going into shock, but then I realize I'm laughing.

"Are you sure? You know the falciparum might not show up in the blood smears because he's been on prophylaxis. And if it's the early stages, the count might be too low...."

The doctor is totally pissed. "We didn't just do smears. We tested for antibodies. Your husband has the flu." The doctor turns to the intern, who does not look happy. She does not even look relieved. She is squinting at me as though I've cheated her out of a once-in-a-lifetime experience. When will she ever get the chance to treat cerebral malaria? Probably never. "I want him discharged immediately."

IN BED IN THE MIDDLE OF THE NIGHT, I hit Brian so hard my palm stings.

"You fucking asshole," I hiss. "You stole two days of my sleep."

"Ow," he complains. "I'm still sick."

"You're lucky you're not dead, because I feel like killing you myself."

And I curl happily into the crook of his arm and remember something I once saw at the Lola nursery.

Bandaka was a boisterous six-year-old whose favorite game was terrorizing Lodja. He was bigger than Lodja—she was only three—and in typical six-year-old fashion, he would pull her hair, steal her toys, and generally act like an obnoxious brat. Finally, Bandaka and Lodja were big enough to go to group two, where Maya, the female Claudine rescued just after Mikeno, reigned supreme. Unlike Mimi, who liked to watch conflicts from a distance, Maya had no problem interfering in group politics. She wasted no time teaching Bandaka the place of a "*petit bonobo garçon*," and several of her lessons were pretty brutal.

One day, one of Maya's particularly stern "corrections" left Bandaka crying in the bushes and hugging himself. He was inconsolable. He lay facedown, slapping his palms on the ground and howling. Not wanting to get in trouble with Maya, no one went to comfort him. Then I saw Lodja, little Lodja with her red lips and long eyelashes, creep over and wrap her arms around him. She kissed him and clumsily patted his head. Bandaka collapsed into her lap while she kissed and groomed him all afternoon.

WE DO TERRIBLE THINGS to the ones we love. We cheat and lie and betray them, for thirty pieces of silver or our own selfish hearts. The only way love endures is because of one simple gift.

Forgiveness.

Chapter 26

"Vaneh," Mama Yvonne yells from under her mango tree. "Get over here. We've been waiting for you all morning."

Claudine has brought the Mamas the latest issue of *Marie Claire* from Paris. It is the tenth anniversary of Princess Diana's death, and they are reporting on the inquest, which is still ongoing.

"Who is the man with the princess in the car accident?"

"Oh," I say happily, because Princess Diana is something I know a lot about. "He was Dodi Fayed, whose father owned Harrods, a big store in London."

"Not the prince?"

"No, they divorced."

"Why?"

"You didn't hear about Camilla and the tampon?"

The Mamas think I am charming but stupid. I have the most backward ideas about having children (I prefer dogs), cooking (reheating takeout), and domestic duties (I use the iron as a weapon against insects). They wonder aloud what Brian sees in me and hope he didn't pay too much for my dowry since I'm obviously a dud deal.

Mama Yvonne, in particular, is obsessed with getting me pregnant. I try to explain that I want a baby as much as I want a shard of glass in my food, but Yvonne can't handle it. Every time she sees me, she tries to bully me into making love to Brian, even at two thirty in the afternoon, in the middle of testing.

But now I have something they value—gossip. I have the dirt on every glossy star in the magazine. I take the magazine and hold it as though it's been blessed by the pope and the Mamas lean forward to receive the wisdom within. Mama Esperance stands up and gives me her rattan cane chair—an honor I have never been given before. I tell them about Princess Diana's fairy tale gone wrong, the Jolie-Pitt-Aniston debacle, the anorexic Olsen twin, and Nicole Kidman surviving Keith Urban in rehab.

By the time I'm finished, the vet Anne Marie and the office girls have joined the audience. I'm absurdly pleased with myself. Even Mama Henriette has come up from the huts, where she's been looking after Lomela, the new orphan.

Lomela is the ugliest bonobo I have ever seen. She has kwashiorkor, a type of malnutrition, so she looks like a famine child, with a swollen belly and sticklike limbs. Her head is too big for her body and her eyes bulge out of their sockets. She is completely naked except for a tuft of hair on her head. Pierrot found her in Lodja, a city right in the middle of Congo that is practically a sausage factory for bonobo meat. There were three orphans. Only Lomela made it to Lola.

"We call her Eat-Pee-Poop," says Mama Henriette. "Because that's all she ever does."

"Will she survive?"

It hardly seems possible. She is almost a corpse. Her skin is so close to the bone I can see her veins threading across her skull. Her shoulder blades stick out like angel's wings and every notch of her spine pushes through her naked back.

"Eating like she does? Definitely."

Mama Henriette settles her down in front of a pile of fruit. Lomela picks up a mango, strips the skin back with her teeth, and starts eating. Mama Henriette might be right. There is something of a survivor in the strength of her bite, the carnivorous way she tears off bright orange strips of flesh.

Beside her, Mama Yvonne has a two-year-old bonobo called Mwanda on her back. Mwanda climbs down and sits next to Lomela, gently picks up Lomela's foot, and kisses it. Lomela watches her. It is hard to know what she's thinking. Her eyes are strangely vacant. Mwanda cuddles up to Lomela. After a while, Lomela's scrawny arm curls around Mwanda's shoulders, and they sit side by side for the rest of the afternoon.

I leave them to it and walk back down to the house. I pop open a cold Coke and sip it on the porch, beads of icy moisture condensing under my fingers.

Lola is starting to feel like home. Although our official residence is Germany, we've probably spent four months there in the last two years. The rest of the time is split among the United States, Australia, and dozens of conferences, where I sit, bewildered, in the back while the mess of our experiments is somehow transformed into straight, clean graphs with only stubby little error bars and significant results.

In these conferences, there is always a girl or two at the front with soft eyes and deep cleavage. They watch Brian hungrily. He is something of a niche fetish for aspiring primatologists. Apparently, at Yale, the undergraduates have made a calendar of him. I'm bewildered. Brian? A sex symbol? I puzzle over this until my head hurts.

If they figure out who I am, I get various looks of envy and contempt. I want to laugh and slap them at the same time. I love the guy but I'm all too familiar with his nail-biting, hair-splitting, obsessive-compulsive worst. *Girls,* I want to say, *you wouldn't last ten minutes.*

The constant traveling has given us gold frequent-flyer status and permanent jet lag. Lola is the only place where I feel like I've stopped.

As soon as we arrive, clouds of butterflies scatter in front of us like confetti. There is a sweetness on the breeze, of lilies and ripe fruit. My mother, the feng shui fascist, would be hard-pressed to fault Lola's wind-water harmony. The lush green forest is perfectly balanced with the coiling path of the river and the mirror calm of the ponds. Sunrise and sunset are marked with the bonobos calling and the Mamas singing.

This year, Brian has brought a secret weapon—Tory Wobber. Tory is Richard Wrangham's graduate student, and she is analyzing the levels of hormones in bonobos and chimps. In the behavioral data that says bonobos are more sexual than chimps, there is no hormonal data that might help reveal why the differences exist. We can say that bonobos use sex during our tests to defuse the tension so they can cooperate better, but until people believe bonobos are more sexual than chimps, this is a moot point.

But Tory knows from studies of humans and animals that levels of testosterone are strongly related to sex drive. As we age, we have lower levels of testosterone and therefore lower sex drives. So testosterone plays a large role in driving libido. Tory is going to compare the testosterone in the saliva of chimps to that of bonobos. It is a harmless procedure—she gives them cotton wads covered in powered Sweet Tarts, then collects the sodden cotton when they spit it out, sloppy with drool. She analyzes the saliva back at Harvard to determine the hormone levels in each individual. If Tory finds hormonal differences between the bonobos and chimpanzees living in sanctuaries, it will help us understand whether the differences we are observing in their behavior are being driven by their physiology—which is not going to change overnight because they are living in a zoo or sanctuary. If we find hormonal differences, it is likely these same differences exist in wild bonobos too.

This year I also have a secret weapon—Suzy Kwetuenda. We met Suzy on our first trip to Lola. She was just hanging out with the bonobos, watching them and taking notes. This was unusual behavior for anyone, much less a young Congolese woman. In all her years, Claudine had never had anyone come watch the bonobos every week for the hell of it.

Suzy's father was a professor in Uvira before the war. He was an ichthyologist and studied the fish of Lake Tanganyika. Suzy's family was comfortably middle-class and she and her siblings lived in a nice house and went to good schools.

When Suzy was seventeen, she and her two brothers were on

holiday in Bujumbura, a port town on Lake Tanganyika in Burundi. On the day they were supposed to go home, war broke out in Congo. Rebel soldiers took over Uvira and went from home to home, killing, raping, and pillaging.

Suzy and her brothers stayed for three months without any news of their parents. They were sure their parents were dead. Finally, a letter arrived. Her parents were safe, but they had lost everything. Their home, their possessions, almost all of their money. They had just enough cash to buy Suzy and her brothers plane tickets to Kinshasa, where they have lived ever since.

"My father still has no work. He was a respected professor, with many friends and colleagues. Now he sits at home all day, staring at nothing. Even now, when so much time has passed."

Suzy is destined to become the breadwinner for her family. She is getting close to her final exams for her master's degree in biology at the University of Kinshasa, but she never misses a Wednesday at Lola. She sits by the red porcelain roses and watches the bonobos with the rapt attention of someone who is escaping her reality.

She has two dreams. She wants to see the bonobos released into the wild and to become a university professor. "I want to give my father something to be proud of again," she said.

We hired her on the spot. And from that day on, I've never had to do another day's testing. Suzy listens eagerly to Brian's hour-long monologues. She thoughtfully pauses, then asks intelligent questions. She knows the bonobos inside and out and extensively discusses their potential for testing.

Brian is in heaven. He can't wait to get to work. After the tests are done, he comes home beaming. One afternoon I pass the testing building. I hear Brian yell something. I pop my head in and see Suzy and Brian hanging from the bars three feet in the air.

"Suzy has never climbed a tree," he says, as if this explains everything. "I asked her how she was going to escape the bushpigs at the release site."

"Eh, Vaneh, I have never thought of the bushpigs."

"So now we're in training. At any time during the tests, I yell, 'Bushpig!' and we both have to climb something to escape."

Semendwa is in her hammock, inspecting her nails. She gives me a look that says, *I thought the test was supposed to be about me.*

"I hear you," I say to her, and I leave Brian and Suzy congratulating themselves on their fine and cunning plan.

Soon neither Brian nor I can imagine life without Suzy. Her smile is brighter than a camera flash, and she is always cracking jokes about Brian's test choices.

"Why do you choose Kikwit to do your test? Kikwit is *zoba*."

"Why is everyone so mean to him? He's so sweet. I believe in him."

"Your Kikwit's head is *empty*. Even your love won't save him."

Every time I pass the building I hear laughter. I would probably be ragingly jealous if I didn't like her so much myself.

CLAUDINE FUSSES AND CLUCKS over us as though we're another couple of orphans to take care of. We join the menagerie of rescued animals that pass through Lola: the three dogs, nine cats, three African gray parrots, two monkeys, and a galago. We stay at her house in Ma Campagne and eat crepes on Sunday mornings. She takes us to art exhibitions and introduces Brian as her "*petit bonobo garçon.*" Victor is in booming health. The cancer turned out to be a stomach ulcer the size of his head that he knocked out with a round of antibiotics. He takes us to Kinshasa's finest restaurants, with cuisine worthy of any chef in Paris. We meet their other children, Giselle, Thomas, and Phillipe, and receive Fanny's kisses from Nice (she has dumped her musician, to everyone's relief, but has still not found her life's calling).

But despite Kinshasa and all her splendor, as soon as we leave the sanctuary, we are aware of suffering. The war is still raging in the east and there are unsettling rumors about the new president. According to a Human Rights Watch report, Kabila has been subtly encouraging the torture and murder of his opposition. In March, two hundred of Bemba's supporters were killed. Government troops executed five hundred people without trial and imprisoned a thousand more. The Kinshasa jail is once again full, with stories of electrocuted genitals, beatings, and mock executions leaking into the world outside.

Bemba, after skulking around Kinshasa menacingly for months and refusing to disarm his five-hundred-strong army, fled after a riot in April, just before Kabila accused him of treason. In Belgium, the screams of Bemba's past caught up with him. The International Criminal Court issued a warrant for his arrest for the war crimes he committed in the Central African Republic in 2002–2003. From his sprawling mansion in Portugal, Bemba denies everything.

In the east, a new enemy is rising. His name is Laurent Nkunda, and he fought with Kabila Senior on his march to Kinshasa but is now waging war against his son. Nkunda has the long, predatory look of a praying mantis. He is rarely without shades, providing a barrier between the public and whatever is behind his eyes. He occasionally wears a white robe and leads a snow-white pet lamb around on a leash.

Rumors of the new general filtered down to Kinshasa in 2004 from Bukavu in the east of Congo. Almost on the Rwandan border, the sprawling city has fingers of land that reach into Lake Kivu. Lush mountains rise in the west, where Dian Fossey began her mountain gorilla studies.

On May 27, 2004, the year after the war ended and Kabila was installed as interim president, government troops under a general called Mabe rounded up six Congolese Tutsi students and brought them to a major traffic intersection. The soldiers forced the young men to undress and tied them together. To avoid nearby U.N. peacekeepers, the soldiers led the students to a field and beat them to death.

This was the beginning of an attack on Congolese Tutsis in Bukavu. Soldiers tied up two teenagers and opened fire. When the boys fell to the ground, the soldiers gave a cheerful thumbs-up to horrified bystanders.

They went from house to house, rounding up Congolese Tutsi

men, women, and children. Some were shot on sight. Some were taken to a shipping container in the center of town and then executed. Some were allowed to pay a ransom and escape across the border into Rwanda. More than three thousand Congolese Tutsis fled Bukavu, some of them with wounds from guns, knives, and machetes.

In retaliation, Nkunda, himself a Congolese Tutsi, proclaimed himself a savior and marched his army of four thousand into Bukavu. Nkunda's troops were a formidable fighting force. Unlike the unpaid, starving government soldiers, Nkunda's men were fed on the rich cheese from his farm in Masisi. Rwanda-trained and Rwanda-financed. Nkunda's troops stormed into the city barely a week after the initial attacks.

On June 3, Jean Mbuzi was in his home when Nkunda's soliders burst in and demanded $500 at gunpoint. Jean had only $75. So the soldiers locked Jean and the other men in his family in a room and raped his seventeen-year-old sister. Jean could hear her screaming through the wall. When the soldiers unlocked the door, one of them said, "Until you accept Congolese Tutsis as truly Congolese, there will be no calm in Bukavu." The next day Nkunda's troops gang-raped a mother in front of her husband and children. They then raped her three-year-old daughter and looted the house, taking almost everything. And so on and on it went. U.N. troops saved as many people as they could but they did not prevent Nkunda from taking over the city and setting himself up in the governor's mansion overlooking Lake Kivu.

Two years later Nkunda is slowly but surely taking over the east of Congo. His legend has reached Kinshasa. They say he beheaded 150 of his own men for mutiny and threw their bodies into the Congo River. They say no child is safe from being conscripted into his army.

Cool and media-savvy, Nkunda swears to every reporter from Anderson Cooper to Ben Affleck that he is protecting the Congolese Tutsis from massacre and that all he wants is a unified, prosperous Congo. He has a smooth, calm voice, not the voice you would expect from a madman. He denies committing crimes against humanity and modestly hints about running the country someday.

Kabila is threatening to cooperate with Hutu rebels to fight Nkunda's Tutsis, which may provoke a counterattack from Rwanda. The U.N. refuses to talk to Nkunda and accuses the Rwandan Tutsi government of funding him. Angola is stirring. Uganda, as watchful of Congo as ever, may make a move. Nkunda could spark off Congo's third war.

I KNOW WHAT IS GOING ON outside the electrified fences of Lola. I know more than a thousand people die a day and children are being forced to become soldiers who then recruit other child soldiers. I know rape is still a weapon and no one will ever know the extent of its physical and psychological devastation.

But that's what paradise is. A refuge from reality. Where you can sit on the porch and drink a cold Coke and watch the river flowing past. Paradise is where you pretend that everything you see is everything that exists.

Until the outside world throws a piece of itself, like debris, against your door.

Chapter 27

🕸️

*K*atako-kombe arrives in a wooden crate. It is an ordinary wooden crate, one that might hold apples, milk bottles, or something that needs to breathe.

Staring between the pine-board slats are two huge eyes framed by wispy black hair. I hold my hand out. She reaches out, fist closed. An open hand is a gesture of friendship. A closed hand is a greeting without trust.

Pierrot stands nearby, relaxed and crisp in a pressed patterned shirt, talking to an official from the Ministry of Environment. When Claudine started confiscating bonobos at the bushmeat market in Kinshasa, the animal traffickers slashed her tires. After that, she decided to let the government do its job. Since then, there is no storming into army headquarters and demanding the general hand over his pet bonobo without question. No raiding market stalls and making a run for it with a terrified bonobo under her arm and the vendor screaming after her.

An official from the Ministry of Environment is present at every confiscation. It is this official who informs the sellers they are breaking the law and are under arrest. The message is clear: If people want to break the law and traffic in bonobos, it is the Congolese government they must answer to, not Claudine André.

. . .

"WHAT'S HER NAME?" I ask Pierrot.

"Katako-kombe. After a village in Equateur."

"Katako-what? I'm never going to remember that. I'll call her Kata for short."

Pierrot is too polite to say anything but Mama Henriette snorts as she walks past.

"That sounds like 'caca,'" she says. "Why are you calling that baby poop?"

Brian comes out of the building, glowing. He has spent the morning collecting drool from Malou, his girlfriend. Apparently she won't let anyone else do it, and Brian is giddy with the privilege of still being her favorite. So he comes out of the building triumphantly holding an entire test tube full of Malou drool. He stops dead when he sees me cooing in front of Kata.

"Oh no, not again."

I look up innocently. Brian grabs my arm and drags me away from the crate.

"Skippy, remember what happened last time?"

"Yes. You stopped me from taking that little bonobo and he died."

Brian gapes silently.

"You practically killed him with your cold-blooded ruthlessness. I was the one who wanted to bring him in the house, and you stopped me."

Brian throws up his hands, laughing. "Okay, okay, you win. You look after that little baby if you want. But she could be carrying all sorts of diseases; do I need to go through them again? So don't come anywhere near me until you're completely sterilized. Then at least one of us will have a mouth that can explain to the doctors why your face is falling off."

. . .

KATA DOESN'T REALLY NEED ME. After Bolombe died, there was no more talk about an isolation period. Anne Marie lifts Kata out of the box, takes her to the sink, and gives her a bath to get rid of skin parasites. Kata shrieks but she is too weak to protest. When Anne Marie finishes, she wraps Kata in a towel and hugs her close. Kata looks directly into her eyes and shrieks the sex shriek, where they want you to rub their genitals and make them feel better. Kata wriggles her little bottom, shivering and scared.

"*Reste tranquille, ma petite,*" says Anne Marie. "You're safe now."

In the vet room, Crispin gives her a shot and takes blood to send to a lab in Kinshasa that will test her for other diseases. Kata covers her face with her hands and whimpers.

Mama Henriette brings a bottle of warm milk. Kata refuses to drink it.

"She has lost the taste for her mother's milk. She must have been a long time without it."

Anne Marie strokes her head and says, "Try again this afternoon; maybe she will not be so afraid."

CLAUDINE CRADLES KATA in front of the nursey so "her spirits can be lifted." But Kata is not interested in the bonobos. Instead, she is fascinated, as we all are, with Claudine's red hair. She lifts it up gently, lets it fall through her fingers, touches it with her lips. She takes a handful and presses it against her face. Then, as though the effort has exhausted her, she curls into Claudine's bosom, closes her eyes, and rests her chin in the crook of Claudine's arm.

"She is a very sad bonobo," Claudine says. "She has seen too much already."

"What can I do?" I say.

She has the same advice as last time. "Try to make her drink."

SO EVERY MORNING AFTER BREAKFAST, I go down to the little row of bungalows by the river. The third door from the end is open. *Soukous,* the upbeat music of Congo, drifts from a radio. I recognize the tune.

Staff Benda Bilili is the latest craze on the music scene. The band is made up of paraplegic musicians who used to live outside the Kinshasa Zoo. Their instruments are made of milk cans, fish baskets, and wire. Their melody is at once silly and haunting.

Inside, Mama Henriette dips sugarcane in milk and coaxes Kata to suck on it. Beside her, Lomela sits on a landfill of mango peels, banana skins, and chewed-up sugarcane.

"*Bonjour,* Mama Henriette."

"*Bonjour,* Vaneh *babote.*"

"*Babote*" is "beautiful" in Lingala but I'm not sure it's a compliment. They also call Mama Micheline *babote*, and she has only three teeth and is about a hundred years old. With my knotty hair and dirt-streaked face, I suspect they are being ironic.

"Still hasn't drunk?"

"Still nothing."

I sit down and Kata makes her greeting cry. The first day she doesn't even approach me. The second day she shrieks and offers her clitoris, keeping her hands well away. By the fifth day, she sits on my lap and rubs her clitoris on my tummy, squealing. I take over from Mama Henriette, dipping the sugarcane in milk. I take the chewed pieces that have been drained of sugar juice and let the fibers soak up the milk before I dribble it into her mouth. She sucks on it a little. She has drunk only an ounce and a half today, the equivalent of two fingers of scotch. Most of it lies in drips on her fur. Lomela has already drunk three full bottles.

"Lo-me-la," Mama Henriette croons. "Eat, pee, and poop."

It is ten A.M., and Lomela has already eaten six mangoes, three bananas, two sticks of sugarcane, and half a papaya. Her flesh is filling out and she is starting to resemble a living creature rather than Gollum from *The Lord of the Rings.*

I settle in with Kata on my lap, and Mama Henriette tells me the morning gossip.

"There was a fire in the village last night."

"Where?"

She points with her lips. "There. A man there had a son by his first wife. The son dropped in on the man's third wife and her two children last night. They knew the son well; the children called him Big Brother. Then he took them down to the basement and slit their throats."

"No!"

"Yes! Then he poured gasoline over the house and set it alight. The next-door neighbor saw the fire and bashed down the door to drag the son out. He was bleeding from his mouth and nose and his whole face was burned up."

"The children?"

"Dead."

"Why did he do it?"

"His mother told him to. That is why it is bad to have more than one wife. Nothing but trouble."

"Are women allowed to have more than one husband?"

"More than one? Why would you want more than one? Isn't one enough trouble already?"

"More than enough trouble," I agree.

Anne Marie stops in. "Did she drink?"

Mama Henriette shows her the full bottle. "Wait here," she tells Anne Marie. "I have to go to the kitchen. Get more mangoes for Eat-Pee-Poop."

Kata gets up to follow her. I rub her tummy and press my face close to hers. She decides to stay.

"Did you hear about the fire in the village last night?" I ask Anne Marie.

"Tell me."

I tell her the story. She is suitably outraged.

"Does your husband have more than one wife?"

She looks sad. "I don't have a husband."

"Oh, I'm sorry," I say, flustered. I knew she had two children; I assumed she was married.

She waves away my apology with her hand. "It's fine. We were separated when the war came. He was in Goma at the time, all the way in the east, and I was in Kinshasa. The planes were grounded and the roads were shut down. There was no way I could get to him, or for him to reach me. There were no phones, no mail, nothing I could use to find him. My two children were with me, and we waited, hoping for some news. We sent messages to Goma, tracked down friends and relatives. I thought if he was not dead, then he would come home.

"Two years later, he called me. He was married with a new family."

"What a jerk," I breathe.

Anne Marie shrugs. "I'm over it. I have my children."

Mama Henriette returns with a basket full of fruit. Lomela squawks happily and starts on her seventh mango. She holds it in one hand and rips the peel off with her teeth while holding a banana in her other hand and a mango in each foot, in case Mama Henriette changes her mind and takes the basket of fruit away. Kata burps in greeting but does not leave my lap.

BEFORE I GO TO SLEEP I think about Kata rubbing her clitoris on my stomach. It wasn't sexual; it was more interesting than that. It was as though she was trying to soothe herself, to make herself feel better.

Next to me, Brian is reading a paper. I poke him.

"Babe?"

"Hmm?"

"You know how Tory's study is looking at testosterone levels? Won't that help us see if bonobos really have a higher sex drive than chimps? Kata rubbed her clitoris on me today. She is so young, only about three, and even she is using sex as kind of a handshake. I wonder if we can study that. In the nursery."

Brian lowers his paper past his nose and stares at me, shocked. "Did you just propose a study?"

"Well, we could compare the Lola nursery to the chimp nursery in Oleti. The nursery groups are isolated from the adults, so they can't learn their sexual behaviors from adults."

"And they are wild-born," he says slowly. "We can observe them in the context where the most sexual behavior occurs, when they eat together. Skippy, that's a great idea."

We work out the details. I will go to the nursery every morning, half an hour before the food, then half an hour during the food, then half an hour after the food.

I dream of Kata drinking a full bottle of milk.

Chapter 28

❧

"Wow." Brian looks stunned.

I've drawn a highly scientific diagram of the different ways I've seen the babies have sex. Using PowerPoint, I created stick figures, then added smiley faces for orientation and also to make it clear that the sex is consensual.

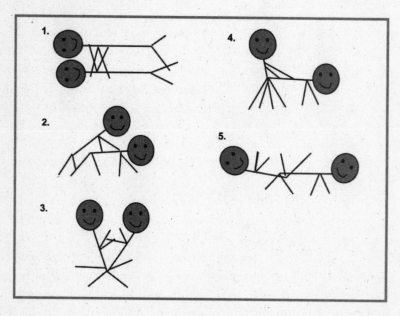

"I did it so you could see which end was which. It doesn't have to be exact, does it?"

Brian kisses me on the forehead. "It's a great histogram, Skippy. Your very first study."

EVERY MORNING, I eat breakfast early and go into the nursery enclosure thirty minutes before the babies get their big fruit salad. I sit on a small hill the size of a pitcher's mound and watch and take notes. Nothing much happens during the first half an hour, except as soon as she sees me, Mwanda wraps herself around my head and tries to stick her clitoris in my mouth. I have no idea why she does this. I am still amazed by the bonobo clitoris. Even on a three-year-old like Mwanda, it is curled, pink, and hard. I can feel it wriggling against my lips as Mama Yvonne, laughing, tries to peel her off my head. Of course I can't laugh. I can't even scream. I just have to be still and resist the entry of that persistent little toggle.

There is a lot of play-wrestling, chasing, and tickling. Then Mama Yvonne gives the signal and Mama Esperance comes up the hill carrying a large basket of food on her head. Boyoma, a three-year-old male who looks like a goblin, is crazy about food and as soon as he sees it, he must, at all costs, have his penis rubbed. He rubs it on anything he can reach—Luozi's bottom, Mwanda's arm—and if no one will touch it, he simply leans backward and thrusts his penis as high as he can, as though he is trying to spear something with it. Then he squeals at an ear-splitting pitch until someone can't take it anymore and rubs it for him.

Tchilenge, a five-year-old female, clasps Mwanda tightly to her breast. The sex is quite impressive, almost double-jointed, as their groins take on a life of their own. Their clitorises grasp each other, two pink worms, butting heads, coiling and uncoiling, then releasing so they can butt heads again.

The strange thing is, the sex isn't erotic. There is no penetration with the little boys, no orgasms (that I can see) with the infant girls. Sexual behavior in the nursery is not a calculated negotiation tactic where they exchange sex for food. They don't see the food and become horny. It is as though they see the food, become incredibly anxious, and then have to rub their genitals on something to make themselves feel better.

After everyone has eaten, they resume their games. Luozi invariably steals my pencil. It kills me the way he manages to get the pencil every single day. He lurks in the bushes, pretending he is playing with his friends and has not the slightest interest in the shiny yellow instrument I move with such concentration over my paper. Like a curveball, he sneaks around at an angle, knowing I can't see him as he approaches. He waits until I am distracted by the activity of the other bonobos, then, at the speed of light, he flashes past me, swipes my pencil, and runs off to hide his booty. Mama Yvonne calls his name furiously, and he drops his spoil someplace where it is impossible to retrieve, preferably in a big pile of poop. Then he scoots away, chuckling.

Yolo has never liked me, with that peculiar decision that bonobos make as soon as they see you. What is it about me that he doesn't like? Is it the way I look? Is it because I sit too close to his Mama Yvonne? Whatever it is, his favorite activity is standing on his hands and kicking me in the head.

But one day, Luozi, the pencil thief, bites Yolo's foot so hard it bleeds. Yolo screams and clutches his foot. I'm the closest one available, so he hops toward me, crying piteously.

"Yolo, you poor thing, come here."

In a second he flings himself against me, breathing hard from the playground trauma. It is the first time he has touched me, but his surrender is so complete that I feel his grudges melt into my lap. He lies there for hours and refuses to move, which is weird because he is usually so hyper. His bottom lip is pushed out in the biggest pout I have ever seen. When the study is over and I get up to leave, he whimpers and holds me tighter, so I give up and sit there for another hour, grooming him. From then on, Yolo is my number one fan. When I enter the nursery, he runs and wraps himself around my knee, quickly climbing to encircle my waist with his legs and my neck with his arms.

Afterward I go back to the house and Brian asks me, "How did your session go, my little researcher?"

I tell him the day's antics, stripping off my nursery clothes, which are covered in poop and mango slime and brown banana streaks. I take a quick shower, washing myself thoroughly with soap, cleaning my hands and arms with antibacterial sanitizer. I put on fresh clothes, then go down to the row of green bungalows that lines the river.

Chapter 29

❧

*T*he days become all about making Kata drink. We put her in front of Lomela so she can watch her chug three full bottles of milk. I dip my fingers in warm milk, then try to put them in her mouth. She presses her lips together and closes her eyes.

I wonder why she resists.

"She doesn't know if she wants to live," says Claudine as Kata buries herself in her hair.

I wonder what will make her want to live. She is warm and safe. She curls up at night next to Lomela's warm body, which is now covered in peach fuzz. She spends all day in the bungalow with Mama Henriette, and Anne Marie and I are always popping in to visit. She is loved.

The power of sadness has always amazed me. My father was a manic-depressive and I could almost see his misery wrapping him in a diaphanous net. No one knows the mechanisms, but long-term sadness really messes you up. It causes physical pain that has no source. It attacks your heart. Gives you cancer. Sometimes, people can be so sad that they die.

Someone has to make Kata laugh, and I am a good tickler. There's a sinewy muscle in the space between the collarbone and the neck, and another one where the thigh meets the groin. I can have anyone, human, chimp, or bonobo, cackling in seconds. I can make them laugh so hard they start to wheeze.

But Kata does not laugh. She doesn't even smile. I try everything. I tickle her gently, then hard. She grimaces. I blow raspberries into her stomach. I let my hair down and let her get tangled in it. It becomes my mission to get the tiniest smile out of her. But I never can.

She loves bread. It is the only thing she eats with any enthusiasm.

"Eh, Katako," says Mama Henriette. "Who baked you bread every morning in the forest?"

She prefers her mandarin and orange segments peeled, with the skin taken off and the seeds removed, like I did when I was little. Claudine makes sure she gets the smoothest mangoes, the sweetest sugar bananas, the juiciest sugarcane. I sneak her green apples from South Africa. But no matter if the milk is warm or cold, cow milk or formula, she will not drink it.

I spend so much time with my hands in milk that my fingers become soft and wrinkled. I wait until she's drowsy on my lap, then bring the bottle to her lips. I blow into her face, so she opens her mouth to catch my breath, then I pour milk into her mouth. It always ends with milk dribbling down her chin into her fur.

I feel helpless. What she needs is her mother.

I GET UP EARLY IN THE MORNING and creep down to the night boxes. Kata has her arms wrapped around a hot water bottle. She is sprawled over it, the way she would sleep on her mother. Her eyes are clenched shut. She doesn't want to wake up. She doesn't want to admit she is here.

IT IS A HOT, SWELTERING MIDDAY. My clothes are sticky and clinging. Kata is sprawled over my legs, maximizing her surface area in an attempt to cool off.

"And she just took his penis right off," Mama Henriette says.

There have been several penis-snatching incidents in Kinshasa. Penis theft is quite common in West and Central Africa. Witches cast a spell on a man by bumping into him or touching him with a magic object.

"It's those Nigerians," says Mama Yvonne sagely.

"Wait a minute," I interrupt. "You can't really believe this."

"What's not to believe?" Mama Henriette puffs up her magnificent bosom. "It happened to my third cousin, in Equateur. My sister saw it with her own eyes."

"No way. What did it look like?"

"There was nothing. Just a bump."

"Like a Ken doll?"

Mama Henriette looks perplexed. I explain the nether regions of Barbie and Ken.

"*Exactly* like that."

Mama Yvonne puts her hand in her pocket, covering her groin. "Men all over Kinshasa are walking like this. Make sure Brian doesn't go into town."

"Oh, don't worry. He won't care if it's true or not. That is one thing he's not messing with."

"Ha!" says Mama Yvonne. "Not that he's using it by the look of things."

"Don't start," I squeak.

Mama Yvonne narrows her eyes. "Did you make a baby last night?"

"That's none of your business."

"It's just you're so old."

"Yvonne, I'm thirty."

"Like I said, so old."

"I'm on the pill."

"The pill gives you cancer."

"It does not."

Here the Mamas nod seriously and chime in unison, "Mmm, yes, cancer."

"Will you all shut up already?" I push my face into Kata's tummy. "I already have a baby right here."

. . .

KATA GETS AMOEBAS IN HER STOMACH. Her poop is a thick, yellow mucus that runs in rivers out her bottom. She has cramps that make her little face scrunch up in pain. Anne Marie medicates her almost immediately. The drugs are powerful and fast. She would be fine, except for the major side effect of diarrhea—dehydration.

And she still isn't drinking any milk.

I'M SITTING IN THE BUNGALOW on a mattress. Jacques stops by to visit.

"How are you?"

"I'm too hot to move."

He takes in my lank hair, my sagging shoulders. Kata is curled into my chest in a fetal ball. Her eyes are squeezed shut in pain. The cramps must be terrible.

"Tell me a story."

Jacques sits down. "Did I ever tell you about the mama in our village who was going to a wedding? She knew the bride very well so she brought a goat as a gift. The wedding was a long walk away, and she had to pass through a big forest. When she was deep in the forest, far from anyone, a leopard came down from the trees and stole her goat.

"The mama was upset—she was poor and had no money for another goat—so she cried and wailed as loud as she could for help. Some bonobos came in a big group and they followed the leopard. They chased him, screaming, and he was so frightened he dropped the goat and ran away."

"No shit? Do you hear that?" I chuck Kata under the chin. "I'm going to take you into the forest with me as leopard protection."

"In Equateur, our hunters say that if you aim your gun at a bonobo, they clap. They hold out their arms in front of them and clap twice. In this way they beg the hunters for their life."

Kata falls asleep and her body goes limp.

"Does it work?"

Jacques shakes his head and looks at Kata. "No."

. . .

IT'S DARK, HOT, and sticky. I lean my head against the wall and Kata lies facedown on my chest, so her heartbeat is above my heartbeat. Mine is strong. It pushes against her so she vibrates. I can barely register hers. Every now and then I feel a brief tap-tap. The beating of butterfly wings.

I pick up her hand and groom her. I slide my fingers through her hair. She is so thin. Her skin is dry and leathery. I can feel the contours of her bones. Her muscles are a few threads woven into her limbs. Her arms are matchsticks. If I took them between my index finger and thumb I could break them with a snap.

When I used to hold her, there was a weight in my hands. A form. A being. Now there is nothing. Almost no existence at all. I go over every square inch of her, from the top of her head all the way down to her little toes. I comb my fingers through the wisps of black hair that frame her face. It falls almost to her shoulders.

Lomela has amoebas too, but with her three bottles of milk a day, she can afford to shit rivers for a while. Lomela has a smooth chest that swells out to her tummy. Her skin glistens and her eyes are bright.

Kata is ribs all the way down. When I turn her over, in the light I can see her rib cage, the knuckles of her spine. Her cheeks hollow out. When she pulls her lips back and squeals, she looks like a skeleton.

Death is coming for her.

"I DO NOT THINK she will make it," says Claudine. "It is too much. She is too sad."

I know she is telling me to prepare myself. She is trying to cushion me, even though her losses have been so great.

Isiro leaps off the log into the water. She is dancing again. She catapults herself into the air and spins with her arms folded to her chest. Her head is thrown back and her eyes are closed, as though she is somewhere else.

"I don't know how you do it," I say for the hundredth time.

Fizzi chases Tembo across the log. They wrestle each other until they fall into the water, laughing.

"They look happy," she says slowly. "Don't they?"

And that is her answer.

KATA'S SKIN HANGS SLACKLY from her bones. There is not much time left. The amoebas have carried away the little sustenance she had. She no longer smells like fruit salad and coconut. She smells like rotten milk and shit. She is hollowed out. Empty.

Her eyes are dead. Like Bolombe's the night before he died. You never forget that look once you have seen it. They are the eyes of the Rwandan refugees who saw their families hacked to pieces. They are the eyes of children from the east, arms stretched over the bodies of their mothers sprawled in the street. She has given up.

I hold Kata's hand. It is always open toward me now. She trusts me, even though it isn't enough. It is something I will hold on to when she is gone.

Chapter 30

*In the morning, I do not go to the nursery for my sex study. Instead I go to the building where the babies sleep. Everyone has had their bath and they are already in the playground. I have not seen Mama Henriette or Kata.

I have a bad feeling. I pass Jacques; he says nothing. He doesn't look at me. I go to Kata's night box. It is empty.

They must have taken her body away.

I hear laughter from inside the infirmary. It amazes me how the Congolese can laugh in the face of death, but I guess they have seen so much already.

I don't feel well. I feel sick to my stomach and I have cramps. I hardly slept and I just want to go back to bed and lie down.

On impulse, I open the door.

The first thing I see is Katako-kombe with a bottle of milk tipped up against her face. Milk is running down her chin and pooling in a puddle around her. It's dripping from her hair and all over her hands. She drinks as though she's walked through a desert and has fallen into a river. She holds the bottle with both hands and gulps.

She drains the bottle and gives it to Mama Henriette, wiping her mouth with the back of her hand. She exhales a great breath with the satisfaction you get from a cold drink after a long run on hot pavement.

"Hey, Vaneh!" cries Anne Marie. "Look at your *petite*. It's a miracle."
I can't answer. I am crying.

Now I KNOW there is something more human than the desire to die.
The will to live.

Chapter 31

There are six of us in the bungalow: Mama Henriette, Mama Yvonne, Mama Esperance, Lomela, Kata, and me.

"But, Vanessa," Mama Esperance says melodically, her voice soft and chiding, "Brian is a good man."

"He's a shit. In fact, if a rich, hot Congolese man walked in here now I would run off with him immediately."

Mama Henriette and Mama Yvonne fall over themselves laughing. Mama Esperance is outraged.

"You can't say that."

"I can and I mean it. He's making me live in America, a million miles away from my family, with no friends."

Brian has accepted a position at Duke University in North Carolina. I'm terrified. Germany was strange but transient. America is about to become my home.

"But America is wonderful. We would all love to live in America."

"Well, I want to live in Australia with my mom and my sister and my brother and my friends."

"But it is for the woman to move. You must follow him."

"And give him a baby," Mama Yvonne chimes in.

"Ha! I'm not giving him anything until I know for sure that some rich Congolese guy won't rescue me. Then I can stay here and our babies can play together."

"Yes," whoops Mama Henriette. "You can stay here, with us."

"And be Kata's mama." I nuzzle my face into her neck and she tightens her arms around me and wriggles her clitoris. "And then my baby will be good-looking, not like any baby of Brian's. He was such an ugly baby, you don't even know. He had these buggy eyes, and he was so fat."

"You can't call Brian ugly!" Mama Esperance is upset.

"What? You think a baby with him is going to be pretty? That big forehead. That giant nose. I just hope it's not a girl. And the way he looks at Malou."

"Malou?"

"*Oui*, Malou!" crows Mama Henriette. "Tell Esperance about Malou."

"Well, for one thing, he pays more attention to her than to me. And he would ditch me in a second if it meant he could hold her forever. Imagine! Competing with a bonobo for my husband."

Brian's head appears in the doorway.

"*Où est* Vaneh?"

"Ah, Brian!" the women cry. Kata squeals.

"*Je cherche* Vaneh."

"She is here! She is here!"

"I'm not here," I retort. "You cheating shithead. I am leaving you for a Congolese man."

The women howl, but Brian doesn't understand my French. "I'm not going to America to have your fat ugly babies when all you care about is that hussy Malou. I'm going to find me a rich Congolese man and stay here with my friends."

Brian frowns and pretends to be angry. "Vaneh, *donne moi un bébé!*" He wags his finger, scolding me. "*Donne moi un bébé!*"

Out of nowhere, Kata leaps up, a ball of fury running straight for Brian. She is puffed up and screaming at him. She alarm-calls, waa-barks, then runs back and jumps into my arms. She runs to Brian again, yells at him, and then bolts back onto my lap.

Even I am laughing by now.

"Katako is angry with Brian!" Mama Henriette says, collapsing with laughter. "She is defending Vaneh from Brian."

The Mamas hoot and slap each other. I tickle Kata in the space between her neck and her collarbone. To my surprise, she smiles.

I AM FISHING SIX WAYS UNTIL SUNDAY but Claudine will still not tell me what I want to hear: that Kata will be okay.

Claudine shakes her head.

"I don't know. I just don't know."

The Mamas are optimistic.

"Katako *va mourir ce soir,*" Mama Henriette chants cheerfully. *Katako will die tonight.* My Chinese superstition kicks in and gives me a heart attack every time I hear it.

"Mama Henriette! You can't sing that! It's bad luck."

"No. I am singing it because she is safe."

I am not so sure. She has lost her ghoulish pallor, and she moves with more vigor, but she is still heroin chic under her hair. Her tummy has swollen, and I know this fat will soon melt into her arms and her legs and fill out the bones on her fingers.

But she doesn't laugh. Every bonobo here, from the tiniest to the largest, seems full of joy. Isiro as she leaps off logs. Kikwit as you are chasing him up and down the fence. Malou as Brian reaches out to tickle her. Even Tatango gives up a smirk once in a while.

As long as Kata doesn't have enough joy to spill over into laughter, I can't believe she is here to stay.

IT IS THREE DAYS until we leave. Tory has enough bonobo drool to fill a swimming pool. As soon as she gets back she will start analyzing the hormone content and compare it to that of the chimpanzee.

I have completed the bonobo sex study and will finish it with the chimps next summer. But I already know I will see not one bonking session at Oleti, and definitely not in any of the creative positions of the Lola nursery group.

Today is October 15, the start of the rainy season. It has been muggy and hot all week. The low-hanging clouds create a feverish haze that presses in so close you can't breathe.

"It's not going to rain today," I complain to Mama Henriette.

"It will rain."

"It's been like this all week."

"It will rain."

I tip the contents of a full bottle of milk down Kata's parched throat. Lomela has already had two bottles and she has more of a milk beard than a milk mustache. In the dim light outside I can see that Lomela is covered in fine downy hair. It's the hair of a newborn baby. Soft, even, thick. I look at her luminescent coconut-colored skin and her buggy eyes. She is going to be a beautiful bonobo. Almost as beautiful as Malou.

Full after her milk, Kata crawls into my lap. A peal of thunder shakes the bungalow. It makes me jump, but Kata lifts her eyes outside. The sky has grown dark. Like clockwork, the first few drops splatter on the roof, but in no time at all, they have multiplied into a full downpour.

The rain pelts down, and the crisp smell of it cools the bungalow, a fresh wind whipping into the corners. I'm nervous at the ferocity, but Kata seems brighter. She has heard this sound before.

She sits up and lifts my hand. I run my fingers through her hair. She lifts my hand again, puts my finger gingerly in her mouth, looking at me with those huge chocolate eyes. She bites down gently.

I make a play face. I wiggle my finger between her neck and collarbone. She smiles and squirms. She bites my finger again. I pick her up and blow a raspberry into her stomach. Her stomach trembles, as though she is holding something inside her.

I tickle the muscles between her thigh and groin. I poke her. Her mouth is shut but she's breathing fast, her lips shut tight as though something might escape. Then I plunge my fingers into her neck again and it bursts out of her, loud and free. She cackles. She squirms, I keep tickling her, and she laughs. She flounders away, then throws herself back onto my lap, leaving herself open, sprawling at the mercy of the tickle monster.

I use all my skill to find the tickle nerves. I wriggle my fingers around and dig in deep. I pin her to my lap and resist her attempts to writhe away.

Her laughter is louder than the rain, louder than the river, louder than Mama Henriette crooning in triumph, "Katako *va mourir ce soir*!"

Chapter 32

❧

I am sitting in a café in Chapel Hill, North Carolina, checking my e-mail. It is a lazy day in spring. The dogwoods are bursting with white and pink blossoms. The breeze smells like honeysuckle.

Brian is an assistant professor of evolutionary anthropology at Duke University, so we have moved to America for good. After years in rainy, cold Germany, we are in love with North Carolina. The people are as warm as the weather. Brian's fellow professors are chilled out, with pretty houses and cute kids.

The anthropology department gives me a position in the faculty as a research scientist. I squirm around in the title, pleased but nervous that someone will find out that a few years ago the only experiments I did were with my hair.

An e-mail pops up in my in-box. My father is coming to visit next fall. We have been talking over the phone every month, and he e-mails a couple of times a week.

Two things happened that convinced me it was time to make peace. The first was that Jacques, the keeper at Lola, got fired. He was living with a friend who owned a bar and every month, Jacques blew his paycheck getting drunk. At first it was only on his days off. Then it was after work. Then it got to the point where he couldn't make it through his overnight shift without sneaking off to get hammered.

He disappeared a few nights while we were at Lola and came staggering back in the morning. Brian was furious. What if something had happened while he was gone? What if we needed help? But I convinced him not to tell Claudine. When I tried to talk to Jacques, he said he just drank to relax. It was the only time he came close to telling me to mind my own business.

Then one night, Claudine was staying at Lola when the electricity went out. She waited for thirty minutes in the pitch-darkness. Finally, she crawled around until she found a flashlight, then went to find out why Jacques hadn't turned on the generator.

The night guards covered for him, but Claudine can sniff a lie like a bloodhound. Jacques came reeling back at four in the morning. At six, he was still so drunk he could barely let the bonobos out. Claudine had no choice. She fired him.

Everyone was shocked. Employment in Congo does not usually come with job security and benefits. The pay was good. The hours were fair. And Jacques loved the bonobos. No one could understand how he could throw it all away.

I could. My father was an alcoholic. And if there is one thing I know about alcoholics, it is that they break everything they care about, starting with what they love most.

I want to find Jacques. I want to give him money and a place to live and someone to talk to. But no one knows where to find him. And even if I did, it wouldn't do any good. The road to recovery is long and he still has too far to fall.

I know where Dad is. And through his one-line e-mails and the occasional presents of Laotian silver, I know he is reaching out. That he is trying to make amends.

The second incident was after we moved to America and our car was broken into. I went to get the car window fixed at a glass-repair shop in Durham, a neighboring town to Chapel Hill, in the scariest neighborhood I have ever seen. All the shops had chain link on the windows. A stray dog was chewing on a used syringe.

The biker who owned the shop tipped some pills into his palm, threw back his head, and swallowed them dry. He shook his head.

"Goddamn Vietnam. All I got to show for it is five pills a day."

He was not talking to me; he was talking to the wall, and I could barely understand his thick Southern drawl. But sitting in my New York designer pants, red shoes from Paris, and Tiffany necklace, I felt compelled to say something that would make me seem more like him and less like a brightly plumed bird he might like to shoot.

"My dad was in Vietnam."

"Your daddy?"

"Yes, he was a sergeant."

It was as though I said the secret password. The biker leaned back in his chair and started talking directly into my eyes.

"Worst thing about Vietnam was the kids. I remember these two little boys were messing around, and one of them took my ration tin with my camera."

"I know," I added, still mistaking this for a conversation. "Dad says during the war the kids in Vietnam were always picking his pockets."

"Well, I tole 'em, 'Don't you mess with that,' but they kept touchin' it and messin' with it. Then wun uv 'em took it and started to run."

I got ready to laugh. I felt a punch line coming. Like one of Dad's old stories where he and a mate rafted down the Mekong River and the village kids had to save them from crocodiles.

"So I shot 'im."

My smile froze on my face. The biker watched me carefully. Dad never talked about the people he killed. But I found a poem once, buried in the garage, about an eight-year-old boy holding a hand grenade in the jungle. How dad shot him in the groin, then stood watching the small body empty its blood into the dirt.

I was tearing up inside because I wanted the man to stop. My face was begging him to shut up, but he couldn't. His eyes were blank and he just kept talking.

"The government done send us in sometimes, to villages they

said was aidin' and abettin' the enemy. And we had to kill 'em. All of
'em. Women, little kids, all of 'em. We shot 'em where they was stan-
din', runnin', or screamin'. We done killed every one. Jes like they tole
us."

I wonder what it would do to you to arrive at a small village with
emerald fields and jagged mountains covered in mist, where cooking
fires were burning and women were carrying their babies on their
backs, and have to approach, without faltering, and take every single
life. What you must become at that moment to follow through. What
you must do afterward to endure your memories.

The biker kept going. He told me about coming home, the anti-
war rallies, how two young men jumped him to see how tough he
was. And how without thinking he threw one of them to the ground
and stomped on his head so hard his eyeball popped out. He told me
about his ten-year-old son who was killed by a woman who bent
down to tune her radio while she was driving. About the grandson
with leukemia who will die next year.

I have come a long way since I read the story of Zainabo, the
Congolese woman who watched men eat her two daughters in front
of her. I no longer think of her as an alien living in a strange part of
the planet where shit like that just happens. I no longer read news
stories of horror and bloodshed and assume it will never happen to
me or the ones I love.

Since we arrived in America, two people were shot up the road.
Four people have been held at gunpoint in Durham, someone was
knifed, several girls were raped, and a student was shot not far from
Brian's office. A graduate student had a man break into her house, slit
her throat, then leave her crying in her own blood.

We all carry our own tales of violence. The distant war going on
over there is not so different from the war we fight here. I don't know
why some people, like the Mamas and Suzy, can survive a war and still
find enough joy to laugh as if their whole life has been blessed. Or
why others, like my father, like the biker, like Jacques, never recover.

"I think it has to do with what kind of person you are before you experience violence," my father says when I ask him. He is calling from Vietnam, and the next day he will visit one of the bloodiest scenes from his past, just outside Saigon. "If you have a strong sense of who you are and what's important, you can live through it. People like me, we never knew who we were, so we became the war. And because I was the war, I could never let it go."

We are who we are, but our circumstances shape us. It is never nature versus nurture. It is always nature *and* nurture. My father is who he is because of what was done to him. I'm sure if he had the choice he would have been the father I wanted. I'm sure, if he could have, he would have been a better man.

It is time to forgive him. It is time to move on.

ANOTHER E-MAIL IN MY IN-BOX. It is from Maria at Oleti. Brian underestimated her when he said she wouldn't last six months. She will probably grow old and die at Oleti. She is more at home in Congo than in Spain. She would rather listen to the chimps bashing the building than Chopin. She even prefers manioc to chocolate.

With Debby's help, she has turned Oleti into somewhere I actually want to visit. The first thing they did was drill for water. It turns out there is a natural spring beneath the sanctuary with water cleaner than that at our house in Chapel Hill. Solar paneling provides hot water for showers and electricity around the clock. There is wireless Internet. A solar fridge. They have a new house that overlooks the savanna with a wraparound porch that catches the afternoon breeze.

Baboo, the killer monkey, has been released into a forest reserve. I must admit, I miss him glaring at me while I eat my breakfast, raking his fingernails down the chicken-wire fence.

The islands are almost ready. There are three of them, and the largest is 250 acres, twice the size of Ngamba Island in Uganda. The jungles that cover them seem so prehistoric, you almost expect a pterodactyl to burst from the foliage. I think of the chimps roaming through the trees, like the ones they slept under so long ago. They will not have to worry about farmers and their crops, or hunters and their dogs, or village women on the way to the markets. In these forests, they can truly be chimps at last.

Brian has not forgotten FS3, the chimps at Yerkes. Together with the Humane Society, he is trying to get chimps classified as endangered in the United States. By some loophole, chimps are endangered when they are in Africa, but as soon as they are born in or smuggled into the United States, they lose their endangered status. Classifying chimps as an endangered species on U.S. soil will make it difficult, but not impossible, to carry out medical tests on them. No frenzied breeding to cure a disease chimps don't even get. No leaving hundreds of chimps to rot in metal cages for sixty years.

Brian does not want to shut down biomedical centers. Medical testing on chimps could lead to breakthroughs that save millions of people. He just wants the biomedical community to behave responsibly toward an animal that is, genetically, almost human.

And if research is necessary, when the chimps have finished the tests, they should get the same respect we would give anyone who has helped save human lives. They should be able to live somewhere with trees, where they can see the sky, where they finally have choice.

Brian's experiments have proven that sanctuaries are a viable place to carry out noninvasive research on ape psychology. His steady stream of papers has caught the attention of the mainstream media, who are thrilled he is finally on East Coast time and they don't have to wait until midnight to call him in Germany. *Smithsonian* magazine names him one of the top thirty-seven scientists under thirty-six. National Geographic does a documentary on the cooperation experiments. *Time* magazine runs a feature on him.

Excuse me, I want to say to the reporters in his office. *Who do you think actually* did *all his experiments? Bonobos don't trust* men. *He doesn't even speak* French.

But in the end, I just roll my eyes. Maybe my ego is less important than his dream. Maybe I am just a little proud.

Last month, Dominique, the president of Friends of Bonobos, asked me to be on the board of directors. I look after the Web site, the blog, and the adoption program, which is growing steadily. I'm not a grant-writing powerhouse like Dominique. And I don't have Claudine's charisma, which hypnotizes you into reaching into your pockets and handing over all your spare change. But I work hard, as often as I can. If I ever get tired of working on Sundays or bored of formatting yet another grant, I think of Kikwit, shouting an alarm at nothing or Isiro "correcting" one of the little boys, and I smile to myself and keep going. After all these years, I feel like I am getting back what I left behind at Ngamba Island with Baluku. I feel like I matter. Like what I do makes a difference.

As for Brian and me, the two of us have passed into the no-man's-land that movies and romance novels avoid at all cost—the married couple. Our most passionate moments are arguing about who forgot to put the butter away or the quickest way to Whole Foods. He no longer leaves me the last bite of his dessert. In fact, he usually steals half of mine. And I haven't said a romantic word to him in years.

So since I will never say this to his face, let me say it once, here, to thousands of strangers.

We may not be perfect, but we are perfect for each other. The Chinese say that love is balance. He is the water to my fire. The chimpanzee to my bonobo. And when I am mired in life's ugliness, when I can see only what's decaying both inside and outside my own head, he is the blindness I need, the mindless faith in happy endings.

MY PHONE RINGS IN THE CAFÉ, and I barely hear it above the music. It is Brian.

"Skippy?"

His voice sounds strange.

"Hang on, babe, let me go outside."

I go outside, where a warm wind takes the chill off the April morning. Across the road, the branches of a blossoming dogwood hang heavy under the weight of its flowers.

"It's Malou."

"Your girlfriend? What's she done now?"

"Skippy." I hear what is wrong with his voice. He is crying. "Malou died. They don't know why. It was sudden. Maybe a virus."

"That can't be right," I say. "Suzy sent me photos last week. I posted her on the blog—"

"She's dead. Skippy, she's dead."

I can't speak. On the end of the line, Brian sobs.

I LOVE CHIMPANZEES. I love their stubbornness and their strength. I love the way they dig their fingers into life and never let it get the better of them. I love the tenderness beneath their wild tempers. I love them because they refuse to apologize for who they are.

For bonobos, I feel something different. It's like I am *in* love with them. I can't tell you why, despite all our experiments and papers and conference presentations. But when I try to explain it, I always think of Malou.

Brian used to play this game where he threw her high into the air, as high as he could. He would fling her toward the sky with all his strength and she would laugh so hard I thought she was going to wet herself.

I used to do the same thing with Baluku. But the difference is, Baluku never relaxed when I threw him. He contorted himself like a cat, to land on his feet in case I dropped him, and when he came down, *he* caught *me*.

When Brian threw Malou, she went completely limp. If he had dropped her, she would have cracked her head open. But she knew he would never, ever drop her. That no matter what, he would catch her as she fell.

At summer camp we used to play this game where we stood in a circle and fell back into each other. For it to work, you had to fall straight back, without using your hands or sticking your butt out to break your fall. Trust is about letting go.

Bonobos are far more trusting than it is reasonable for anyone to be. Which is strange because they are so shy and so scared of risk. But once they trust you, they trust you with their everything, with their lives.

The death of a bonobo weighs heavy on your heart. The death of a bonobo like Malou is enough to break it. I know Brian will never again love a bonobo like he loved Malou. I'm so sad I'll never get to stroke her hair while she is wrapped around Brian's head, even though she would slap my hand and try to bite me. I'm so sad I'll never get to tell her that I never meant any of the mean things I said about her and that really, I thought she was beautiful.

When I think of Lola's bonobos going back to the wild, I hope they fill the empty forest with laughter. I hope they sleep safely, with soft branches wrapped around them under a sky full of stars. I hope one day there will be another little Malou, with her skin unblemished by the burns of a human fire, cradled in her mother's arms and smiling her impish grin.

Chapter 33

❧

March 8, 2009, and it is Congo versus Ghana in the African Nations Championship. In Congo, soccer is more than a sport, it's a national obsession. Drive through any city or village and you will see a bunch of kids huddled around a ball. The ball is usually improvised out of tightly packed paper or plastic bags wrapped in string. It doesn't necessarily have to roll as long as it can be kicked. When the national team, the Leopards, play a game, the whole country comes to a standstill. A thousand people huddle around a single radio as news of each play ripples through the crowd.

Rivalries between African teams run fierce and deep. Players are not above hiring witch doctors to smear the blood of a pig in their opponent's locker room or burying a cow in front of the goalposts.

Congo's Leopards were once legendary. With their uniforms the color of a bright sun in a blue sky, in 1974 they won the African Nations Cup and were the first black African team to qualify for the World Cup. Mobutu, who was once a goalkeeper himself, gave each team member a car and promised them a sack of cash if they won.

But 1974 was their last good year. Since then they have quietly slipped down the ranks and the soccer world turned its eyes to more promising teams—like Ghana's.

Known as the deadly Black Stars, the Ghana soccer team has

qualified for the Olympic Games five times in a row. They won the African Nations Cup four times, making them the second-most successful African team in history.

It is a miracle Congo even made it to the finals. Most are attributing this feat to the Leopards' coach, Santos, who is nicknamed Obama because when asked if his team has a snowball's chance in hell of winning, his reply is, "Yes we can." But even Santos wishes they were playing anyone but Ghana, who beat Congo just eight days ago 3–0.

In front of a crowd of thirty-five thousand people, the Leopards face the Black Stars. The grass is slippery and wet, and the atmosphere at the stadium in the Ivory Coast is electric. From the first minute, the Congolese team keeps control of the ball. Ghana, to everyone's surprise, can't seem to find their rhythm. Toward the end of the first half, Ghana breaches Congo's defenses several times, but Congo is always quick to counterattack.

In the first minute of the second half, Congo scores. Less than fifteen minutes before full time, they score again.

When the game ends, no one is more shocked than the Congolese. There is a half beat of silence before the whole country explodes into one raucous cheer.

As Brian and I step off the plane at the Kinshasa airport, for a moment I think we have landed in the middle of a coup. Armed men are shouting and waving their guns. Airport officials are punching each other and chest-bumping like gorillas. In the distance I hear thousands of voices raised in a war cry. Everywhere I see nothing but bared teeth.

I recognize the roar for victory. I have never seen the immigration officials look so happy. They wave us through, and not a dollar changes hands. One of them even *hugs* me.

The streets are swarming. It is as if all of Kinshasa's eight million people are out celebrating. It is nine P.M., and hundreds of men run half-naked in packs down the street. They run because there is nothing else they can do with their joy. It is bursting out of them. They look like they are flying. They thump on cars and raise their hands in a V for victory, but also for 2, because the score against Ghana was 2–0.

"You see, madam," says our driver. "Always we are in the news because of the war. People in the West think we are animals, always fighting and killing each other. But now, you can see, we are champions. Now we are proud."

THE FIRST BONOBO I SEE IS ISIRO, napping. I look at my watch. It's only ten A.M. She never naps in the morning. This is her patrol time, when she watches the little boys like a traffic cop, counting on infringements to spice up her morning. But here she lies, with her arm flung over her face. Her coltishness has filled out to enviable curves. She has breasts now, and her swelling will soon give Semendwa a run for her money. She rolls over and exhales cute, breathy snores.

Isiro, Semendwa, and Semendwa's baby, Elikia, have been moved to Max's group because they will be released back into the wild in a few months. Lomami, the bonobo who arrived with his fingers cut off, approaches Isiro shyly. He tucks her hair behind her ear and gently grooms her, occasionally pressing his lips to her head. Where is the cowering shadow of 2005? The Lomami who flinched if you clicked your fingers? He has the awkward body of a teenager, but with a new confidence. He moves the stumps of his right hand as deftly as the unharmed fingers on his left hand.

Semendwa has Lukaya's head pinned to her lap. Lukaya is a teenage female and she is getting this season's hairstyle. Every year, Semendwa decides it's time for a makeover and then proceeds to force one on the entire group. Lord knows where she gets her ideas; maybe one of the Mamas throws a *Vogue* over the fence every now and then. But every time we come, all the bonobos have a new do. Last year it was a Mohawk. The year before it was a bald head with a ducktail, and the year before that it was a kind of pageboy-cum-monk creation where Semendwa plucked a bald circle on top of the head with a long bob surrounding it.

This year, Semendwa is getting ambitious. She appears to be deriving inspiration from Mercedes-Benz Fashion Week, reviving the eighties with a stunning waterslide of hair that sweeps from the top of the head around the right shoulder.

Semendwa hunches over her reluctant participant, tense with concentration, determined to transform Lukaya's hair into a masterpiece.

Occasionally, Semendwa looks up from her handiwork to glare at Max, who, just like he does every year, refuses to let anyone near his hair. Beside Max, I see a strange bonobo and it takes me a while to realize it's Lomela. She is unrecognizable as the bald little Skeletor from last year. She is huge. Not huge as in fat, huge as in *big*. When she arrived we thought she was three, but she must have been more like six, because a year later, she has a prepubescent swelling emerging between her legs. No wonder she ate like a T. rex in a meat locker. She had three years of growing to catch up on.

I walk up the hill to look for someone I have missed terribly.

"Vaneh *babote!*" call the Mamas.

Mama Micheline says something in Lingala. The Mamas stare at me.

"You got fat," Mama Henriette states flatly.

"What? I did not!"

The Mamas nod vigorously. Mama Micheline, the wise one, speaks again.

"Your ass is definitely bigger," translates Mama Henriette. "Your boobs are huge."

"Is there something you want to tell us?" asks Mama Yvonne slyly.

I finally get it. "I'm not pregnant!"

They are crestfallen.

"You'd better get busy," Mama Yvonne warns me. "This trip for sure." She shakes her head. "How can you have gotten that fat and not be pregnant?"

"Where's my baby?" I say, desperate to change the subject.

Crouched in the very back of the nursery is the one I've been looking for. A pair of eyes peeps out from behind the bushes. I crouch down and hold out my hand. The eyes look from side to side nervously. Then they lock onto mine. Slowly, she comes out. She has a wrinkled little face, as though she is squinting. She takes my hand and climbs onto my lap. She wraps her arms around my neck and hugs me, her whole body pressing against mine. The sun is hot, and her skin is damp under her hair. She is heavy, so deliciously heavy, and I know what I'm holding in my arms won't disappear. She presses her head to my mouth so I kiss her and murmur her name.

"Mama Henriette's baby is *so* ugly!" croons Mama Yvonne in triumph. "Katako is the ugliest bonobo I've ever seen."

Mama Henriette is impressed that Kata has even come out of the bushes. "I've never seen her do that. Usually she is shy."

"She's not shy, she's embarrassed because she's ugly!"

"At least she's not stupid like your baby Kikwit!"

Mama Yvonne and Mama Henriette go at it while Mama Micheline and Mama Esperance kill themselves laughing. Kata squeals and rubs her clitoris all over me in her special bonobo handshake.

AT LUNCH, Claudine gets a call from her husband, Victor. A man has turned up at Victor's truck yard wanting to give up an orphan bonobo. This has been happening more frequently over the years. Some dumb country hick thinks they can make a heap of cash by selling a bonobo in Kinshasa. Once they arrive, they discover the bonobo market has gone underground. Thanks to Lola's education program, no one in Kinshasa will even look at a bonobo. They might order bonobo steak surreptitiously in a restaurant but no one is stupid enough to keep one in their backyard. They know it is illegal, and what with Kinshasa being one big village, someone will call the cops.

So the hick from Lukwe or Masumuna, or wherever he is from, can try to find a wildlife trafficker. But in the meantime the baby bonobo is eating into the hick's meager finances and is probably sick and dying to boot. So someone from Kinshasa, often a child who has visited Lola, takes pity on the hick and tells him to get in touch with

Claudine, who will give him only $25 for transport—but at least it is something.

I'm collecting videos for the Web site, so I ask if I can go and film the rescue of the orphan. I jump in the car with Clemence, the new vet nurse who arrived at Lola the year before. She is a sweet girl with a moon-shaped face and a shy smile. The babies in the nursery adore her and she can persuade even the most stubborn of them to take their medicine.

I haven't had the chance to speak to her much, so I ask her where she is from.

"Goma, in the east. We moved to Kinshasa after the second war." In 2002, Clemence watched from her house as the rebels attacked.

"Who were they?" I ask.

She shrugs. "I don't know," she said. "They all looked the same."

The rules were the same as Jacques had outlined—stay in your house and they might leave you alone, but anyone who ventured outside was shot. Clemence huddled with her family in her house, watching bombs and rocket fire destroying houses across the street.

"We could hear people screaming, all the time screaming. We were so scared. But we had nowhere to go."

Her neighbor was dragged outside his house. Rebels slit his throat, then cut off his penis and stuffed it in his mouth.

"After that we came here. We had nothing, but then I got this job. Lola saved us."

We drive through Kinshasa, which pulses like a giant dust-covered heart. Boys shake and twist to the *soukous* playing on a nearby radio. Slender girls sashay past, their hips and breasts tightly wrapped in their *kanga*s. Old men tap out their memories onto plastic tables and watch the people go by.

We pull up to Victor's truck yard. Men weave between the metal beasts and the air vibrates with the noise of motors, generators, electric saws. We get out of the car and a man appears. He is wearing a white T-shirt with a picture of sea turtles. Beside him, a bonobo walks upright, holding his hand the way a child might. The bonobo is a three- or four-year-old male. My gut contracts because he is the spitting image of Kata when she first arrived at Lola, wisps of long black hair framing the face but, beneath it all, thin, terribly thin.

Clemence crouches on the floor and holds out her arms. He wrests his hand from the man and runs to her and clings as tight as he can. He doesn't make a sound. He looks at the man with the sea turtle shirt but Clemence kisses him and strokes his hair and he buries himself into her breasts.

The man is staring, waiting. I get back in the car, assuming that we are leaving now, but the man says something to our driver. Our driver translates. The man wants $150.

This was not the plan. The man was supposed to hand over the bonobo. If Claudine had known the man wanted to *sell* the bonobo, neither Clemence nor I would be here. A car full of ministry officials and police would have arrived and arrested the man and confiscated the orphan.

The man says he has been walking for days. He shows us his swollen feet. He says he sold his bike and his shoes. He says he has been feeding the bonobo for a month.

Something is not right. The man's eyes are squinted and bloodshot. He is smiling and joking with our driver, as though this is a business transaction.

Victor calls Claudine.

"No," she says. "We don't buy bonobos. The most we can give him is twenty-five dollars for his travel."

The man knits his brows together. He growls that he could sell the bonobo for $600 in the market.

"Go ahead, my friend," says Victor. "No one will buy it."

"Come with us to Lola," says Clemence. "You can talk to Madam Claudine. You can see for yourself."

The man shakes his head.

This is the moment for me to intervene. The bonobo looks so much like Kata. I have $120 in my pocket. I know if I give it to him, he will let the bonobo go. Or I could snatch the bonobo and run.

There must be twenty men in this truck yard who work for Victor. If I pick a fight, I am sure they will cover for me.

DIAN FOSSEY, the famous researcher who wrote *Gorillas in the Mist,* was an incredible woman. At more than six feet tall, she had blazing eyes, a mass of dark curls, and balls the size of Texas. She studied gorillas for eighteen years and was the first person ever to be accepted into a mountain gorilla community.

Unfortunately, she was not such a great hit with the locals. Occasionally, Fossey or one of her students would stumble on the dead body of one of her gorillas. Hunters had cut off their heads and hands and shot them multiple times in the chest. Understandably, Fossey went a little nuts. She raided poacher camps, wearing Halloween masks and setting off firecrackers to make them think she was a witch. She tied up hunters and spat on them and once even kidnapped one of their children. She shot the back legs off their cattle, leaving them moaning and lowing in pain.

I can imagine how easy it would be to give in to rage. I want so much to punch this man's smug, squinty-eyed face in.

But I can't. Because, as Fossey found out, you won't win.

Fossey was found brutally murdered in her cabin the day after Christmas 1985. Her head had been sliced open by a machete that she had confiscated from a hunter years before. No one knows who killed her, but her vigilante justice was not appreciated by the pygmies who hunted in the forest, the traditional Batwa who used the mountains for grazing, or the park officials.

Claudine has worked for fifteen years without a single paycheck. Like a true bonobo, she has carefully cultivated ministers and police officials until finally, she has their support and their trust. The last thing she needs is a crackpot foreign researcher from her sanctuary beating people up or starting a $150 trade in bonobos. I can't steal the bonobo. I can't buy him either. So I stand and watch.

Clemence is holding the baby, who has started to eat a little piece of orange. He is wrapped up tightly in a pink blanket and every now and then he stops eating to gaze into Clemence's warm brown eyes.

The man pulls the bonobo by the neck. I break down and start yelling. One of Victor's men holds my arm.

"Let him go, madam. Let him go."

The bonobo shuts his eyes and clenches his fists into Clemence's clothing and whimpers. But he is too weak to hold on for long. He goes limp. The man takes him roughly by one arm and storms out of the truck yard to try to sell the bonobo in Kinshasa. The bonobo looks back but doesn't cry.

"I had him in my arms," Clemence says softly, bewildered. "I had him safe in my arms."

Victor's man who grabbed my arm says simply, "He had a knife. He told us if you tried to take the bonobo without paying him, he would have slit its throat."

WHEN WE GET BACK TO LOLA, Claudine holds my hands in hers.

"You are sad. But it is better this way."

I show her the footage.

"I know this man. He is a wildlife trader. If you had paid him, he would have been here next week with ten bonobos to sell."

She gives me a hug.

"I remember something someone once said to me. They said, 'When your heart is less in the bonobos, you will do more for conservation.' They are not my children. They are wild animals. And sometimes, I have to let them go."

INSPECTORS FROM THE MINISTRY scour the streets of Kinshasa, but the man has gone underground like a serpent, taking the bonobo with him.

Chapter 34

๑

The next few weeks at Lola are the worst I have ever lived through. If I had known what would happen, I never would have come. I would have stayed safe at home and cried from a distance. But if we could see the future, we would never get out of bed.

In February, a flu went around Kinshasa. For twenty-four hours, people felt so bad they could barely move. Then the next day they got up and were fine.

On Wednesday, March 11, several of the babies in the nursery came down with a cough and a runny nose. No cause for alarm. Just like kids, baby bonobos constantly have runny noses. It's as though there is a reserve of snot in their brains that occasionally spouts like a fountain. And like any mother, the Mamas are all over that shit. They make the babies drink gallons of warm tea with honey and lemon. They harass the keepers to buy oranges out of season for the vitamin C. They administer daily doses of multivitamins in the shape of Flintstone characters. They traipse down to the vet block, looking for soothing salves and eucalyptus rubs to open the air passages and clear the sinuses. Within a few days, the nursery is clear.

But then it hits group one, Mimi's group. Like the nursery, the bonobos get a cough and a runny nose. But the virus quickly moves to the chest and stops the passage of air to the lungs. The bonobos can't breathe. They heave as though their lungs have turned to stone and their throats have tightened to pinholes.

On March 18, Lodja dies. Claudine shifts into emergency mode. The release bonobos in quarantine must be protected at all costs. Lola is closed to visitors. The staff are kept to their assigned enclosures and do not mix with one another during the day. They take showers before and after their shifts. Each day their clothes are disinfected. Everyone's hands smell of antibacterial sanitizers.

The vets isolate the worst bonobos and give them antibiotics to stave off secondary infection. They pull another baby off her mother and give her to Suzy, our Congolese student, to look after. They save the lives of almost everyone they can get under close observation. Mercifully, the release bonobos stay clean.

One afternoon, Kikongo doesn't come in from the forest. Suzy goes out to look for him in the middle of the night. The staff are afraid of the forest because of snakes. Yesterday, one of the keepers killed a Gaboon viper with a body as thick as an arm and a head the size of a clenched fist. But Suzy knows if she waits until daybreak, it will be too late.

She finds Kikongo collapsed beneath the moon, sprawled facedown and breathing so faintly she has to press her face against his mouth to make sure he is breathing at all. She carries him slung across her shoulders all the way to the vet block, stooping under his weight. She sits with him all night long, feeding him fluids and pieces of apple. He is so weak, he has to breathe through an oxygen mask.

Without knowing how, I pray, and it sounds like *pleaseGodnot KikongopleaseGodnotKikongo*.

Kikongo is spared. But not: Lodja with the red lips and black eyelashes. Kisantu's six-month-old baby. Kindu, who liked to play with my hair. Mixa, who could touch his chin with his tongue. Mimi's newborn baby. And worst of all, we lose Mimi.

Mimi did not die of the flu. She died from complications after the birth of her baby. It was such a shock to everyone because she showed no signs of illness after she delivered her baby; she just handed him over the way she did all her others. But a few days later, she died. And in a moment, the empress is gone, and Lola has never looked so empty.

THE FLU IS NOT A NEW THREAT to primates. A virus that is harmless to one host becomes dangerous when it mutates and jumps across species. Bird flu, for example, has little effect on water birds but is deadly to people. Influenza in pigs in Europe and Asia became H1N1, or swine flu, when the genes of the virus rearranged themselves.

Respiratory illnesses are a major problem for zoos, sanctuaries, and wild populations. On March 26, seven chimps in the Lincoln Park Zoo caught the flu and one of them died. In 2006, twelve wild chimps in Mahale, Tanzania, died from a similar virus.

But this is the first time I have seen it. This is the first time I sit in the night building, holding Kikongo's hand and making sure his breath is still fogging up the oxygen mask. This is the first time I get up in the morning and wonder if someone will die today.

And with every death, I know that bonobos are one step closer to extinction. No one knows how many bonobos are left, but it isn't enough to fill Yankee Stadium. If a common cold can do this to Lola, what might a serious epidemic do to the bonobo population? Or a vengeful army? Or a hungry village? All the world's bonobos live in one forest. I am no population geneticist, but it seems to me that eggs and one basket are a bad thing.

But the survival of the species is not why I spend hours looking at photos of those who have died, why I check Kata's nostrils fifty times a day for signs of snot, or why I wake up in the middle of the night crying.

It's because we watched them grow up. Just like I have watched Mama Esperance's face lose its baby fat to reveal high, proud cheekbones and full lips. Her walk has transformed from light steps to a sensuous sway. Her cuteness has unfolded into a magnificent, beating beauty, so it almost hurts my eyes to look at her. When we are alone, she slips her hand into mine and leans close to whisper secrets that mean nothing except that I am important enough to trust.

I love her. It is as simple as that. And that is how it happens. All of a sudden it has been five years. Without knowing it, you have fallen in love with a country and a people and a whole bunch of bonobos, and because you have seen them grow up, you take it for granted that you will see them grow old.

But it isn't always so. If I have learned one thing from Congo, it is this:

If there are those you love, whoever or wherever they are, hold them. Find them and hold them as tightly as you can. Resist their squirming and impatience and uncomfortable laughter and just feel their hearts throbbing against yours and give thanks that for this moment, for this one precious moment, they are here. They are with you. And they know they are utterly, completely, entirely . . .

Loved.

Chapter 35

❧

When my friend's brother overdosed on heroin, she said the worst thing was that he vanished. Her family held a tiny funeral because they were ashamed of the way he died. Afterward, people were so anxious not to upset her that they never mentioned his name. It was as if he never existed.

The Congolese cope with death differently. When someone dies in Congo, no matter how shameful or terrible the cause, everyone who has ever known the person turns up for the funeral. And they dance. They dance all night to celebrate the life the person lived, the people the person touched.

There are no funerals for the bonobos, but the staff don't talk about them as if they are gone. They talk as if the bonobos have decided to move to Australia and may call any minute.

Crispin, the vet, catches me crying at the stadium in front of Kikwit, who is hiding six apples under his bottom. I always count the apples out exactly so that everyone will get one. This morning I automatically counted out eighteen, forgetting that six have died. I tried to cut the spare apples into smaller pieces to share but I started shaking, so I gave up and threw them all to Kikwit.

Crispin sits with me for a while in silence and then he says, "You know, Kikwit, he is so gentle and kind. When Kikwit grows up, he will be a lot like Mikeno."

I feel like he has just slapped my face. I don't want to think about Mikeno. If I think about Mikeno I will think of Mimi and Lodja and Bolombe and the others who have died, and I am already trying as hard as I can not to miss them.

Later in the day, the Mamas tease me about how jealous I was of Malou.

"Vaneh," they say, "do you remember how you chased Brian around the sanctuary because he loved Malou more than you?"

I take a deep breath and remind myself they are not trying to be cruel. Then I say slowly, "She pulled my hair. That little witch pulled my hair and kicked me in the head whenever Brian was within a hundred kilometers."

"A hundred kilometers!" they cry. "Even from here to Bandundu, she would kick you in the head!"

We talk and laugh about Malou and how much Brian loved her. And though I feel guilt and sorrow and heartbreak, I also feel relief. I think she would be happy no one has forgotten her.

"My last memory of Mimi is best," says Mama Henriette. "We brought her into the nursery when she was pregnant, because she had lost two babies already and we wanted to be careful this time. Mimi was so nice with all the kids. She would hug them and kiss their scratches and protect Kata from the boys and save treats for Lomela. One day Yvonne left the nursery gate unlocked. Mimi stood up, pushed the gate open, and walked outside. She didn't go anywhere. She didn't run into the kitchen and steal sodas like Mikeno or knock dishes off the table like Kikongo. She just walked over to the hose that one of the gardeners had left on. And she picked it up and started watering the flowers, like she had seen him do. That is how I will remember her, watering the flowers like a grandmother while the other babies played in the sun."

"*MA CHÈRE*," Claudine says when she sees me in the vet block, looking at the night box where Kindu used to sleep as a baby. "Are you all right?"

"Yes, fine," I say, my eyes welling up with tears. I hate crying in front of Claudine. I want to be composed and dignified like her but instead I'm a puffy-eyed, blotchy-faced wreck.

Claudine invents a flimsy excuse and packs me off to her house. She and Brian go to Lola every day while I sit at home and stare at her exquisite collection of African art or curl up in the corner with a book.

Brian is sweet but wary. He treats me like I'm an epileptic rabbit who can't handle loud voices or sudden movement. He is sad about the dead bonobos, but being male, he squashes his emotions into a box and files them away for processing at some later date. My female histrionics make him nervous.

I don't blame him. He has to keep it together, because the bonobos have done something incredible.

In 1988, a crane operator called Joe Honner was digging out telegraph poles on Darrell Tree's farm in South Australia. Joe's three-year-old son was sitting with him in the cabin while Joe maneuvered the crane.

Suddenly, the crane swung into live telegraph wires. More than nineteen thousand volts of electricity shot through the broken wires into the crane, which, being made of metal, was a superb conductor. Joe jumped clear, but his son was stuck in the cabin. Joe rushed forward to get his son, but he was held back by the farmer, Darrell. The little boy was fine, Darrell said, as long as he didn't move. The electricity wound around the crane, creating a perfect circuit, but the leather interior of the cabin was untouched. The boy was frightened and started to cry. As Darrell turned to get a rope to rescue him, Joe rushed forward. As soon as he touched the crane, he tapped into the circuit and electricity shot through his body, arcing him backward and rooting him to the spot.

Darrell charged Joe, pushing him clear. Both of them were knocked unconscious. When Darrell came to, he saw the boy lying curled on the ground beside the crane. Electricity was shooting through his head near his right ear. Darrell charged again and pulled the boy away from the crane. Again, the voltage knocked him unconscious. This time when he revived, Joe and his son were away from the crane, but neither of them was breathing. Darrell gave them both mouth-to-mouth and CPR. The boy lived, but Joe died before the ambulance arrived.

As for Darrell, the force of the electricity fused his spine and cracked his vertebrae. He had to have sixty-six stitches all over his body and the electric shock burned off his little toe.

Whatever you want to call it—heroism, altruism, temporary insanity—everyone from psychologists to economists claims that intentionally helping an unrelated individual at a cost to yourself is uniquely human. Despite Lassie, Flipper, and the other animal heroes, no one has solid evidence that any creature besides humans has altruistic tendencies, hence the word "*human*itarianism."

Even though not all of us would rush to take on nineteen thousand volts of electricity to save a child, most of us perform small frequent acts of altruism, like donating to charities or giving blood. Thousands of experiments have been designed to try to figure out where it comes from. What are the psychological and emotional mechanisms that allow us to put the welfare of someone else before our own?

The Dictator Game is one of the more famous experiments that prove our innate benevolence. Say you have $100. There is someone in the next room, a stranger you have never met before and whom you will never see. You can give her as much of your $100 as you want, or, like an evil dictator, you can keep all the money and give the stranger nothing.

According to hard-bitten economic theory, you would give the other person zero. You don't know him. You will never see him again. Why would you give the stranger anything?

But economists have found over and over again that many people give as much as half. This kind of altruism has been found all over the world in all different cultures. It has even been found in eighteen-month-old babies. This, say the economists, is what makes us human.

All of us are capable of these small acts of kindness that occasionally lead to the heroic acts of people like Darrell Tree.

Ever since Mimi threw herself over Lipopo's dead body, Brian has been obsessed with finding evidence of altruism in bonobos. So he is playing the Dictator Game with bonobos, but instead of money, he uses food.

Semendwa sits up straight, her eyes focused on a pile of food in the next room. She hasn't eaten this morning, and the mound of food has papaya, cucumbers, pineapple, and her favorite—green apples. Semendwa loves green apples so much she will cut your heart out if she even suspects you are hiding them from her.

In the other room is Kikwit. He is also watching the apples, but he is behind a door that can be opened only by Semendwa. Brian opens Semendwa's door. She comes into the room with the apples. Kikwit calls out.

Then, without even touching the apples, she goes to Kikwit's one-way door, unlocks it, and lets him in.

Bingo. Semendwa has effectively given Kikwit half of her $100. She didn't do it because she just enjoys his company—she could have eaten the food *first,* or at least the apple, before she let Kikwit in. She didn't touch the food. They didn't even have sex. She didn't have a fetish for opening doors, because on the other side of the room is another door that connects to an empty room. No. Before eating any of the food, Semendwa let in Kikwit so she could share with him.

Brian is ecstatic. It's the strongest experimental evidence of altruism in a primate other than a human, and he has found it in bonobos. There is no way a chimp would do the same thing. Brian has already tested the Ngamba chimps in a similar experiment and the results were conclusive—if the chimps didn't need help to get the food, they wouldn't share it.

He tries the same experiment with Semendwa and Sake, a baby female in the nursery who arrived only a few years before. Sake and Semendwa are in separate groups. They are strangers. They have never met or touched. But still Sake lets Semendwa in.

In a way, it is not surprising. All these precious traits we cling to as uniquely ours—empathy, altruism, morality—they have to come from somewhere. They didn't just appear as soon as the first human plopped out of his or her mother's womb. Evolution is a journey. One tiny change links to the next. Our unique forms of empathy, altruism, and morality are built on the foundations of what we share with other apes.

SIX MILLION YEARS AGO, our last common ancestor with apes split into three different lines, which would eventually become chimpanzees, bonobos, and us. Along our journey, something extraordinary happened. We grew big brains. We tamed fire. We started to talk. But all that would have been for nothing if not for one simple thing—tolerance.

Tolerance is what allowed us to cooperate so flexibly. Every one of our great accomplishments comes from sharing ideas, building on the thoughts and concepts of others.

In our very first experiments, we found chimps could cooperate, but only after we controlled for tolerance. Intelligence wasn't the problem. They were smart enough to know they needed help from someone else, but their emotions got in the way. Somewhere during our evolution, human emotions changed so that even on a battlefield, two groups of enemy troops can come together to share simple gifts and songs.

Of course, tolerance isn't always something we excel at. From the ear-temperature and picture studies, we know that chimps have an involuntary physiological reaction when they hear or see a stranger. To a certain extent, we have the same reaction. Even as babies, we prefer faces we recognize to those of strangers. As we grow older, we tend to have negative reactions to people we identify as "them" and not "us."

There are many people who are uncomfortable with the suggestion that there is a biological basis for aggression. They want to believe that aggression is something that crops up as a result of mental illness or guns or drugs or bad parenting. But if a biological basis for aggression exists, isn't it our responsibility to learn how it works so we can develop strategies to manage it?

In a way, we already have. We have a police force and a justice system and other regulatory structures to make sure we can't act like chimpanzees on a rampage whenever we feel like it. Surely it isn't weakness to admit to our imperfections and strive to overcome them. Isn't that, in the end, what makes us human?

And what of bonobos, our long-lost cousins? What have we discovered about them that makes them important?

Our comparisons between bonobos and chimpanzees have given us some of the answers. The sexual acrobatics Frans de Waal observed at the San Diego Zoo were not exaggerated. Tory's hormone results are back and baby bonobos have incredibly high testosterone, which probably modulates their sexual libido. The highest testosterone level found in the 2007 tests was in Masisi, a two-year-old female.

In the wild, bonobos may have less sex than in a zoo, but the sexual mechanism is there, and it is not present in chimpanzees. Data from my baby-sex study at Lola indicates that bonobos have sex when they need to resolve tension, but this behavior is totally absent in infant chimpanzees. In the wild, kicking back with heaps of food and space, there may not be any reason to fight. But in a zoo, where space is confined and feeding times restricted, sex enables tolerance. In the temperature studies, we found that bonobos do not have a negative response to strangers. They don't seem to care whether someone is part of "us" or one of "them."

So if bonobos are more tolerant in some ways than humans, why did they never develop our level of intelligence? If they are so tolerant, why isn't Kikwit replacing Steve Jobs at Apple or Isiro running the White House? Why aren't bonobos ruling the world?

The answer is, they don't need to. As humans, our quest for food and resources drove us to come up with ingenious ideas. We had to fight the enemy, defend ourselves from predators, hunt down meat. Eventually, we became more sophisticated, until here we are, flying like birds, diving like fish, and touching the stars with the tips of our fingers.

Bonobos have enough food. They don't hunt each other like chimpanzees. The females are safe. Babies aren't killed by their own kind. Why would they want to change anything?

We began these experiments because we wanted to find out what makes humans so smart, what it is that bonobos *lack* that makes the crucial difference between them and us. But in the end, who would you rather be? In our modern miracle of a world, life is pretty sweet. We can be sipping margaritas in the Caribbean one minute and shopping in Los Angeles the next. When we get bored of real life, we can escape into a book or a movie. Everything we need is on the Internet. Even our phones can play music, take photos, and guide us via GPS to our favorite restaurants.

Except that you and I are the lucky ones. More than 80 percent of people live on less than $10 a day. More than twenty-five thousand children die a day from poverty. More than forty million people have HIV. Since 1945, there have been only twenty-six days without war. Every year, half a billion people get malaria. More than a billion people have no clean water. Even in America, the land of dreams that I am coming to love as my own, one in ten people lives in poverty.

In the end, if fate is just a roll of the dice and you could be born anywhere, to any family in the world, if you look at the odds, who would you rather be? Most of the time, bonobos have no hunger, no violence, no poverty. And for all our intelligence, all our *things,* bonobos have the most important of all possessions—peace.

And that is why bonobos are important. Because they hold the key to a world without war. We have already learned so much from chimpanzees. Yet our other closest living relative, the one who has no war and lives in peace, we have kept at arm's length, as strangers.

If we lose bonobos, we will never learn their secret. And even more tragically, because they share so much of what makes us human, we will never understand ourselves.

Chapter 36

❧

While Brian spends all day with Semendwa and Kikwit, Claudine picks up Belgian nobility at the airport. Like most of the English-speaking world, I had never heard of Claudine André, so it is easy to forget that to the Francophones, she is a hero. She has received the Legion of Honor, the highest possible award for a civilian, from both Belgium and France. She has been declared one of the "women of the world" by the French magazine *GEO*. Carla Bruni-Sarkozy, the wife of the French president, wrote to say she loved her memoir. The editor of the French edition of *Elle* magazine (more powerful than Meryl Streep in *The Devil Wears Prada*) fondly calls her "cousin."

I'm sure she is dazzling to all of them, resplendent in evening gowns as she receives her awards, charming and gracious as she replies to Madame Sarkozy. But to me, she is just Mama Claudine. She frowns when I don't eat enough food and fusses if I don't get enough sleep. And though she has sixty other orphans to take care of and a thousand e-mails to answer, at the end of each day she comes home, kisses me three times, searches my face, and says, "*Ma chère,* how are you?"

If I were an angel, I would paint the sky the color of her eyes.

I DRAG MYSELF OUT OF BED at nine thirty A.M. and appear as a swamp monster at the breakfast table.

"Sorry I'm crashing your house again," I say to Victor, who is clean-shaven and smoking a cigar over the radio.

"Sorry, why? Are you not family?"

Victor has been so kind that I start using his bear hugs as a kind of biofuel to get me through the day. I crunch on a piece of toast.

"What are you listening to?"

"Kabila is making a speech. Stop playing with your hair."

Kabila has ended up being a bit of a disappointment. Since his election in 2006, his promise of creating a united, strong, and prosperous Congo has largely gone unfulfilled.

The war in the east has not ended. The most brutal crimes are still, as always, against women and children. The number of reported rapes has risen from forty thousand in 2004 to more than two hundred and fifty thousand in 2009. The testimonies gathered by various NGOs flow in a steady, horrific stream. Like the three-year-old girl in South Kivu who died after being raped with her twelve-, fourteen-, and seventeen-year-old sisters. Or the twenty-seven-year-old from Masisi who was kept as a sex slave by the Congolese army for a month. Or the forty-year-old from Kalehe who miscarried her four-month-old baby while she was being gang-raped.

Rape has always been used as a weapon of war. After World War II, the Russian soldiers raped thousands of East German women, although the women were not allowed to talk about it, because it didn't fit with the propaganda of Soviet heroes saving Germany from the Nazis. Similar strategies were used in East Timor, Afghanistan, Sierra Leone, Kosovo, and Algeria. Bemba's "Operation Clean Slate" was presented almost as a vaccination campaign—every house looted and every woman raped.

In third-world countries, it is women who till the fields and tend to the crops. If they are trapped in their homes, too terrified to emerge, there is no food. If they are ostracized from their families because they have been raped, if they are infected with HIV, if they are forced to take care of the children they bear from their trauma, how can they hold the community together?

As harrowing as this is, what has followed is worse. Rape is no longer just a military tactic. Now soldiers from all sides see rape almost as an entitlement. They take sex from women the way they might buy milk in a supermarket, as something that requires little thought and even less regret.

It is not just the rapes. On April 17, 2009, Rwandan militiamen burned five young children to death. On May 9 and 10, dozens of civilians were killed in Walikale. When I first arrived in Congo in 2005, the death toll was 3.9 million. In 2009, it hit 5.4 million.

Kabila claims progress has been made. On March 5, 2009, a Mai Mai warlord and his militia were sentenced to death and their victims awarded up to $300,000 in compensation. On January 22, 2009, Nkunda, the praying mantis general with the pet lamb, was arrested by Rwandan troops. Nkunda is being held in a secret location in Rwanda since everyone, from his wife to Kabila, wants to get their hands on him. It is unclear who will hold the trial, but for now, he is safely out of the way.

During an uneasy cease-fire, rebel groups continue to scratch at the earth for coltan, copper, and diamonds. Unfortunately, minerals are not quite the cash cow they used to be. The effects of the economic meltdown in the United States ricocheted through Congo. The production of copper, one of Congo's most abundant resources, fell by 50 percent in July 2008. Katanga, a mining province larger than California and rich in cobalt, copper, and diamonds, has all but shut down. At the end of 2008 alone, three hundred thousand miners lost their jobs. By spring 2009, hardly a soul was employed at all. The Congolese franc has plummeted and government spending has been slashed by half.

Kabila wants to sign a $9 billion deal with China that would exchange minerals for hospitals, railways, universities, and airports. The Chinese will triple the paved road network and rebuild almost 1,900 miles of railway, most of which have been rotting since the Belgians built them more than a half a century ago. The International Monetary Fund (IMF) is protesting. It was on the brink of signing off on

$11 billion of debt relief to Congo but argues that the falling price of minerals on the world market could plunge Congo into more debt. In 2009, $9 billion can buy a hell of a lot more copper than it could in 2008, when the deal was made. The IMF says that if the value of minerals stays low, Congo may never be able to repay the money, keeping it indebted to the Chinese. The IMF, in which the United States has the most voting power of any other country, is worried about China's increasing power and influence in Africa.

Kabila figuratively gives the IMF the finger, saying the IMF's twin institution, the World Bank, just gave a $12 billion loan to Romania, which has a population of 22 million, and yet gave Congo, with a population of 68 million, only $0.3 billion. He threatens to add North Korea and Russia to his list of business associates.

Although Kabila isn't an evil dictator, he isn't quite the heroic prince Congo was hoping for. He is more the fill-in guy, the one you kick around with while waiting for the real Prince Charming to show up.

The next elections are in 2011. Congo can only wait and see. And hope.

FANNY TURNS UP AT NOON. She brings a gust of cool air swirling around her Japanese patterned skirt.

"You're staying all week, right?" she demands. "I'm working on something I want you to see."

Fanny is back in Kinshasa. She doesn't know why except that she just wanted to come home. She has a gorgeous new Congolese man and together, they want to rebuild their country, although they are both still a little nebulous on the details.

Fanny has started painting. She has a studio in the back and I watch her shadow furiously working thick, textured strokes onto her canvas. Her artwork is riveting and chaotic. Claudine proudly hangs a bright red sculpture that looks like a bursting artery in the dining room and we contemplate it while we eat.

I hope Fanny becomes famous. I hope her paintings are hung in the best galleries in Paris. Congo needs a voice like hers. There are so many tourists like me who turn up in a country and spend a few months or a few years and think they can tell its story. But we can't. I don't know what will become of Congo. I know that for all our meddling we have not been able to help because, unlike Semendwa, our intentions are not truly altruistic. There is always an ulterior motive to our benevolence. A hidden agenda to our gifts.

I could despair, like almost every foreigner who understands a fraction of the challenges that have yet to be overcome. I won't. Because I know the spirit of the Congolese. The Mamas, Suzy, Fanny— all of them have been through so much and yet they are not the walking dead. They are living, and they are living as though they believe they will become free.

Almost half the population of Congo is under fifteen years old. The children will bring Congo her future. And I hope it is a bonobo one.

As FOR ME, the Mamas are right. I should shut up and have a baby.

If it's a girl, I'll call her Malou.

Epilogue

Ekolo ya Bonobo

⚫

*B*asankusu is a small town with tight-packed dirt roads. As you go down the main street, a right turn takes you to the local market. Opposite the market is a dilapidated concrete building. Black mold runs down the side and rust from the corrugated iron roof seeps through the walls. Across the building someone has boldly written in blue paint:

NOUS PROTÉGEONS BONOBOS ET BONOBOS NOUS SAUVERA

We protect bonobos and bonobos will save us

During the war, government soldiers loyal to Kabila Senior occupied Boso Ngubu, the capital of the native Pô. The warlord Bemba's rebels set up camp in a village called Elonda on the Lopori River. Both armies marched from opposite directions and met at what became the Battle of Eleke.

The Pô could see what was coming and fled into the forest. For days they watched the Lopori River flow red with blood. Bodies floated down in the hundreds.

Bemba's reinforcements arrived from the south on the Maringa River, which joins the Lopori at Basankusu. After two months, Kabila's government soldiers fled.

Bemba took over. He installed a government and ran Basankusu as a rebel province. When Kabila Junior succeeded his dead father, he invited Bemba to be part of his team of rivals. Bemba became one of four vice presidents and the Pô were left alone once again.

Since the Pô agreed to become bonobo guardians, life has changed. There are five primary schools and two secondary schools with more than a thousand students who have not had new textbooks for twenty years. The bonobos have brought textbooks for every classroom, blackboards, schoolbooks, pencils, and pens.

There is no clinic for miles, so the women gave birth in a dark hut on the dirt floor. The bonobos have brought mattresses, sheets, sanitary equipment, and a room with light for women to bring their babies into the world.

Like every village in Congo, there is a group of ragged kids who play soccer. They had never played a proper game or worn anything but rags. The bonobos have brought them green uniforms with the name of the release site, Ekolo ya Bonobo, written on the back, which means "land of the bonobos." The Basankusu Bonobos, as they are known, went on to win the provincial championships.

There was no medicine. The bonobos brought a clinic and medical supplies. There was no work. The bonobos have given jobs to trackers, housekeepers, and administrative staff.

When outsiders turn up to help the Congolese, it is usually to rub their faces in failure. Your women are being raped, so we have come with a clinic to treat their wounds. You people are killing each other, so we are here to enforce some measure of order and control. Your fields are untended, your children are starving, so here, take these sacks of *foufou* and for God's sake feed yourselves. We have come to help but your cause is hopeless, so we will do what we can, then leave.

Bonobos have given Basankusu back its pride. The rewards that arrive—the schools, the clinics, the soccer uniforms—come because the Pô have done something right. On June 14, 2009, nine bonobos were transferred from the sanctuary to the release site, where they will live from now on among the Pô. The whole village cheered in greeting and escorted them to their new home.

In return, the bonobos will share their secrets. Schoolchildren learn that when bonobos get angry, they hug. Women hear that together, bonobo females are strong. Men understand that it is possible to live a life without war.

The people of Basankusu have something more precious than diamonds or gold or coltan. They have something no one can steal. Something that will cause neither war nor bloodshed. This treasure remains a glimmer of hope, an outline of night through the trees.

ISIRO SLOWLY WAKES UP. She is a little sore, as though she has been lying cramped for many hours. She turns her head and sees Semendwa, Lomami, Lomela, and Max. They are stirring, stretching their limbs, sitting up and blinking.

The air smells different. An almost-forgotten memory. A spicy fruit. Her mother's breath. Near her head is a forest snail the size of her curled hand. The sight of its meaty foot leaving its glistening trail is at once strange and familiar.

It is darker here. Cool. The sun is shielded by a high green canopy pierced now and then by a red leaf glittering like a jewel.

Beyond the fallen trunks covered in wispy moss there is a river wider and deeper than forever. The river reflects the light sky but its waters are as black as her eyes.

She takes a deep breath. A million leaves whisper her name. The earth is soft and damp beneath her feet.

The others fall in behind her and together they fill the forest.

They are no longer frightened or abandoned or lost.

They are home.

They are free.

Acknowledgments

❧❧

The orphans of Lola ya Bonobo survive because of the generosity of people like you. If you would like to sponsor a bonobo or make a donation, please visit Friends of Bonobos at
www.friendsofbonobos.org.

Checks can be sent to :
Friends of Bonobos
P.O. Box 80254
Minneapolis, MN 55408, USA

To help orphan chimpanzees, visit the Jane Goodall Institute at
www.janegoodall.org.

To help women who have been raped in Congo, visit Heal Africa at
healafrica.org.

If you would like to e-mail me, please contact
bonobohandshake@gmail.com.

You can follow the stories of Lola's bonobos on the blog
bonobohandshake.blogspot.com.

For bonobo photos, videos, and stories, visit
www.bonobohandshake.com.

. . .

I COULD NOT HAVE WRITTEN this book without the love and enduring patience of my husband, Brian Hare. Thanks, babe, for hugging me through all those breakdowns.

Thank you, Mom, for taking me to the beach house, and thank you, Sara Gruen, for being the best friend to bonobos ever, and Sheril Kirshenbaum, for being the best writing buddy. Thank you, Kara Schroepfer and Adamou Hamadou, for patiently transcribing the interviews. Big hugs to Sammy and Bronnie for weeding out the bad jokes and horrible bits. And to the dashing Richard Wrangham, the fabulous Debby Cox, and the inspirational Dominique Morel for proofreading, sharing our adventures, and generally being awesome.

Thank you, Lauren Marino, your excellent editing skills turned the book from a garbled mess into a story. Thank you to my agent, Max Brockman; you're the best. For the blog followers and adopted parents, thank you so much for your support over the years—I read all your comments, and they prop me up and make me smile.

Kinshasa wouldn't be the same without Fanny and Victor, who took us in and made us a part of the family. Thank you to the keepers, the staff of Lola, and especially the Mamas, whose spirit I will always treasure.

No book will ever do justice to the courage and kindness of Claudine André. Thank you, Mama Claudine, for drying my tears, fattening me up, and showing me that there is such a thing as a selfless heart.

And finally, to the bonobos of Lola, living and gone. I know there's no way for me to tell you how much you mean to me, how much I love you, or that I carry you with me, every day. The best I can do is make a gift of my memories, so everyone will know how special you are. I hope they will come to love you as I have, and that this love will ensure your future.

Further Reading

There aren't many books on bonobos, but anyone who speaks French should read *Une Tendresse Sauvage* by Claudine André.

For English readers there is Frans de Waal's *Bonobo: The Forgotten Ape*. Takayoshi Kano is probably the world's most respected bonobo researcher, and his *The Last Ape* is a crucial study of their behavior and ecology. Sara Gruen is writing one of the first fictions about bonobos, tentatively called *Ape House*.

Anyone interested in the origins of human violence should read *Demonic Males* by Richard Wrangham and Dale Peterson.

The landmark text on Congo is, of course, *King Leopold's Ghost*, by Adam Hochschild. One of the most fascinating and brutal memoirs in the last few years is *All Things Must Fight to Live* by Bryan Mealer. The Pulitzer Prize–winning play *Ruined*, by Lynn Nottage, is a must-see. For a history of Congo, *The Troubled Heart of Africa* by Robert Edgerton is a great read. Finally, *The Congo: Plunder and Resistance* by David Renton, David Seddon, and Leo Zeilig is a moving account of the Congo war and our part in it.

Bibliography

Books

André, C. (2006) *Une Tendresse Sauvage*. Paris: Calmann-Levy.

Axelrod, R. (1984) *The Evolution of Cooperation*. New York: Basic Books.

Axelrod, R. (1997) *The Complexity of Cooperation*. Princeton, NJ: Princeton University Press.

Butcher, T. (2008) *Blood River: A Journey to Africa's Broken Heart*. London: Grove Press.

Clark, J. F. (2002) *The African Stakes of the Congo War*. New York: Palgrave Macmillan.

Collier, P. (2007) *The Bottom Billion: Why the Poorest Countries Are Failing and What Can Be Done About It*. New York: Oxford University Press.

Conrad, J. (1963) *Heart of Darkness*. New York: W. W. Norton & Company.

De Waal, F. (2005) *Our Inner Ape: A Leading Primatologist Explains Why We Are Who We Are*. New York: Riverford Books.

De Witte, L. (2001) *The Assassination of Lumumba*. New York: Verso.

Edgerton, R. B. (2002) *The Troubled Heart of Africa: A History of the Congo*. New York: St Martin's Press.

Fouts, R. (1997) *Next of Kin: My Conversations with Chimpanzees.* New York: Avon Books Inc.

Furuichi, T., and Thompson, J. (2008) *The Bonobos: Behavior, Ecology, Genetics and Conservation.* New York: Springer.

Hochschild, A. (1998) *King Leopold's Ghost: A Story of Greed, Terror and Heroism in Colonial Africa.* New York: Houghton Mifflin.

Kano, T. (1992) *The Last Ape: Pygmy Chimpanzee Behavior and Ecology.* Stanford, CA: Stanford University Press.

Mealer, B. (2008) *All Things Must Fight to Live: Stories of War and Deliverance in Congo.* New York: Bloomsbury.

Messinger, D. (2006) *Grains of Golden Sand: Adventures in War-Torn Africa.* Fine Print Press.

Nest, M., Grignon, F., and Kisangani, E. F. (2006) *The Democratic Republic of Congo: Economic Dimensions of War and Peace.* London: Lynne Rienner Publishers.

Nzongola-Ntalaja, G. (2002) *The Congo: From Leopold to Kabila—A People's History.* New York: Zed Books.

Peterson, D., and Ammann, K. (2003) *Eating Apes.* Berkely, CA: University of California Press.

Prunier, G. (2009) *Africa's World War: Congo, the Rwandan Genocide, and the Making of a Continental Catastrophe.* New York: Oxford University Press.

Renton, D., Seddon, D., Zeilig, L. (2007) *The Congo: Plunder and Resistance.* New York: Zed Books.

Savage-Rumbaugh, S. (1994) *Kanzi: The Ape on the Brink of the Human Mind.* New York: John Wiley and Sons, Inc.

Tayler, J. (2000) *Facing the Congo: A Modern Day Journey into the Heart of Darkness.* New York: Three Rivers Press.

Turner, T. (2007) *The Congo Wars.* New York: Zed Books.

Wrangham, R., and Peterson, D. (1996) *Demonic Males: Apes and the*

Origins of Human Violence. New York: Houghton Mifflin Company.

Wrong, M. (2000) *In the Footsteps of Mr. Kurtz: Living on the Brink of Disaster in Mobutu's Congo.* New York: Perennial.

Yerkes, R. M. (1925) *Almost Human.* New York: The Century Co.

Journal Articles

André, C., et al. (2008) "The Conservation Value of Lola ya Bonobo Sanctuary." In *The Bonobos: Behavior, Ecology, and Conservation,* ed. T. Furuichi and J. Thompson. New York: Springer.

Autesserre, S. (2006) "Local Violence, National Peace? Postwar 'Settlement' in the Eastern D.R. Congo (2003–2006)." *African Studies Review* 49(3): 1–29.

Boesch, C., Crockford, C., Herringer, I., Wittig, R., Moerius, Y., and Normand, E. (2008) "Intergroup Conflicts Among Chimpanzees in Taï National Park: Lethal Violence and the Female Perspective." *American Journal of Primatology* 70:519–532.

Boesch, C., Head, J., Tagg, N., Arandjelovic, M., Vigiland, L., and Robbins, M. (2007) "Fatal Chimpanzee Attack in Loango National Park, Gabon." *International Journal of Primatology* 28:1025–1034.

Chiwengo, N. (2008) "When Wounds and Corpses Fail to Speak: Narratives of Violence and Rape in Congo (DRC)." *Comparative Studies of South Asia, Africa, and the Middle East* 28(1): 78–92.

Clark, J. F. (1998) "The Nature and Evolution of the State in Zaire." *Studies in Comparative International Development* 32(4):3–21.

Clark, J. F. (2002) "The Neo-colonial Context of the Democratic Experiment of Congo-Brazzaville." *African Affairs* 101:171–192.

De Waal, F. B.M. (1988) "The Communicative Repertoire of Captive Bonobos (Pan Paniscus) Compared to That of Chimpanzees." *Behavior* 106:183–251.

Draulans, D., and Van Krunkelsven, E. (2002) "The Impact of War on Forest Areas in the Democratic Republic of Congo." *Oryx* 36(1): 35–40.

Farmer, K. H. (2002) "Pan-African Sanctuary Alliance: Status and Range of Activities for Great Ape Conservation." *American Journal of Primatology* 58:117–132.

Fehr, E., and Fischbacher, U. (2003) "The Nature of Human Altruism." *Nature* 425:785-791.

Fehr, E., Fischbacher, U., and Gaechter, S. "Strong Reciprocity, Human Cooperation, and the Enforcement of Social Norms." *Human Nature* 13(1):1–25.

Fehr, E., and Gaechter, S. (2002) "Altruistic Punishment in Humans." *Nature* 415:137–140.

Fehr, E., and Rockenbach, B. (2003) "Detrimental Effects of Sanctions on Human Altruism" *Nature* 422:137–140.

Frushone, J. "New Congolese Refugees in Tanzania." United States Committee for Refugees (USCR). December 24, 2002.

Goossens, B., Setchell, J. M., Dilambaka, E., Vidal, C., and Jamart, A. (2003) "Successful Reproduction in Wild-Released Orphan Chimpanzees (Pan troglodytes troglodytes)." *Primates* 44: 67–69.

Goossens, B., Setchell, J. M., Tchidongo, E., Dilambaka, E., Vidal, C., Ancrenaz, M., and Jamart, A. (2005) "Survival, Interactions with Conspecifics and Reproduction in 37 Chimpanzees Released into the Wild" *Biological Conservation* 123:461–475.

Haney, C., Banks, C., and Zimbardo, P. (1973) "Interpersonal Dynamics in a Simulated Prison." *International Journal of Criminology and Penology* 1:69–97.

Hare, B., Melis, A., Woods, V., Hastings, S., and Wrangham, R. (2007) "Tolerance Allows Bonobos to Outperform Chimpanzees on a Cooperative Task." *Current Biology* 17(7):619–623.

Kabemba, C. (2005) "Transitional Politics in the DRC: The Role of Key Stakeholders." *Journal of African Elections* 4(1):165-180.

Kassa, Michael. "Humanitarian Assistance in the DRC." In *Challenges of Peace Implementation: The UN Mission in the Democratic Republic of the Congo*, ed. Mark Malan and Joao Gomes Porto. Pretoria: Institute for Security Studies, 2004.

Knight, R. (2003) "Expanding Petroleum Production in Africa." *Reviews of African Political Economy* 30(96):335–339.

Langford, D. J. (2006) "Social Modulation of Pain as Evidence for Empathy in Mice." *Science* 312:1967–1970.

Laporte, N. T., Stabach, J. A., Grosch, R., Lin, T. S., Goetz, S. and J. "Expansion of Industrial Logging in Central Africa." *Science* 316:1451.

Marsh, N., et al (1997) "The Gaboon Viper, Bitis Gabonica: Hemorrhagic, Metabolic, Cardiovascular and Clinical Effects of the Venom." *Life Sciences* 6(8):763–769.

Medana, I. M., and Turner, G. H. (2007) "Plasmodium Falciparum and the Blood-Brain Barrier—Contacts and Consequences." *Journal of Infectious Diseases* 195: 921–923.

Melis, A., Hare, B., and Tomasello, M. (2006) "Chimpanzees Recruit the Best Collaborators." *Science* 311(5765):1297–1300.

Merckx, M., and Vander Weyden, P. (2007) "Parliamentary and Presidential Elections in the Democratic Republic of Congo, 2006." *Electoral Studies* 26:797–837.

Montague, D. "Stolen Goods: Coltan and Conflict in the Democratic Republic of Congo." *SAIS Review* 22(1):103–118.

Ngolet, F. (2000) "African and American Connivance in Congo-Zaire." *Africa Today* 47(1):65-85.

Nishida, T., and Kawanaka, K. (1985) "Within-Group Cannibalism by Adult Male Chimpanzees." *Primates* 26(3):274–284.

Olsson, O., and Congdon Fors, H. (2004) "Congo: The Prize of Predation." *Journal of Peace Research* 41(3):321–336.

Reyntjens, F. (2001) "Briefing: The Democratic Republic of Congo, From Kabila to Kabila." *African Affairs* 100:311–317.

Ron, J. (1994) "Primary Commodities and War: Congo-Brazzaville's Ambivalent Resource Curse." *Comparative Politics* 37(1):61-81.

Schatzberg, M. (1997) "Beyond Mobutu: Kabila and the Congo." *Journal of Democracy* 8(4):70–84.

Stanford, C. (1998) "The Social Behavior of Chimpanzees and Bonobos: Empirical Evidence and Shifting Assumptions." *Current Anthropology* 39(4):399–420.

Talley, L. Spiegel, P. B., and Girgis, M. (2001) "An Investigation of Increasing Mortality Among Congolese Refugees in Lugufu Camp, Tanzania, May–June 1999." *Journal of Refugee Studies* 14(4): 412–427.

Tratz, E. P., and Heck, H. (1954) "Der Afrikanische Anthropoide 'Bonobo,' eine Neue Menshenaffengattung." *Saugetierkundliche Mitteilungen* 2:97–101.

Tutin, C. E., Ancrenaz, M., Paredes, J., Wacher-Vallas, M., Vidal, C., Goossens, B., Bruford, M. W., and Jamart, A. (2001) "Conservation Biology Framework for the Release of Wild Born Orphaned Chimpanzees into the Conkouati Reserve, Congo." *Conservation Biology* 15(5):1247–1257.

Uenzelmann-Neben, G. (1998) "Neogene Sedimentation History of the Congo Fan." *Marine and Petroleum Geology* 15:635–650.

VandeBerg, J. L., and Zola, S. M. (2005) "A Unique Biomedical Resource at Risk." *Nature* 437:30–32.

Walton, G. E., and Bower, T. G. R. (1993) "Newborns Form 'Prototypes' in Less Than 1 Minute." *Psychological Science* 4(3):203–205.

Watts, D. (2004) "Intracommunity Coalitionary Killing of an Adult Male Chimpanzee at Ngogo, Kibale National Park, Uganda." *International Journal of Primatology* 25(3):507–523.

Weiss, H. F. (2007) "Voting for Change in the DRC." *Journal of Democracy* 18(2):138–151.

White, B. (2005) "The Political Undead: Is It Possible to Mourn for Mobutu's Zaire?" *African Studies Review* 48(2):65–85.

Wilke, D. S., and Carpenter, J. F. (1999) "Bushmeat Hunting in the Congo Basin: An Assessment of Impacts and Options for Mitigation." *Biodiversity and Conservation* 8:927–955.

Wilson, M. L., Wallauer, W. R., and Pusey, A. E. (2003) "New Cases of Intergroup Violence Among Chimpanzees in Gombe National Park, Tanzania." *International Journal of Primatology* 25(3):523–549.

Wrangham, R., and Wilson, M. L. (2003) "Intergroup Relations in Chimpanzees." *Annual Review of Anthropology*. 32:363–92.

Wrangham, R., and Wilson, M. L. (2004) "Collective Violence: Comparisons Between Youths and Chimpanzees." *Annals New York Academy of Sciences* 1036:233–256.

Wrangham, R., Wilson, M. L., and Muller, M. N. (2006) "Comparative Rates of Violence in Chimpanzees and Humans" *Primates* 47: 14–26.

Reports

"Addendum to the Report of the Panel of Experts on the Illegal Exploitation of Natural Resources and Other Forms of Wealth of DR Congo." *UN Security Council*, November 10, 2001.

"Children at War: Creating Hope for Their Future." *Amnesty International*, October 2006.

"Chimpanzees in Research: Strategies for Their Ethical Care, Management, and Use." Committee on Long-Term Care of Chimpanzees, Institute for Laboratory Animal Research, Commission on Life Sciences, National Research Council, 1997.

"China's Commodity Hunger: Implications for Africa and Latin America." *Deutche Bank Research*, June 13, 2006.

"The Curse of Gold: Democratic Republic of Congo." *Human Rights Watch*, 2005.

"D.R. Congo: War Crimes in Bukavu." *Human Rights Watch Briefing Paper*, June 2004.

"Democratic Republic of Congo: Torture and Killings by State Security Agents Still Endemic." Amnesty International, 2007.

"First Assessment of the Armed Groups Operating in DR Congo." Letter dated April 1, 2002 from the Secretary-General addressed to the President of the Security Council.

"From Kabila to Kabila: Prospects for Peace in the Congo." International Crisis Group, March 16, 2001.

"Interim Report of the Panel of Experts on the Illegal Exploitation of Natural Resources and Other Forms of Wealth of the Democratic Republic of the Congo." *UN Security Council*, May 22, 2002.

"Mass Rape: Time for Remedies." *Amnesty International*, 2004.

"Mortality in the Democratic Republic of Congo: An Ongoing Crisis." *International Rescue Committee*, 2007.

"Seeking Justice: The Prosecution of Sexual Violence in the Congo War." *Human Rights Watch*, March 2005.

"Struggling to Survive: Children in Armed Conflict in the Democratic Republic of the Congo." *Watchlist on Children and Armed Conflict*, April 2006.

"Supporting the War Economy in the DRC: European Companies and the Coltan Trade." *International Peace Information Service*, January 2002.

Myers, K. "Petroleum, Poverty and Security." Chatham House, June 2005.

Pendergast, J., and Thomas-Jensen, C. "Averting the Nightmare Scenario in Eastern Congo." *Enough*, September 2007.

"Situation in the Central African Republic: In the Case of *The Prosecution v. Jean Pierre Bemba.*" *International Criminal Court,* May 23, 2008.

Stenberg, A. "D R Congo: Presidential and Legislative Elections July–October 2006." Norwegian Centre for Human Rights, February 2007.

"The War Within the War: Sexual Violence Against Women and Girls in Eastern Congo." *Human Rights Watch*, June 2007.

"'We Will Crush You': The Restriction of Political Space in the Democratic Republic of Congo." *Human Rights Watch*, 2008.

News articles and newswires

"Africa's Unmended Heart." *The Economist.* June 11, 2009, 20–22.

Argetsinger, A. "The Animal Within." *The Washington Post*, May 24, 2005.

Blomfield, A. "I Played Piano for Congo Warlord Laurent Nkunda." Telegraph.co.uk, November 4, 2008.

Carroll, R. "US Chose to Ignore Rwandan Genocide." *The Guardian*, March 31, 2004.

"Deal with Rebel General." *Africa Research Bulletin*, July 1–31, 2007, 16936.

"DRC: Call for Investigation into Fire That Destroyed Presidential Candidate's TV and Radio Station." *International News Safety Institute*, September 20, 2006.

Elliott, F., and Elkins, R. "UN Shame over Sex Scandal." *The Independent*, January 7, 2007.

"Epidemic of Rape." *Africa Research Bulletin*, October 1–31, 2007.

Gettleman, J. "Mai Mai Fighters Third Piece in Congo's Violent Puzzle." *The New York Times*, November 21, 2008.

Hutcheon, S. "Out of Africa: The Blood Tantalum in Your Mobile Phone." *The Sydney Morning Herald*, May 8, 2009.

Hutchinson, E. O. "Clinton Kept Hotel Rwanda Open." Alternet.org, January 3, 2005.

Kron, J. "Kinshasa Walking a Tightrope to Rebuild Economy." *Daily Nation*, May 15, 2009.

Parker, I. "Swingers." *The New Yorker*, July 30, 2007.

Polgreen, L. "Congo's Riches, Looted by Renegade Troops." *The New York Times*, November 16, 2008.

Price, S. "Why Trouble Flared in Bukavu." *New African*, July 2004.

Repke, I., and Wensierski, P. "Lost Red Army Children Search for Fathers." *Spiegel Online*, August 16, 2007.

"Rogue General Wreaks Havoc: Laurent Nkunda Is Making Himself Master of the Kivu Region." *Africa Research Bulletin*, July 1–31, 2007.

Todd, B. "Congo, Coltan, Conflict." *Heinz College*, March 15, 2006.

"U.N. Says Congo Rebels Carried Out Cannibalism and Rapes." *The New York Times*, January 16, 2003.